MW00773650

HASIDIC COMMENTARY ON THE TORAH

THE LITTMAN LIBRARY OF
JEWISH CIVILIZATION

The Littman Library of Jewish Civilization is a registered UK charity
Registered charity no. 1000784

HASIDIC
COMMENTARY
ON THE
TORAH

◆

ORA WISKIND-ELPER

London
The Littman Library of Jewish Civilization
in association with Liverpool University Press
2018

The Littman Library of Jewish Civilization
Registered office: 4th floor, 7–10 Chandos Street, London WIG 9DQ

in association with Liverpool University Press
4 Cambridge Street, Liverpool L69 7ZU, UK
www.liverpooluniversitypress.co.uk/littman

Managing Editor: Connie Webber

Distributed in North America by
Oxford University Press Inc., 198 Madison Avenue,
New York, NY 10016, USA

Catalogue records for this book are available from the
British Library and the Library of Congress

ISBN 978–1–906764–12–8

Publishing co-ordinator: Janet Moth
Copy-editing: Agnes Erdos
Proof-reading: Norm Guthartz
Index: Sarah Ereira
Design, typsetting and production by
Pete Russell, Faringdon, Oxon.

Printed and bound in Great Britain by
TJ International Ltd., Padstow, Cornwall

Acknowledgements

I WOULD LIKE to thank Elie Holzer, Carmi Horowitz, Ziva Kosofsky, David Roskies, and Don Seeman for their insights on how I might make this a better book. Connie Webber, Janet Moth, and Ludo Craddock of the Littman Library offered valuable advice at many crucial junctures. Thanks, too, to my copy-editor Agi Erdos for her careful attention to the manuscript. As this project came closer to completion Susan Handelman's wisdom and support were essential. And for guiding me through the final stages, Simi Peters has my deep gratitude. Beyond all this, there are no words to describe the love and support of my children and family during the many years over which this book came into being.

July 2017   O.W.-E.

Contents

Note on Transliteration and Conventions Used in the Text

THE TRANSLITERATION of Hebrew in this book reflects consideration of the type of book it is, in terms of its content, purpose, and readership. The system adopted therefore reflects a broad approach to transcription, rather than the narrower approaches found in the *Encyclopaedia Judaica* or other systems developed for text-based or linguistic studies. The aim has been to reflect the pronunciation prescribed for modern Hebrew, rather than the spelling or Hebrew word structure, and to do so using conventions that are generally familiar to the English-speaking reader.

In accordance with this approach, no attempt is made to indicate the distinctions between *alef* and *ayin*, *tet* and *taf*, *kaf* and *kuf*, *sin* and *samekh*, since these are not relevant to pronunciation; likewise, the *dagesh* is not indicated except where it affects pronunciation. Following the principle of using conventions familiar to the majority of readers, however, transcriptions that are well established have been retained even when they are not fully consistent with the transliteration system adopted. On similar grounds, the *tsadi* is rendered by 'tz' in such familiar words as barmitzvah. Likewise, the distinction between *ḥet* and khaf has been retained, using *ḥ* for the former and *kh* for the latter; the associated forms are generally familiar to readers, even if the distinction is not actually borne out in pronunciation, and for the same reason the final *heh* is indicated too. As in Hebrew, no capital letters are used, except that an initial capital has been retained in transliterating titles of published works (for example, *Shulḥan arukh*).

Since no distinction is made between *alef* and *ayin*, they are indicated by an apostrophe only in intervocalic positions where a failure to do so could lead an English-speaking reader to pronounce the vowel-cluster as a diphthong—as, for example, in *ha'ir*—or otherwise mispronounce the word.

The sheva na is indicated by an *e*—*perikat ol, reshut*—except, again, when established convention dictates otherwise.

The *yod* is represented by *i* when it occurs as a vowel (*bereshit*), by *y* when it occurs as a consonant (*yesodot*), and by *yi* when it occurs as both (*yisra'el*).

Names have generally been left in their familiar forms, even when this is inconsistent with the overall system.

All translations in this book are my own unless noted otherwise.

Place Names

Because this book deals largely with Jewish literary sources written in eastern and central Europe before the Second World War, some of the place names used in the text reflect the Yiddish names used by Jews at that time. Thus we have Polonnoye, not Polonne, and Vilna, not Vilnius. Readers may find it useful to note the current names and locations of these places, and also the current locations of places whose names haven't changed.

Name as it appears in the book	Current name	Current location
Aleksandrow	Aleksandrów Łódzki	Poland
Amdur	Indura	Belarus
Apta	Opatów	Poland
Berdichev	Berdychiv	Ukraine
Brest-Litovsk	Brest	Belarus
Brody	Brody	Ukraine
Chernobyl	Chernobyl	Ukraine
Chmielnicki	Khmelnytskyi	Ukraine
Ger	Góra Kalwaria	Poland
Grodno	Hrodna	Belarus
Grodzhisk	Grodzisk Mazowiecki	Poland
Homel	Gomel	Belarus
Husiatyn	Husiatyn	Ukraine
Izbica	Izbica	Poland
Kopyczynce	Kopychyntsi	Ukraine
Korets	Korets	Ukraine
Kotsk	Kock	Poland
Kozienice	Kozienice	Poland
Kraków	Kraków	Poland
Kutow	Kuty	Ukraine
Lantset	Łańcut	Poland
Linits	Illintsi	Ukraine
Lizhensk	Leżajsk	Poland
Lyady	Lyady	Belarus
Myropil	Myropil	Ukraine
Mezhirech	Mezhirichi	Ukraine
Międzybóż	Medzhibozh	Ukraine
Mogielnica	Mogielnica	Poland

Name as it appears in the book	Current name	Current location
Monastyrishche	Monastyryshche	Ukraine
Noviye Mlini	Noviye Mlini	Ukraine
Ostropol	Ostropol	Ukraine
Piaseczno	Piaseczno	Poland
Pinsk	Pinsk	Belarus
Polonnoye	Polonne	Ukraine
Praga	Praga	Poland
Przysucha	Przysucha	Poland
Radomsk	Radomsko	Poland
Radoshitz	Radoszyce	Poland
Radzyn	Radzyń Podlaski	Poland
Ruzhin	Ruzhyn	Ukraine
Ryczywół	Ryczywół	Poland
Shinova	Sieniawa	Poland
Skalat	Skalat	Ukraine
Slutsk	Slutsk	Belarus
Sudilkov	Sudylkiv	Ukraine
Uman	Uman	Ukraine
Vilna	Vilnius	Lithuania
Żelechów	Żelechów	Poland
Zhitomir	Zhytomyr	Ukraine
Zinkov	Zinkiv	Ukraine
Zlochow	Zolochiv	Ukraine
Żółkiew	Zhovkva	Ukraine

Introduction

'He came to the place and rested there, because the sun had set. He took from the stones of that place and arranged them around his head, and lay down there. And he dreamt' [Gen. 28: 11]. 'The stones of that place'—they are the letters of the Torah, traces of holiness that reside hidden everywhere. For there are parts of the Torah that can be understood simply, but other parts need explanation ... In the effort, 'these stones which I have set up shall become a house of God' [Gen. 28: 22]—from the letters that he had placed again in order, he built a home. (*Sefat emet*, 'Vayetse' 5645)

Fugitive, far from home, as night falls the biblical Jacob draws together scattered stones. In gathering up those emblematic shards of meaning, recombining them into new forms of truth, his figure teaches a way of contending with confusion and estrangement in a dark world. This is R. Judah Leib Alter of Ger's reading of the Torah's familiar story. Originally delivered in a talk in Yiddish to a group of his followers one sabbath in the late autumn of 1884 in Góra Kalwaria, Poland, it is a reading meant for 'generations like ours', spiritually displaced, in exile.[1] The hasidic master clearly recognized that the task of translating the biblical text in the hope of making it speak in a meaningful way to readers in his own day required a variety of interpretative tools. Some of these are traditional exegetical moves; others are innovative and strikingly modern. As the talk unfolds, the master weaves together midrashic phrases and fragments of verses, subtle allusions, threads of kabbalistic symbols entwined with his own reflections. Slowly, the scattered stones are drawn together, their traces of holiness restored, refined. His words beckon, inviting us inside, into a refuge suffused with light. This is a retelling that enacts the message it seeks to convey.

---

[1] With these words the author refers to his own times, in the diaspora, after the destruction of the Temple: 'like our own generations, who have been exiled from our "House of Life"' (*Sefat emet*, 'Vayetse' 5645, 130).

Approach, Method, Aims

Hasidism, a movement of religious awakening, spiritual innovation, and social reform, originated in mid-eighteenth-century Ukraine. After two and a half centuries of crisis, upheaval, and renewal, it remains a vital presence. In the early 1770s hasidism came under attack: religious opponents (*mitnagedim*) saw it as a heretical sect threatening traditional rabbinic authority, while enlighteners denigrated it as a primitive and subversive cult. Hasidic masters nonetheless continued to draw a growing, enthusiastic body of adherents. They established thriving communities throughout eastern Europe and gradually produced a vast array of texts of varied literary expression. From its origins until today, hasidism has been observed, embraced, or calumniated as a cultural, social, historical, religious, and mystical phenomenon. By the mid-nineteenth century, as east European Jews struggled to become part of modern society, its nature and significance were fiercely debated. In Allan Nadler's words, these were the burning questions:

What is modern, enlightened Jewry to make of Hasidism? What is its authentic message, historical significance and current relevance? What, if any, are the merits of Hasidism when contrasted to the Rabbinic Judaism which it came to challenge, and to the enlightenment which it so forcefully resisted? And, most pertinently, was Hasidism a progressive force which helped pave the way for the liberation of the Jewish nation from the ghetto? Did Hasidism contribute theologically to the modernization of Judaism, or socially to the emancipation of the Jewish people? Or was it, quite the contrary, a regressive, superstitious, anti-rational, and thoroughly anti-modern movement which served only to reinforce the ghetto walls and to keep the Jews all the more isolated from the wider European society?[2]

Academic interest in hasidism began in the late nineteenth-century Wissenschaft des Judentums school. Its foundational tenet was historical positivism; its aim, to reach scientific, objective truths. Since then, the critical study of contemporary documents—polemical literature, archival records, journalism, belles-lettres, hasidic tales, and homiletics—has enabled scholars to reconstruct important aspects of Jewish life in eastern Europe. An impressive body of modern scholarship continues to advance our knowledge of hasidic intellectual and social history, thought, and theology.

Yet I must confess that these questions are not my questions, nor are these aims and methods ones that will further my own enquiry. I mention them here because the idea of this book took shape against the background of that

---

[2] Nadler, 'Rationalism, Romanticism, Rabbis and Rebbes', 1–2.

critical discourse. My original goal was to seek an understanding of hasidism 'from the inside', through its own literature and on its own terms. Hasidic teaching is formed and informed by creative interpretations of the Torah— that is, the sacred oral and written sources of Jewish tradition. Many hundreds of volumes of hasidic literature containing such teachings have been written and published over the past 250 years. Scholars have recognized them as a primary form of Jewish creativity, and have mined certain works for useful information in a wide range of fields. But few have explored their exegetical and literary dimensions or plumbed their experiential and spiritual depths.[3]

This book emerged from a different set of questions. I wanted to understand how this body of writing and commentary works, and to discover how it has remained such a compelling aspect of Jewish experience—for spiritual seekers, for hasidim of all times and places, and for academics of varied persuasions. Equally urgently, I wondered whether an attentive reading of hasidic teachings written over more than two centuries might truly enrich our understanding of hasidism—from its origins to its so-called late historical phase. How, through their creative interpretations of the Torah, did hasidic masters confront the challenges of their times? As they struggled with problems of faith and doubt, suffering and disaster, how did their readings of sacred texts help them make sense of the world, history, and their own lives?

The genre of hasidic interpretation of, or commentary on, the Torah is most commonly referred to in English as 'homiletical literature', and is composed of sermons or homilies usually based on the weekly scriptural reading. These English equivalents of the Hebrew word *derashah* are, however, neither accurate nor elegant, and have quite a few misleading connotations.[4] In Hebrew, *derashah* (plural *derashot*) stems from a richly allusive root, *d-r-sh*, meaning to seek, enquire, investigate, search out meaning—in this case,

[3] The term 'exegetical' and the related term 'hermeneutics' figure prominently in my discussion. Exegesis is the practice of searching out the deeper meanings of a text; in the case of Scripture, these meanings would be theological, ethical, mystical, and existential. Hermeneutics is a broader term; in a general sense, hermeneutics concerns the methods or principles used in the interpretative process. But as Jean Grondin notes, the notion of hermeneutics has evolved over time: 'Traditionally understood as the art of interpretation (*ars hermeneutica*) that provided rules for the interpretation of sacred texts, hermeneutics today serves to characterize a broad current in contemporary continental philosophy that deals with the issues of interpretation and stresses the historical and linguistic nature of our world-experience' ('Hermeneutics', 987.)

[4] I present these words with some unease, as they are borrowed from non-Jewish cultural contexts in which homiletics, sermons, exegesis, and commentary have connotations that do not fit the Jewish conceptual universe. The term *derashah* (like *derash* and *derush*) can also be used to describe the entire genre of homiletical teaching which, as Naftali Loewenthal points

meanings concealed in Scripture. This alerts us to something essential: the mode of reading that the hasidic masters developed in their *derashot* has much in common with rabbinic midrash. But there are deeper lines of kinship than the grammatical root that *midrash* and *derashah* share. With the Second Temple's destruction, amidst national devastation, exile, and untold suffering, the Rabbis engendered a method of interpretation to 'underwrite' the Torah's survival and authority and to ensure the continuity of Jewish identity. Scholars have highlighted the radical nature of rabbinic interpretation: the tension between continuity and rupture, allegiance to the text and alienation from it.[5] In midrash, the Rabbis struggled with the enigmas and gaps of Scripture and, equally, with the problem of God's silence, absence, or seeming indifference to human suffering. Hermeneutical engagement with the Torah was a way to catch sight of its secret, concealed intent, to glimpse the unfolding of revelation in history, to give meaning and direction to everyday life. In the attempt, the Rabbis seem to break apart syntax, defy immediate semantic meaning, and draw unlikely associations between far-flung elements—a reading practice that, on the face of it, would seem to prove 'either the naïveté or hermeneutic bad faith of the rabbis'.[6] Yet we know that these radical 'disruptions', as Daniel Boyarin puts it, were profoundly creative and regenerative, for in this way alone could the potentialities of the Torah be brought to light. The interpreter—rabbinic and hasidic, past and present—thus takes on a powerful role, making connections and discerning hints in the most minute details of Scripture.

Writing this book has taken me on an exciting, unanticipated intellectual journey. There were blocks and unsettling dead ends as well as certain illuminations along the way that changed my thinking and guided me as its chapters developed. As I wrote, the question of audience was a constant concern. I wanted to appeal to a broad readership but was also aware of the expectations and demands of academic readers. Bringing these two discourses together without losing my own voice has not been easy. And so I will not engage just yet with the extensive body of research on hasidism, its history, and its literatures. Further down I will present the relevant aspects of scholarship on hasidism, consider the dominant attitudes and methodological assumptions on which it is founded, and frame my discussion against that background. Before addressing all these concerns, though, I would first like to touch on

out, might be found in virtually any Jewish literary context, hasidic or not. See his 'Midrash in Habad Hasidism', 429.

[5] Rawidowicz, 'On Interpretation', 47–8. The notion of 'underwriting' as a metaphor is George Steiner's: see *Real Presences*, 41.   [6] Boyarin, 'Old Wine in New Bottles', 542–3.

certain ideas that have deeply informed my own approach. I will also describe the hasidic writings that are the subject of this book and explain how I will be reading them and to what ends.

Michael Fishbane's work on the 'vast Jewish cultural enterprise of interpretation' and the crucial interface between spirituality and hermeneutics was a formative influence on my thinking as this project took shape. Certain (biblical) texts, Fishbane suggests, 'presuppose a new sensibility in which Scripture has become the vehicle of new revelations, and exegesis the means of new access to the divine will. Thus, complementing the divine revelation now embodied in a written Torah, the sage seeks from God the grace of an *ongoing revelation* through the words of Scripture itself—as mediated *through exegesis*.'[7] He emphasizes the ethical and existential dimensions of understanding sacred texts, not only for interpreters in times past but also for readers here and now: 'the role of interpretation is neither aesthetic illumination nor aesthetic judgment, but rather the religious duty to expound and extend, and so to *reactualize* the ancient word of God for the present hour'.[8] Fishbane's own incisive readings of biblical, rabbinic, and kabbalistic sources are an inspiring model. His work has guided my efforts to re-envision hasidic commentary on the Torah and to find a voice and a mode of reading that could help unlock its mystery.

While I gathered and ordered my material a daunting problem, breathtaking in its simplicity, troubled me. What is it really that the hasidic masters are trying to interpret? True, their sermons are filled with words from sacred texts, which they read and transform in endlessly creative ways. Yet the meanings they convey, and the experiences that concern them, go far 'beyond the verse'; they come to bear on the most fundamental aspects of being. Here, Paul Ricoeur's work enabled me to think about hasidic teaching in a wider context. Ricoeur taught that human experience is inherently interpretative: throughout our lives, we engage in creative dialogue in our search for meaning. Hermeneutics, or the work of interpretation, for Ricoeur, 'is not confined to texts nor to authors of texts; its primary concern is with the worlds which these authors and texts open up. It is by an understanding of the worlds, actual and possible, opened up by language that we may arrive at a better understanding of ourselves.'[9] Many of Ricoeur's most influential insights have made their way into the pages of this book.

---

[7] *The Garments of Torah*, 67; Shonkoff, 'Michael Fishbane: An Intellectual Portrait', 23. In an interview with Hava Tirosh-Samuelson, Fishbane speaks of the 'vast Jewish cultural enterprise of interpretation': *Jewish Hermeneutical Theology*, 227.

[8] *The Garments of Torah*, 37–8. [9] *A Ricoeur Reader*, 490.

There is one more important encounter that I need to note. The social and intellectual history of hasidism, its dynasties, schools of thought, and organizational strategies have been analysed in a number of important large-scale studies. Historians of the late nineteenth century have charted a process of decline and 'ossification' in hasidic creativity, as religious leaders grew entrenched in battle against the aggressive modernizing influences of the outside world. Yet we know that a complex mix of powerful cultural forces was at work in those years, changing the face of traditional Jewry. How did these forces affect the way in which hasidic masters encountered reality? Were there hasidic thinkers who continued to engage in a constructive way, through their commentary on the Torah, with the challenges posed by modernity? Carlo Ginzburg's work caused a shift in my sensibilities. As a cultural historian, Ginzburg has focused on broader forms of dialogue—comprehending art history, literary criticism, philosophy, psychology, and other disciplines—which models an important alternative approach. His notion of microhistory, the unique social and cultural experience of individuals, offers a compelling way of seeing into the past. Both in attitude and in rhetorical tone, Ginzburg's studies shaped my attempt to reach a more nuanced understanding of hasidic creativity—above all in that emotionally charged period of modern Jewish history.

The Commentaries

This book spans some 200 years of hasidic commentary on the Torah. It begins with a foundational document written by the Ba'al Shem Tov in the late 1740s and ends with a sermon by R. Kalonymus Shapira, the Rebbe of Piaseczno, from 1943. My original plan was to cross the 'great divide' and continue to a discussion of hasidism in the post-Holocaust era. At some point, however, I realized that the complexity of those years, which witnessed seismic cultural and religious changes in the Jewish world, would demand many more pages than I have available. Hasidic commentary on the Torah from the decades after the Holocaust and up to our own times is an important topic well worth further study.

The *derashot* that I will discuss contain central elements of hasidic teaching and the ethos it embodies. I have selected each of them to illustrate some element of the genre as a whole, and the ways in which ideas are brought to the fore through the interpretation of Scripture. The authors of many of these expositions are celebrated figures, and their homiletical works are widely recognized as important collections of hasidic commentary. Some of the passages that I present have already received generous scholarly attention, but a good number of them have not, to the best of my knowledge, been discussed by academics. They appear in English translation here for the first time. Selecting the texts that would carry my discussion was a long and arduous process. I looked for passages with some sense of a personal voice and attitude —be it irony, humour, affection, tension, pain, uncertainty, or resolve. Moreover, the *derashot* I sought needed to address evident exegetical questions and to treat them in an accessible and translatable manner. The ones that I finally chose are jewels—each of them an exceptionally insightful reading, a moment of greatness and rare vision. These texts serve as touchstones; they enable us to explore innovative dimensions of hasidic teaching and its resources of historical tradition.

In Chapter 1, I will discuss some dimensions of self-understanding in the early generations of hasidism. What interests me here is how that collective self-image is expressed through the hasidic masters' choice of motifs and themes. There is a cogent subtext at work in their discourses as well: an understated, at times ironic, response to opponents of hasidism and a strong assertion of identity.

Chapter 2 explores the modes of relating to Scripture that the hasidic masters developed: their sense of metaphor and poetic language, the roles of imagination, cognition, and the self, and the dynamics of translation and interpretation. My discussion here unfolds on a thematic axis. It begins with a closer look at each of those elements. I then consider the ways in which they are manifested in the relationship between teacher and student—here, between the *rebbe* and his hasidim—and highlight how the hasidic masters created that interpersonal connection by rhetorical means. The *derashot* in this chapter represent a full century of hasidic creativity in a broad range of schools and trends. They speak of transformative learning and its experiential dimensions, of the notion of personal redemption, and of the power of hasidic teaching to engender a spiritual awakening.

In Chapter 3, I attend to facets of historical awareness in hasidic commentary on the Torah. After presenting certain foundational themes in hasidic teaching related to Torah study, innovation, revelation, and religious experience, I turn to some masters of the late nineteenth and twentieth centuries and consider the ways in which they address contemporary concerns such as modernity, secularization, the forces linking political revolution and divine providence, personal identity, trauma, and catastrophe. What did they teach about God's presence in a dark world, the meaning of the covenant, living as a Jew? How did they perceive their role, and the role of hasidic teaching, in the larger process leading to redemption—not by mystical, magical, or theurgic means, but through acts of 'reading otherwise'?

Rather than isolating themes, models, concepts, or doctrines, I will study continuous sections of discourse and offer close readings that take note of textual layers, exegetical questions, and rhetorical effects. This reading practice can help us see how meanings shift, merge, and resurface in new and compelling forms. Finally, to understand the resonances of the *derashot* more fully, I will try to distinguish facets of their social, cultural, and historical contexts.

Certain renowned hasidic masters do not appear in these pages. Some of them did not give discourses in the form I am considering, or we have no written records of them; in other cases, their teachings have already received a great deal of attention.[10] The amount of material is vast, and my discussion is not intended to be a comprehensive survey. Rather, it is a close examination of elements of hasidic commentary that have not been studied before, using examples that illuminate particular features and which are accessible to the general reader. There is much more to do here and many unexplored areas still remain. Finally, I have not attempted to present a taxonomy of hasidic groups, dynasties, or schools of thought, or to compare and contrast ideas or trace their historical influences. Rather, I have sought to present each *derashah* as a unique, insightful reading framed within its author's larger concerns and responsive to the needs of his time and place.

*

In this book I have tried to give name and form to a manifold sense of presence: the presence of an author—here, the hasidic masters who engendered these *derashot*; their summons to us as readers, if we are to understand anything, to make ourselves wholly present, attentive, and responsive to what their teachings are saying. God is there, too, in the details most of all. Implicitly, my approach also challenges what many scholars have argued: that the hasidic works we are reading are no more than the lifeless remnant of an original momentary revelation gone forever; that the *rebbe*s, their authors, are

---

[10] Two notably absent figures are R. Nahman of Bratslav and R. Tsadok Hakohen of Lublin. On the hermeneutical aspects of R. Nahman's teachings, see work by Shaul Magid, David Siff, and my *Tradition and Fantasy in the Tales of Reb Nahman of Bratslav*. On R. Tsadok's teachings see Brill, *Thinking God*, and Liwer, 'Oral Torah in the Writings of R. Zadok Hakohen of Lublin' (Heb.).

absent from the written word, and that the faces of their audience have been lost in time. George Steiner first touched on the sense of what he called 'real presence' in his own appreciation of literary, musical, and artistic 'master-texts' of our age.[11] The hasidic teachings that appear in this book are, I believe, indeed master-texts of their age and of ours. What matters, crucially, is the questions we ask and the understanding we hope to find.

One last thought. Susan Handelman remarks, 'In academia, we often forget a simple truth: that one needs to love texts in order to read them well, just as we need to love other people in order to understand them well'.[12] 'Love' is a dangerous word, I know. But at the risk of sounding clichéd or naive, what I'm getting at is the ethical relation that I believe we must have with the works that we study. As readers, we need to respect their integrity and attend, with utmost seriousness, to what their authors meant to say and do. Through our encounters with them—learning, translating, interpreting them and allowing them to change us—we grant these works an 'afterlife'. We enable them to live beyond their original enclosed historical moment, on into our own generation, and we mediate their passage to generations to come. In the pages of this book I have tried to enable these hasidic voices to be heard once again without getting in the way too much.

The Hasidic Background

In this section I will outline the historical context in which hasidic homiletical literature developed, introduce some of the terms and concepts that figure most prominently in my discussion, and set out the issues that have concerned scholars and influenced attitudes in academic discourse. I will not attempt to summarize the scholarly treatment of any of these very large topics here, nor will I review the vast bibliography of research on hasidism in general and on its place in Jewish history and tradition. Both of these are important and arduous tasks that many capable scholars have already masterfully undertaken.[13]

---

[11] Steiner, *Real Presences*, 264–5.

[12] *Make Yourself a Teacher*, 5, 10–11. In her own engagement with rabbinic tales, Handelman (p. 14) evokes Walter Benjamin's idea of life and afterlife in works of art; see Benjamin, 'The Task of the Translator', 71.

[13] As this book went to press, *Hasidism: A New History*, ed. David Biale et al., was published. This comprehensive study reviews scholarship in the field and sheds light on many of the historical topics raised in my discussion.

The Birth of a Movement

Among devotees, R. Israel ben Eliezer (the Ba'al Shem Tov; 1700–60) has always been known as the founder of hasidism. From its origins, the movement was associated with 'spiritual awakening, mystical inspiration, and charismatic authority. These led in turn to new forms of leadership, spiritual autonomy, and a highly articulated body of literature presenting mystical conceptions, spiritual intentions, and social goals—a great wealth of original intellectual ideas and spiritual creativity.'[14] Historians in the early twentieth century, influenced by the modernizing and Marxist tendencies of their day, constructed the image of the Ba'al Shem Tov as a popular and radical reformer who rallied the ignorant, oppressed masses to revolt against the rabbinic elite. In the 1960s scholars started to question the Ba'al Shem Tov's identity and historical role. Examining the social texture in which hasidism evolved, Gershom Scholem, Ben-Zion Dinur, Abraham Joshua Heschel, and Joseph Weiss demonstrated the existence in the early eighteenth century of 'circles of pneumatics' made up of social equals—hasidic thinkers who belonged one and all to the rabbinic elite. Though contemporaneous with the Ba'al Shem Tov, these circles functioned independently or semi-autonomously, in clear nonconformity with the schematic 'master–disciple' hierarchy. Moreover, scholars have found that some members of these circles were individuals who continued to perpetuate the practices and values of old-style mystical and ascetic hasidism; others adopted the modified new-style, so-called Beshtian, hasidic practice.[15] Opposition to new-style hasidism erupted in the 1770s. Gestures of self-definition were made throughout the following decades; 'the process of differentiation of Hasidism from hasidism', as Moshe Rosman puts it,[16] was long and difficult—not only for academics but for the players themselves. Some more details from that vital first chapter in the history of hasidism now require our attention.

Critics

In 1772 leaders of the Vilna community, the bastion of traditional Lithuanian

[14] Elior, *The Mystical Origins of Hasidism*, 206.

[15] Reviewing early scholarship on this topic (e.g. Joseph Weiss and Ben-Zion Dinur), Ada Rapoport-Albert concludes: 'Finally and most convincingly, A. J. Heschel provided abundant evidence to show that several of the Besht's early associates, who had been considered by later Hasidic biographers and historians as his devoted pupils, were, in fact, independent Hasidim who, in some cases, commanded their own following and regarded the Besht as their equal, if not, indeed, as his rival or as inferior to themselves' ('God and the Zaddik', 310).

[16] *Founder of Hasidism*, 39.

Torah study, opened an aggressive attack on hasidism with an act of excommunication. In the following months the elders of Brody, Pinsk, Grodno, Slutsk, and Brest-Litovsk followed suit. Over the next forty years, opponents of hasidism (*mitnagedim*) strove to eradicate what they saw as a dangerous, heretical sect through economic and social sanctions, public debates, and written diatribes. Hasidic books were burnt, hasidic leaders were publicly chastised, and some were expelled from their rabbinic position. Polemical writings from this stormy period document the major points of contention against the hasidim: their move to separate from established prayer houses and found private hasidic quorums; changes in the liturgy and set times of prayer; changes in the methods of prayer; changes in ritual slaughter, such as the use of honed knives; neglect of Torah study and disrespect for Torah scholars; bizarre actions; suspected Shabateanism; and merrymaking, greediness, and miracle-working by *tsadikim*.[17] Justifiably, academic treatment of the historical conflict between hasidim and *mitnagedim* has concentrated primarily on these declared issues, which were evident mainly in the social and ritual domains. The ideational content of hasidism, by contrast, has received a great deal less attention. Few scholars have investigated the role that the particulars of hasidic teaching—its theological, ethical, and exegetical aspects—may have played in the conflict.

This is rather surprising. Mordecai Wilensky, a leading scholar of the polemical literature, observes that the appearance in print of hasidic homilies was, in fact, an important catalyst in arousing alarm among the *mitnagedim*. As a case in point he notes that a second wave of this intense conflict was caused in 1781 by the publication of the first book of hasidic teachings, *Toledot ya'akov yosef* by R. Jacob Joseph of Polonnoye. Indeed, as Yeshayahu Shahar asserts, the express objective of this seminal hasidic work, published during its author's lifetime, was to contest the influence of the *mitnagedim* and win recognition for hasidism by citing hundreds of teachings in the name of the Ba'al Shem Tov.[18] Fifteen years later, the vital formulation of hasidic thought in the *Tanya* by R. Shneur Zalman of Lyady, then the most prominent hasidic leader in eastern Europe, combined with the rapidly spreading popularity of hasidism, ignited a third phase of hostility.[19] Beyond social, economic, and

[17] Wilensky, 'Hasidic–Mitnaggedic Polemics', 247. See also Polonsky, *The Jews in Poland and Russia*, ii. 288 ff.; Nadler, *The Faith of the Mithnagedim*, 11–28, 151–70.

[18] *Criticism of Society and Leadership* (Heb.), 62.

[19] Wilensky (*Hasidim and Mitnagedim* (Heb.), i. 188–9 n. 22) posits that 'heretical' passages from the *Tanya* had come to the Vilna Gaon's attention some years earlier, as they had already

halakhic concerns, then, it seems that the spiritual awakening and religious path that hasidism taught—in the written word as well as through the behaviour of its adherents—was indeed perceived by its opponents as threatening.

Nonetheless, until the late 1790s the polemical writings of the *mitnagedim* did focus almost exclusively on hasidic behaviour and practices, and raised hardly any theological concerns. But in the key passage of a letter written by R. Elijah ben Solomon Zalman, the Vilna Gaon, in the autumn of 1796, Gershon Hundert notes that the Gaon names the 'heresy' of the hasidim as their disparagement of Lithuanian-style Torah scholars, their bizarre behaviour during prayer, and—most significantly for our purposes—'their perversions of the meaning of mystical texts'. Hundert's discussion brings him to a far-reaching conclusion: 'Hasidism ultimately involved the masses, but it had no agenda of political or social revolution, or even dramatic reform of any kind. It taught a particular way to worship God, and it was on that level that the Vilna Ga'on responded to it with such ferocity.'[20] It seems, then, that by the end of the eighteenth century both *mitnagedim* and hasidim had come to recognize homiletical activity, in both printed and oral form, as an influential medium for communicating the ethos called hasidism.

The death of the Vilna Gaon in 1798 brought on a sharp escalation of the conflict, and drew fresh attention to hasidic homiletical works. Among other measures, opponents issued a series of polemical missives calling on community leaders to renew and intensify the battle against hasidism. R. David of Makov, a long-standing antagonist of deviant, heretical sects and one of the most prolific and virulent of the *mitnagedim*, scoured the nine hasidic works that had been published up to his own day in search of 'heretical' teachings. He presented their contents in two diatribes. Using partial and distorted citations, R. David showered hasidic teaching with ridicule, cast aspersions on its authors, declared holy war on its followers, and entreated his readers to ban the printing of hasidic books and obliterate those volumes already published.[21]

How did the hasidim respond publicly to all this? Wilensky cites 'a paucity of written reaction' overall. Documents in the polemical literature of the entire period include a few letters that R. Shneur Zalman of Lyady, the

appeared in an epistle written before 1788 by R. Menahem Mendel of Vitebsk and widely circulated among his followers. On the connection between the appearance of *Toledot ya'akov yosef* and the second wave of conflict see Wilensky, *Hasidim and Mitnagedim* (Heb.), ii. 30 and n. 61.

[20] *Jews in Poland-Lithuania*, 204, 209. Cf. Wilensky, *Hasidim and Mitnagedim* (Heb.), i. 187–8, ii. 144.   [21] Wilensky, *Hasidim and Mitnagedim* (Heb.), ii. 49, 144 ff.

primary hasidic spokesman, wrote during the conflict. Some were addressed to his adversaries; others, dating mostly from the early stages of the controversy, were directed at his followers. More hasidic leaders made similar restrained gestures of defence—among them, R. Samuel Shmelke Horowitz, R. Elimelekh of Lizhensk, R. Menahem Mendel of Vitebsk, and R. Israel, the Magid of Kozienice. But it was during his second internment in a St Petersburg prison in 1800 that R. Shneur Zalman was compelled to present a far more direct and thorough account of hasidism. His answers, recorded in Russian translation, to a long list of accusations submitted to the court by the *mitnagedim* who had initiated his arrest, offer a rare apologetics for hasidic social ideology and moral values, this time meant for non-Jewish ears.[22]

The conflict between hasidism and its mitnagedic opponents began to fade in the 1840s as both groups confronted the growing threat of secularization and religious reform.[23] Raphael Mahler, a pioneering scholar of that period, puts it bluntly: 'the very rise of the Haskalah served as evidence that Hasidism had become outmoded. Rather than a progressive force, it became a stumbling block on the road of development.'[24] Marcin Wodziński, in his discussion of the Haskalah in the Kingdom of Poland, offers a more nuanced picture of attitudes towards hasidism in the 1850s and 1860s, ranging from the modernizing camp of traditional *maskilim* (a minority) to radical assimilationists, and a moderate group that favoured Polish acculturation but wished to preserve the status of Judaism and religious traditions. In the eyes of the assimilationists, many of whom had cut their own ties with Judaism, hasidism was 'medieval fanaticism'. The *maskilim* were ambivalent, while the integrationists tended to see the hasidim as their main ideological rival and the central obstacle to the modernization of the Jewish people.[25] The Russian Jewish intelligentsia similarly denigrated the hasidim as the fundamental cause of Jewish backwardness and illiteracy. According to Yohanan Petrovsky-Shtern, 'Due to many a denunciation of Hasidism in the Russian maskilic press, at the turn of the twentieth century such notions as *tsadik* (spiritual leader) came to signify the worst features of the communities in the Pale of Settlement—their scorn of secular knowledge, their medieval superstitions, and their resistance to integration in Russian culture.'[26] Serious intellectual interest in hasidism,

---

[22] Ibid. ii. 271–95. See also Etkes, *Ba'al Hatanya* (Heb.), 257–70, 297–306.
[23] Polonsky, *The Jews in Poland and Russia*, ii. 306.
[24] *Hasidism and the Jewish Enlightenment*, p. xv.
[25] Wodziński, *Haskalah and Hasidism in the Kingdom of Poland*, 154–79.
[26] '"We Are Too Late": An-sky and the Paradigm of No-Return', 94–5.

its history, and its doctrines also began to awaken in the last decades of the nineteenth century, albeit with a marked ideological agenda. By the turn of the century, folklorists and ethnographers were discovering hasidism as an avatar of genuine Jewish folk culture; writers and artists explored the hasidic legacy as a source of neo-Romantic inspiration.

In sum, from its inception hasidism and the people who embodied it—in caricatured, satirized, or nostalgic forms—were richly represented in polemics, journalism, historical studies, literature, and drama. All in all, we have a valuable and variegated body of historical sources portraying the movement from the outside. To complement that perspective, scholars have also sought to describe hasidism as presented in its own literature. Let me now turn to that literature to consider its nature, its social role, and the ways in which it has been discussed.

Hasidic Literature

From its earliest days, hasidic literary activity took a number of forms. Most familiar, of course, are hasidic stories; other genres are conduct literature (*hanhagot*), letters (*igerot*), and homiletics.[27] Since the rediscovery and re-invention of hasidic tales adapted to the spirit of the times, most famously by Michael Levi (Frumkin) Rodkinson in the late nineteenth century and by Martin Buber in the early twentieth century, hasidic narrative tradition has offered a treasure-house of inspiration, appealing to a wide Jewish as well as general audience. These tales have greatly enriched our understanding of hasidic values, concepts, and experience.[28]

Hasidic homiletical works—abstruse and uninviting, obscure in content and awkward in style—came to scholarly attention somewhat later. Gershom Scholem's famed dispute with Buber, which began in the early 1960s, first brought them to centre stage in the intellectual study of hasidism. Scholem recognized the importance of mysticism in understanding the history of Jewish thought and held that hasidic teaching represented its latest, if terminal, phase. He vehemently opposed Buber's neo-Romanticism and his

---

[27] The conduct literature (books of moral instruction) and hasidic epistles are valuable resources for historians. They contain information about hasidic practices and ritual and ethical guidelines, disclose organizational tactics, and at times set out the theoretical basis of those elements in hasidic doctrine. See Gries, *The Book in the Jewish World 1700–1900*; id., 'Hasidism: The Present State of Research'; Barnai (ed.), *Hasidic Letters from the Land of Israel* (Heb.); Karlinsky, *Counter-History: The Hasidic Epistles from the Land of Israel* (Heb.).

[28] See Meir, *Literary Hasidism*. On Buber's hasidic anthologies see Urban, *Aesthetics of Renewal*.

existentialist remoulding of hasidic tales. Scholem introduced a historical-critical attitude to hasidic texts and applied a strict philological method to analysing them. His own approach to hasidism was informed by his affinity with historiography, mysticism, and Jewish messianism.[29]

The next generations of scholars broadened the field with new interest in mapping the social history of hasidism and identifying the innovative aspects of its doctrine and spiritual practices. Hasidic writings—polemical responses to *mitnagedim*, hagiography, epistolary materials, and homiletical works—provide a wealth of relevant information. The results have been impressive. To explain the rapid dissemination of hasidism and its effect on the course of Jewish history, scholars have analysed the strategies of social reorganization, 'propaganda techniques', and folkloristic elements of hasidic teaching that furthered that end. New leadership models and sources of authority, founded on core concepts such as the *tsadik* as symbol and social reality, were instrumental. Transcendent ideas and techniques such as ego-annulment, 'cleaving', ecstasy, divine worship through corporeality, and the transformation of evil to good have also been investigated. Scholars have compared hasidic works to homiletical literature from earlier historical periods to examine the changing roles of kabbalah and messianism in Jewish society. This vast body of scholarship and the diversity of approaches have greatly advanced our knowledge concerning hasidic intellectual and social history, thought, and theology.[30]

Homiletical Activity: Preachers as Agents of Culture

For a fuller understanding of hasidic homiletical literature we need to take a closer look at the traditional genre from which it evolved. Homiletical activity has been a vital part of Jewish life since rabbinic times. Homiletical literature was widely published in the early modern Jewish world, second only to halakhic literature.[31] In eastern Europe in the decades that preceded hasidism,

---

[29] For a recent review of scholarship on the Buber–Scholem controversy and for a critical evaluation of later approaches, see Idel, 'East European Hasidism'.

[30] Important surveys of scholarship and research trends in these areas include: Dynner and Wodziński, 'The Kingdom of Poland and her Jews'; Rapoport-Albert, 'Hasidism after 1772'; Hundert, *Jews in Poland-Lithuania*, ch. 6; Stampfer, 'How and Why Did Hasidism Spread?'

[31] On homiletical literature written throughout Jewish history, see work by Marc Saperstein, Joseph Dan, and Yaakov Elbaum, with references in their studies to earlier scholarship. The title *magid mesharim* ('a preacher of uprightness') probably dates from the sixteenth century. The *magid* often took the role of admonisher (*musar magid* or *mokhiaḥ*). They were widely disliked for their scathing moralizing. Joseph Weiss contended that the sermons delivered by

the preacher—as *magid* or chastiser (*mokhiaḥ*), or his more scholarly and refined variation, the *darshan*—had a primary social role. Some of these fig- ures were itinerant mendicants; they were at times also faith healers or peddlers who lived a life of homeless wandering. Other preachers were stable functionaries or local rabbis. They were variously venerated, tolerated, and resented by the communities that knew them. Some were skilled speakers, perhaps even blessed with a charismatic presence. In less fortunate instances their ineptitude, ignorance, or righteous fury won them more misery than fame. Fulfilling the role of preacher in traditional Jewish society meant taking on the task of addressing the local community whenever occasion required, especially on the sabbath and holidays, and imparting what was supposed to be essential moral, spiritual, and practical religious instruction. Their ser- mons, delivered in the vernacular Yiddish, were customarily directed at a broad audience and sought to combine inventive commentary on the weekly Torah portion or the season of the Jewish religious calendar with issues of current interest, while infusing their message with their own personal con- victions. Preachers in all historical periods and places have served as agents of culture. Wherever and whenever they lived, their sermons, delivered orally, were a vehicle to disseminate ideology. In premodern eastern Europe, they were heralds of popular kabbalah, Shabateanism, and Frankism. It was preachers who brought the tidings of hasidic renewal and preachers who roused hearts to oppose hasidism. It was the preacher who urged his listeners to combine Torah wisdom with worldly knowledge in the early years before the Haskalah in eastern Europe. Most preachers left no written records of their sermons. Those records we have of them are partial, often marked by deliberate self-censorship; their style reflects and imitates traditional homi- letical forms.

From Oral Performance to Written Text

Many hasidic figures in the first generations filled the social role of preacher. We know this from hagiographical sources, from comments in their sermons, and, in some cases, from their appellations: the Mokhiah of Polonnoye, the great Magid of Mezhirech, the Magid of Kozienice, and others. Their activity as preachers was an important aspect of the new image of community leader

---

magidim were generally lacking in literary merit and thus no written records of them were pre- served: 'The Beginning of the Emergence of the Hasidic Path' (Heb.). See also Dan, *Hebrew Ethical and Homiletical Literature* (Heb.), 26–7; Piekarz, *The Beginning of Hasidism* (Heb.), 124, 163–70; Saperstein, *Jewish Preaching*, 44–63.

that gradually took shape in hasidism. The *tsadik* came to embody someone who was not only an inspired speaker with rare access to mystical realms, but also a spiritual and ethical mentor, perceptive teacher, and influential religious authority. The sermons, teachings, and insights these hasidic masters imparted to those who came to hear them—whether a close circle of learned disciples or a general popular audience—belong to the ephemeral, intangible phenomenon of oral culture. We can only speculate about the actual content of their words and try to imagine the lived experience that may have surrounded the event now lost in time, that dynamic meeting between speaker and listeners.

The written records of these oral discourses present scholars with a plethora of difficulties. They were transcribed from Yiddish to Hebrew, often by disciples rather than by the master himself, and put in written form sometime after they were delivered, by perhaps less than gifted writers. Such partial reconstructions, often laced with the scribe's own interpretations, were often not redacted until many years later. Then, editors sometimes compiled the notes of more than one disciple together with other, parallel oral or written sources in preparing a volume for publication. Further problems that complicated the transmission of hasidic teaching from oral to written form included the use of corrupt manuscripts, scribal miscopying, the false attribution of teachings to various authors, and the general purported indifference on the part of the editors to the authenticity of the final product.[32] Printed versions of such dubious making, while they might contain something of the master's original teachings, are clearly not objective, factual reproductions of the spoken word.

Scholars have foregrounded a second, related problem, which stems from the attitudes that some hasidic masters themselves had towards the transcription of their teachings. The figure of the Ba'al Shem Tov, of course, is the critical case in point. As we know, 'the Besht did not leave behind doctrinal writings of his own, and our knowledge of his ideas is drawn almost entirely from the works of his students'.[33] Many scholars ground this fact in an ideological principle: the Ba'al Shem Tov 'insisted that his message was only to be delivered orally, never written down'—as the famous tale about the demon caught red-handed with his notes of them seems to testify so convincingly.[34]

---

[32] Gries, *The Book in Early Hasidism* (Heb.); id., 'The Hasidic Managing Editor as an Agent of Culture'; Reiser and Mayse, 'The Last Sermon of R. Judah Leib Alter' (Heb.); Mayse and Reiser, '*Sefer Sefat Emet*'.   [33] Etkes, *The Besht*, 3.

[34] The tale of the Ba'al Shem Tov's exchange with the demon appears in *Shivḥei habesht* (ed.

Yet Mendel Piekarz offers a more prosaic explanation. Many of the Ba'al Shem Tov's contemporaries—hasidic and non-hasidic, preachers, charismatic leaders, and spiritual luminaries—left no writings either. Their contribution to the 'spirit of the times' is nonetheless inarguable. The books we have, moreover, represent only a small part of what was written. Many manuscripts of sermons were never published, and works that did appear in print were lost or destroyed over time.[35]

Nonetheless orality remains a dominant issue in academic discourse on hasidism. Oral traditions, Zeev Gries argues, 'must have played a more direct, immediate and significant part in determining the nature of the hasidic experience than did any of its written texts'. The hasidic master whose words had been transcribed for eventual publication 'rarely scrutinized, edited, or even approved' the text out of lack of interest, age, frailty, or inability. 'It is unusual for a hasidic rebbe to be involved in writing; most were concerned only with oral delivery, and were often uninterested in publishing their sermons.'[36] The implications, Arthur Green holds, were far-reaching: 'These teachings, spoken around the table, were always offered in a particular context, frequently directed either at an event that had occurred or at the need of a particular hearer. All that was lost once they were written down, translated from oral Yiddish into Hebrew, and published in books. . . . Alas, all we have left of those teachers are their books!'[37]

Regarding more esoteric aspects of the hasidic masters' discourses, Moshe Idel contends that their 'oral activity performed while in a state of union with the divine assumed the aura of a divine revelation'. The words spoken would then belong, fundamentally, to the moment of ineffable experience and only those present could be party to their mystery. As a result, Idel concludes, 'hasidic communities depend not on the written text but on the charisma that compels attention'.[38] All this would suggest that the vast library of hasidic homiletical literature is a shadowy source of knowledge at best—approximate, subjective, perhaps even distorted and unwanted remnants of the master's unique oral performance.

I'd like to look at things from a different perspective. While certain im-

Rubinstein, 230); for an English translation see Ben Amos and Mintz, *In Praise of the Baal Shem Tov*, 170. It figures in nearly every scholarly discussion on orality and hasidic teaching.

[35] Piekarz, *The Beginning of Hasidism* (Heb.), 11–15.

[36] Gries, 'The Hasidic Managing Editor as an Agent of Culture', 142, 154–5; *The Book in Early Hasidism* (Heb.), 28–9, 55, 87; 'Between History and Literature', 115; 'Hasidism: The Present State of Research', 180–1; Siff, 'Shifting Ideologies of Orality and Literacy', 243.

[37] Green, *Speaking Torah*, pp. xv–xvi.   [38] *Absorbing Perfections*, 471, 477.

portant collections of hasidic *derashot* do conform with the models described above, a great many others do not. From the earliest days of hasidism there were prominent masters who delivered their talks orally in Yiddish and wrote them down afterwards in Hebrew. Other masters were aided by their disciples and personal scribes, whose transcriptions they reviewed and edited before publication.[39] These works also need to be included and seriously studied for a more thorough understanding of hasidic literature. We will be reading sections from many of them in the chapters of this book. On a deeper level, I will consider the notion of orality and writing in hasidism in light of the duality of Oral and Written Torah in the rabbinic sense, with an eye to the dynamics of direct, immediate encounter between teacher and student, or between the *rebbe* and his hasidim.

Beyond questions of historical veracity, scholars have been dubious about how much essential literary value and emotional power could still reside in published versions of hasidic discourses. Much, it is argued, has been lost in transmission and translation. 'Only with an experience of the presence of the rebbe, through personal attendance at his discourse, can one fully appreciate the oral word of revelation . . . a unique quality of the written word is the absence of the author.'[40] Disconnected from the charged, dramatic atmosphere of the encounter between master and adherents, the written words, on this view, are pale and lifeless. The printed page, linguistically alienated and depersonalized, cannot speak intimately to anyone in all their uniqueness and so, it is argued, 'in the Hebrew texts of hasidic homiletics the faces of the listeners were lost' as well.[41] As a result, Zeev Gries contends, 'hasidic literature, whether in manuscript versions or in print, never became an indispensable part of the hasidic experience'.[42]

Finally, scholars have critiqued hasidic homiletics by questioning its intrinsic hermeneutical value. Louis Jacobs, for one, was highly sceptical: 'Hasidic Torah can hardly be described as exegesis. The texts are taken

---

[39] Ariel Evan Mayse surveys some 'notable exceptions in which early Hasidic masters wrote their own books', and offers a comprehensive review of the large body of scholarship on questions of orality and textuality in the study of hasidism. *Beyond the Letters*, 41–7. Habad hasidism is surely a notable exception of that order. On the 'communication ethos' and the importance of the printed word, see Loewenthal, *Communicating the Infinite*, 43–54, 145–7.

[40] Siff, *Messianism, Revelation, and the Book*, 245. Siff's objective, however, in proposing that generalized picture is to contrast it to the very different understanding of orality and written texts that he detects in R. Nahman of Bratslav's teachings.

[41] Idel, *Absorbing Perfections*, 480.

[42] 'The Hasidic Managing Editor as an Agent of Culture', 155.

completely out of context to yield the desired conclusions; ideas are read into the texts that by no stretch of the imagination can they possibly mean; grammar and syntax are completely ignored, there is not the slightest indication of any awareness of the historical background.'[43] Norman Lamm saw the tendency of hasidic writers to 'interlace their ideological statements with "words of Torah"' as no more than a largely extraneous detail. He proposed to guide his reader quickly through such 'homiletic exercises' in order to clarify what he held to be the essential message—that is, large topics and themes that would have greater intellectual, theological, or historical bearing than the merely exegetical dimension.[44] A somewhat more inclusive approach, voiced by Arthur Green, recognizes that 'hasidic homilies are highly dependent upon exegesis of Scriptural text and are interwoven with seemingly endless quotations from Talmudic and later literature'. Yet this exegetical activity is rather meagre and limited: 'Bits of exegesis quoted in RaSHI's universally known commentary to the Torah, aggadic statements collected in certain well-worn pages of the Babylonian Talmud, and the basic Midrashic collections (Rabbah and Tanhuma) on the Torah cycle would supply the seeker with by far the larger part of them.' Most of the hasidic masters contented themselves with these sources, Green posits, 'perhaps not only out of their own limitations but out of those of their anticipated hearers. Since most of the homilies were intended, first orally and then in writing, to have a broad-based popular appeal . . . it was best to remain close to the RaSHI passages that much of the audience was sure to remember from study in childhood.'[45]

Others have examined hasidic engagement with scripture through a broader disciplinary lens. Moshe Idel's groundbreaking studies on hermeneutical topics focus on the theory of texts found in certain kabbalistic and hasidic writings, and explore their mystical, magical, and ecstatic aspects. Idel confirms that the huge corpus of hasidic literature is indeed 'paramountly exegetical'.[46] But the hasidic masters, in his view, were not primarily interested in the original semantic content of the classic canonical texts; what attracted them above all was their non-sematic or 'parasemantic' aspects—the 'unknown

---

[43] *Their Heads in Heaven: Unfamiliar Aspects of Hasidim*, 27.

[44] Lamm, *The Religious Thought of Hasidism*, pp. xxx–xxxi. Like Jacobs, Lamm (183 n. 29) held that hasidic commentary has little or nothing to do with the plain meaning of the text. 'Instead, the intent of the verse is universalized and spiritualized by ingenious if often farfetched plays on words.'

[45] *Upright Practices*, 3, 8. Green notes some exceptions to the rule on these points, including the *derashot* of R. Jacob Joseph of Polonnoye, R. Nahman of Bratslav, and of the Habad school.

[46] *Hasidism: New Perspectives*, 19.

ciphers that organize the texts, whose efficacy is a matter of belief'.[47] In the hermeneutics of esoteric reading that Idel recognizes as a central, elitist feature of hasidism, 'the semantic aspects of the text are reduced in favor of a mystical event: cleaving to the divinity found within the sounds related to the liturgical or biblical texts on the one hand, and overlaid by the magical aspects involved in the fact that a supernal power is imagined to be inherent within, or attracted by the hasidic masters, within the pronounced letters'.[48] From this perspective, as Naftali Loewenthal eloquently puts it, Torah study is 'a gateway to mystical radiance, beyond homiletics and meaning as conventionally understood'.[49]

These and other seminal studies have fruitfully explored the interface between hasidism and kabbalah, and have defined elements of continuity and innovation in terms of mystical, theosophical, and theurgic activities performed by the *tsadik* in his enthusiastic recitation of text.[50] While questions of hermeneutics have been central to these discussions, scholars most often focus on more abstract, phenomenological elements. The passages that they select from hasidic commentary on the Torah are those that best demonstrate 'an extreme spiritualization of the biblical text'.[51]

Towards a Reappraisal of Hasidic Commentary

Some years ago Joseph Dan noted with irony that most of those who have dealt with Jewish homiletical literature have exploited it as a means to other ends—as a source of information that can shed light on historical, social, economic, and ideological aspects of Jewish life and thought.[52] These and other research trends have continued to evolve in recent decades. Scholars have focused on the anthropological, psychological, and existential dimensions of hasidic life. A number of studies seek to reconstruct or reimagine the hasidic masters' mystical experiences and examine the theurgic effects or magical powers that were attributed to their teachings. Other studies exploit hasidic sermons to analyse the realpolitik tactics that were used to 'preach the hasidic gospel', neutralize opponents, and further the hasidic conquest of Jewish society.[53]

---

[47] 'White Letters', 170.   [48] 'Hermeneutics in Hasidism', 9.

[49] 'Finding the Radiance in the Text', 299. See also work by Rachel Elior.

[50] Idel, *Hasidism: Between Ecstasy and Magic*, 173.

[51] Green, *Upright Practices*, 7–8.   [52] 'Some Notes on Homiletic Literature' (Heb.), 146.

[53] To 'preach the hasidic gospel' is Petrovsky-Shtern's phrase; see '*Hasidei de'ar'a* and *Hasidei dekokhvaya*', 154. The notion of 'conquest' refers to Dynner's outlook; see *Men of Silk* and 'The Hasidic Conquest of Small-Town Central Poland'.

   This book could not have been written without the vast, rich, and varied body of scholarship that I have reviewed here. I am proposing a different conversation. To define that difference, we might recall a distinction made by the philosopher Hans-Georg Gadamer. In his critique of historical method, Gadamer reflects on what he sees as a deeper problem. Historical consciousness, he notes, is a synthetic, dispassionate, confident enquiry into structures and concepts. And so, 'for the historian it is a basic principle that tradition is to be interpreted in a sense different than the texts, of themselves, call for. . . . It is fundamentally impossible for him to regard himself as the addressee of the text and accept its claim on him. Rather, he examines the text to find something it is not, of itself, attempting to provide.'[54] Gadamer proposes an alternative 'reading consciousness', one that requires us to relinquish the desire for control over the sources that we study. Here, understanding 'does not mean primarily to reason one's way back into the past, but to have a present involvement in what is said. It is . . . about sharing in what the text shares with us.'[55] I believe that hasidic teaching, if we are to understand it fully, requires the same sort of ethical relation that emerges from a sense of answerability and responsiveness.

   The process of writing this book has led me to a number of complementary fields of enquiry. Literary criticism and aesthetics, philosophy and hermeneutics open up important new perspectives, and suggest more nuanced avenues for scholarship on hasidism. The insights and attitudes of thinkers such as Mikhail Bakhtin, Umberto Eco, Hans-Georg Gadamer, Frank Kermode, Emmanuel Levinas, Paul Ricoeur, and George Steiner have been guiding forces as my readings took shape. Michael Fishbane's strong argument that we need to be attentive to 'the personal pathos and spiritual concerns of the text' has accompanied me throughout.[56] My discussion joins a broader cultural dialogue that is taking place in our times. Hasidic teaching and its interpretative dynamics enjoy more attention than ever before, from spiritual seekers and academics, Jewish and non-Jewish. Important work by James Diamond, Sara Friedland Ben-Arza, Arthur Green, Elie Holtzer, Netanel Lederberg, Naftali Loewenthal, Shaul Magid, Ariel Evan Mayse, Nehemia Polen, Don Seeman, Avivah Gottlieb Zornberg, and others continues to enrich the field. I hope this book will open hasidic teaching to a broader horizon of enquiry and encourage new ways of thinking about hasidic thought and creativity.

----

[54] *Truth and Method*, 331–2.   [55] Ibid. 393.
[56] Shonkoff, 'Michael Fishbane: An Intellectual Portrait', 11 n. 24.

ONE

Dimensions of Collective Self-Understanding

Beginnings: R. Israel Ba'al Shem Tov, The 'Holy Epistle'

On Rosh Hashanah of the year 5507 [1746] I took an oath for a soul ascent . . . And in a vision I saw wondrous things, more wondrous than anything I have envisioned all my days on this earth. What I saw and what I learned on that ascent—it is impossible to recount or even express in words. . . . Trembling gripped me. Nearly delivering my soul, I asked my mentor and teacher to accompany me,[1] for ascending to the upper worlds is exceedingly dangerous; never before in my life had I made such a great ascent. I went higher and higher until I reached the chamber of the Messiah. There, the Messiah learns Torah with all the sages and the righteous ones. The happiness there was tremendous, far beyond my understanding. I wondered if, God forbid, it was over my departure from this world. But then I learned that I had not yet died, only that they rejoice on high when I perform unifications here below through their holy teachings. . . . And I enquired of the Messiah himself: 'When will you come, master?' He answered me, 'By this shall you know: when your teaching will become famed and revealed throughout the world, and when your wellsprings will flow forth—all that I have taught you and all that you have attained, that others too may perform uni-fications and soul ascents as you do. Then all the evil husks will be annulled, and it will be a time of favour and salvation.'

Hearing all this, I was greatly dismayed and filled with terrible sorrow that it would take so very long to come about. But then, reflecting on what I had learned there . . . things that can be easily taught and explained, I regained my calm at the thought that others like me will be able to attain what I have as well. But permission was not granted me to reveal this to the end of my life.

Israel Ba'al Shem Tov, of the holy community of Międzybóż

[1] In hasidic tradition the Ba'al Shem Tov's 'mentor and teacher' was the biblical prophet Ahijah of Shilo (1 Kgs 11–12). See *Toledot ya'akov yosef*, 'Balak', 156. Maimonides, in his introduc-tion to *Mishneh torah*, lists Ahijah as a key link in the historical chain of transmission of the written and oral Torah—a direct receiver from Moses himself and the teacher of Elijah the prophet.

These lines are from the 'Holy Epistle' (*Igeret hakodesh*), a personal letter penned by the Ba'al Shem Tov to his brother-in-law that has become one of the most seminal documents for the history of hasidism.[2] It recounts a mystical experience; at its epicentre is an encounter weighty with legend and with urgent contemporary significance. In effect, the momentous question that the Ba'al Shem Tov poses here: 'When will you come, master?' had been voiced centuries before in just those words by a talmudic sage who happened upon the messiah languishing at the gates of Rome.[3] But in contrast to the wistful response in that well-known talmudic scene, with its evident, normative pre-script—'Today . . . if only you will hearken to His voice' (Ps. 95: 7)—now, the messiah's words gesture portentously towards an unknown future. The sign that redemption is near —'By this shall you know'—is bound up with the ulti-mate goal of hasidic teaching. The Ba'al Shem Tov's insights, portrayed here as the fruit of understanding received from on high, yet won as well through personal effort, have been entrusted to him to an end beyond himself. Their trajectory must be outward, towards others. 'Your wellsprings' are to flow from hidden depths into the wide spaces of the world. Somehow they must be

---

[2] R. Gershon of Kutow, the husband of the Ba'al Shem Tov's sister Hannah, had emigrated to the Land of Israel in 1747. Written in Hebrew sometime between the late 1740s and 1751, the letter was first published in 1781, at the end of one of the earliest printed volumes of hasidic homilies, R. Jacob Joseph of Polonnoye's work *Ben porat yosef* (127*b*–128*b*). Two variant versions of the 'Holy Epistle' subsequently appeared in print. A second, shorter, version was published by David Fraenkel in 1923 (*Mikhtavim mehabesht z"l vetalmidav*) and published again from manuscript by M. S. Bauminger, 'Letters of our Rabbi Israel Ba'al Shem Tov and his Son-in-Law R. Yehiel Mikhel to Rabbi Abraham Gershon of Kutow' (Heb.). Yehoshua Mondshine published a third version in 1980, based on a manuscript dating from 1776, which would make his the earliest of the three variants of *Igeret hakodesh*. A synoptic comparison of all three ver-sions, with Mondshine's proposed resolution of the textual and historical difficulties generated by these conflicting versions, appears at the end of his book *Shivḥei habesht*, 222–39. Other schol-ars who have addressed the problems surrounding textual variants of the 'Holy Epistle' include Rosman (*Founder of Hasidism*, 97–113), Etkes (*The Besht*, 79–91, 272–88), and Pedaya ('The Ba'al Shem Tov's "Holy Epistle"' (Heb.)). Additional debated aspects of the 'Holy Epistle' include the role of messianism and its magical components in the history of hasidism; the processes of cosmic, national, and personal redemption, and various perceptions of them. See Moshe Idel's discussion and review of scholarly positions on these issues in 'Hasidism: Mystical Messianism'; ch. 7 of his book *Messianic Mystics*; and his *Ascensions on High in Jewish Mysticism*, 134–66. My translation here, with its many ellipses, contains the parts of the 'Holy Epistle' that are relevant in the present context—those elements that seem to me to reflect the Ba'al Shem Tov's con-ception of his mission and which influenced the self-perception of hasidic masters in later generations. It is based on the first version to be published, as it appears in *Ben porat yosef*.

[3] BT *San.* 98*a*. The messiah's response in that passage, a verse from Ps. 95: 7, is broken in two and incorporated in the talmudic narrative.

communicated, shared, until those waters finally become integrated in the consciousness of those who thirst for them.[4]

Read as a historical-biographical document, the epistle seems to recount 'a messianic endeavor . . . the final link in the Besht's chain of attempts to bring the Messiah'. From such a perspective, with 'the information [he] received when his soul ascended . . . it became absolutely and finally clear to him that he had failed in that task and that he would not be privileged to see the coming of the Messiah during his lifetime'.[5] On another scholarly approach, this is an instance of 'magical mysticism' and it discloses the Ba'al Shem Tov's project to hasten the redemption actively by the use of traditional kabbalistic praxis.[6] A third approach, more attentive to the experiential contours of this account, reads the 'Holy Epistle' as describing a founding event, one that profoundly altered the Ba'al Shem Tov's world-view and informed the innovative path of spirituality that he developed.[7] In effect, hasidic literary tradition tends to relate to the dialogue between the Ba'al Shem Tov and the messiah in more nuanced terms such as these. Scattered allusions to passages from the 'Holy Epistle', found in a wide variety of contexts in hasidic homiletical works, attest to the profound and widespread belief among the loyal that

[4] The water metaphor (from Prov. 5: 16–17) introduced in the 'Holy Epistle' is part of a larger allusion to a passage in BT *Ta'an.* 7a. There, an apparent contradiction is detected in the biblical verses: 'It is written, "your wellsprings will flow forth" [Prov. 5: 16], yet "they will be yours alone" [5: 17].' In the talmudic discussion the issue is resolved simply: 'your wellsprings' should flow forth, but only to students who are worthy of them; if no one worthy is to be found, 'they will be yours alone'. In the Ba'al Shem Tov's account, in contrast, the messiah's words reframe the dialectics of the talmudic passage to set out a radically new mission, imposed from above and entrusted to him, along with all those who will follow his path.

[5] Altshuler, *The Messianic Secret of Hasidism*, 26–7. Altshuler highlights 'the Besht's latent ambition to serve as the herald of redemption'. Citing Aryeh Morgenstern, she posits (p. 9) that printing the Besht's second epistle on a calculated date exposed the messianic purpose behind the publication. In the month of Iyar of that year, 5541 (1781), 'Israel was destined to be redeemed . . . [T]hey published the Besht's *Epistle* in the hope that disseminating the mysteries of the Messiah . . . would consummate the messianic effort that the Besht himself had undertaken.'

[6] This praxis would include mystical unifications, ascents of the soul, nostrums, and magic formulas, similar to the activities of kabbalists and other miracle workers of the period; Tishby, 'The Messianic Idea and Messianic Trends' (Heb.). Similarly, Gries holds that in the 'Holy Epistle' 'there appears to be a tendency to advocate the use of Lurianic *kavanot* among the wider community of Hasidim. . . . [The Ba'al Shem Tov's] regret that the Messiah's appearance will be delayed because of the length of time this will take [suggests] that, in reality, only a very few of the Besht's followers—a small minority within a minority—had the knowledge and ability to use these special techniques of prayer' (*The Book in the Jewish World*, 86).

[7] Cf. Netanel Lederberg's alternative perspective on the experience described in the 'Holy Epistle': *Rabbi Israel Ba'al Shem Tov* (Heb.), 118–33.

the Ba'al Shem Tov's new mode of religious awareness would be the vital key to redemption. At the same time, those references make it clear that, in the eyes of later hasidic masters, 'Your teaching will become famed and revealed throughout the world' is a mission impossible for the Ba'al Shem Tov to realize alone. Only with the cumulative efforts of many followers, through the filter of myriad disparate sensibilities and in an ongoing process of creative engagement with that teaching over time, will the messiah's words ultimately become a reality.

Receiving, Revealing: R. Moses Hayim Ephraim of Sudilkov, *Degel maḥaneh efrayim*

Within a generation the 'Holy Epistle' had become canonical. The passage above, with its imagery and its promise, proved to be a central influence as the collective self-image of hasidic leaders and their respective sense of mission took shape. I'd like to consider some of the reasons that the encounter it describes attained the status of a foundational event in hasidic tradition, and look at some of the ways in which this is manifest in the self-understanding of hasidic masters in later generations. Let me begin with a *derashah* by the Ba'al Shem Tov's grandson, R. Moses Hayim Ephraim of Sudilkov, a late eighteenth-century hasidic master and preacher whose teachings as a whole evoke the image and after-image of his illustrious grandfather with particular intensity.[8]

'And the Children of Israel go out [of the Egyptian exile] with an upraised arm' [Exod. 14: 8]. Onkelos translates thus: 'the Children of Israel will go out *bereish galei*' [lit. 'with head held high'].[9] . . . Now the holy Zohar affirms, 'They will leave exile by merit of this book' [Zohar iii. 124*b*]. Study that passage well, for it explains in great depth that when the book of the Zohar is revealed, the time of exile will come to an end. This, then, is the meaning: 'the Children of Israel [will] go out' of their exile *bereish galei*, that is, by merit of *reish*—alluding to **R**abbi **Sh**imon bar **Y**ohai; *galei*—when his holy book, the Zohar, will be revealed [*yitgalei*].

---

[8]   R. Moses Hayim Ephraim (1748–1800) was born in Międzybóż. The Ba'al Shem Tov's daughter Edel was his mother. He lived in his grandfather's house until the age of 12, when the Ba'al Shem Tov died. On his teachings see Brill, 'The Spiritual World of a Master of Awe'; Goetschel, '*Torah lishmah* as a Central Concept in the *Degel maḥaneh Efrayim*'.

[9]   The reference is to the Aramaic *Targum onkelos*, which translates the Hebrew metaphor *beyad ramah*, suggesting an act done with fearless confidence, with a parallel Aramaic idiom—*bereish galei*. As we will see, the reading of the verse and its Aramaic translation in the Zohar turn on the double meaning of *galei*: figuratively, held high; literally, revealed. *Targum onkelos* reflects the reading also preserved in midrashic tradition; see *Mekhilta*, 'Beshalaḥ', 1.

Or: as the famed and saintly R. Lipa of Chmielnicki taught, and as it says in the 'Holy Epistle' of my grandfather, published in the Rebbe of Polonnoye's book: He asked, 'When will you come, master?' and [the Messiah] responded, 'When your teaching will become famed and revealed throughout the world, and when your wellsprings will flow forth.' All that is hinted in the verse 'And the Children of Israel [will] leave their exile *bereish galei*'—alluding to **R**abbi **I**srael **Ba**'al **Sh**em; *galei*—when his teaching will be revealed [*yitgalei*] and his wellsprings flow forth, then at last 'they will go out of their exile'. Understand this.[10]

At first glance, the section of a longer homily that I've cited here seems to be structured as two parallel, alternative readings of the biblical verse from the weekly Torah portion with which it opens. One small and unassuming word —'Or'—is all that links the two readings in a rather neutral manner. But closer consideration of the Zohar passage mentioned, along with its own textual components, makes it clear that for R. Moses Hayim Ephraim, a much more essential claim is at stake. The larger biblical narrative surrounding that opening verse recounts a formative historical event: the Exodus of the Jewish people from servitude in Egypt. Its dramatic climax comes in our verse: 'and the Children of Israel go out'—this is an illuminated, original, eternally present moment of redemption set against the backdrop of the retrospective narrative. The Zohar passage he cites gestures towards a second, correspondingly weighty event at the opposite extreme of cosmic time: the ultimate advent of the messiah. These two polar moments of first and final redemption are subtly joined together in the lines from the Zohar. With a deft shift in referent, R. Moses Hayim Ephraim's rereading of the biblical verse through the spectrum of this passage makes it speak not only of the eschatological mission undertaken by R. Shimon bar Yohai, the master of the Zohar, but also that of his 'successor', the Ba'al Shem Tov himself.[11] This is a radical statement indeed. What sort of connection is he claiming between the two figures? Just how is that mission meant to be fulfilled?

Note R. Moses Hayim Ephraim's aside to his reader: 'study that passage well, for it explains in great depth that when the book of the Zohar is revealed, the time of exile will come to an end.' On closer examination the passage in question (Zohar iii. 124*b*) does prove to be a core text of vital importance. It is

---

[10] *Degel mahaneh efrayim*, 'Beshalah', 91–2. Little is known about R. Lipa of Chmielnicki; he was a disciple of the Ba'al Shem Tov and R. Pinhas of Korets.

[11] Needless to say, the two figures are linked externally by the acronym that they happen to share, albeit with the letters permutated: Rashbi—**R**abbi **Sh**imon **b**ar **Y**ohai, and Ribash—**R**abbi **Y**isra'el **Ba**'al **Sh**em. I would suggest, though, that the claim being made here goes far beyond that point of commonality.

one of several places in which the author of the Zohar clearly sets out the hermeneutical and, ultimately, the eschatological mission of that entire oeuvre in a strikingly self-reflexive moment.[12] R. Moses Hayim Ephraim seems to pick up here on the rhetorical position that informs significant portions of the Zohar, integrating and expanding it in his own *derashah*. In effect, this same essential moment of self-awareness inheres in the exegetical project of hasidism as a whole.[13]

An attentive reading of this passage and certain other self-referential statements found in the Zohar, along with the textual allusions concealed between the lines, thus needs to be the first step towards discerning some central aspects of that project, its meaning and its purpose. With reflexive statements such as these in mind, we will then have a look at hasidic teachings by other authors and consider how the voices of the earlier texts are manifest in them, and to what end.

*

One biblical source at the heart of the Zohar's overt hermeneutic is from the closing chapter of the book of Daniel. The biblical prophet documents a series of apocalyptic visions; it culminates in a fleeting glimpse of the final End:

'Then, many of those dormant in the dust of the earth will arise—some of them to eternal life and others to endless shame and punishment . . . And the enlightened shall

---

[12] I have chosen to use the phrase 'the author of the Zohar' to refer, for the sake of convenience, to the agent/s who composed the corpus known in academic parlance as the zoharic literature. I will also refer to that heterogeneous corpus as 'the Zohar', in keeping with the practice of the hasidic authors under discussion. While traditionally minded Jewish thinking and popular culture ascribes authorship of the Zohar (as a monolithic work) to the mishnaic sage Rabbi Shimon bar Yohai, modern and postmodern scholarship has identified various authorial bodies and proposed a number of historically contingent compositional processes. Although the literary figure of Rabbi Shimon bar Yohai does not appear in large parts of the zoharic literature, most hasidic thinkers had little use for the historical-critical method, and their readings tend to accept the popular conception of the Zohar as a unified work, with its central hero as its author. Zohar research has proposed a variety of textual models. For a review of attitudes on authorship of the Zohar corpus over the last 200 years, see Huss, 'Admiration and Disgust: The Ambivalent Re-Canonization of the Zohar'; Green, *A Guide to the Zohar*.

[13] I will not engage in detailed biographical and psychological speculations (such as points of identification on the part of the Ba'al Shem Tov with Rashbi), nor will I explore the ideational elements that link his innovations. My focus here is on literary aspects and certain shared motifs. On the role of kabbalistic literature in seventeenth- and eighteenth-century eastern Europe and the 'canonization' of the Zohar in hasidism, see Gries, *The Book in the Jewish World*, 69–90.

shine, radiant [*kezohar*] as the heavens … Now you, Daniel, obscure these matters and seal your book until the end of days; let many wander in search of them, that knowledge may increase.' … I heard but I did not comprehend, so I said, 'My lord, what is the end of all this?' He said, 'Go, Daniel! For these matters are obscured and sealed until the time of the End. They will be clarified and explained and refined by many; the wicked will act wickedly and none of the wicked will understand. But the enlightened will understand.' (Dan. 12: 2–10)

A dialectic of obscuring and revealing, of sealing and releasing from concealment in some unknown future informs these verses. On the Zohar's radical self-reflexive reading of them, that dialectic is enhanced and the vague referents of Daniel's prophecy are redefined in high resolution. The new meanings generated by this innovative exegetical sleight of hand would resonate in later kabbalistic works and in the Ba'al Shem Tov's 'Holy Epistle', and continue to inform hasidic exegetical creativity for generations to come. Here are a few key passages from various contexts in the Zohar that give voice to its author's self-proclaimed project to document and, simultaneously, to enact the realization of Daniel's prophetic vision:

At that time 'the enlightened will understand'—these are masters of kabbalah. Of them it is said, 'The enlightened shall shine, radiant [*kezohar*] as the heavens.' For they expend their efforts in that radiance [*bezohar*] called the book of the Zohar. This light is yours.[14]

'But the enlightened will understand'—they will understand by the grace of Binah, which is the Tree of Life. Thus it is written, 'And the enlightened shall shine, radiant as the heavens': this will come about through your composition [*hibura*]—the book of the Zohar … When Israel will taste the Tree of Life—that is, this book, the Zohar—they will leave their exile by God's mercy.[15]

'By his wounds [*haburato*] we will be healed' [Isa. 53: 5].[16] By the bond [*haburah*] you have bound between us in exile, we will be healed. For you [Moses] are like the glowing sun; although it sets at night, it continues to illuminate the moon and the stars. So your light endures in all masters of law and received wisdom. Secretly, they are watered, like trees irrigated beneath their roots by a hidden spring, until the time those waters well up into the open, as it is written, 'Your wellsprings will flow forth'

[14] Zohar iii. 153*b*. The self-reflective dimension here and in the following citation is created rhetorically: the Zohar's central figure, Rabbi Shimon bar Yohai, is being addressed in direct speech—'this light is yours'.

[15] Zohar iii. 124*b*. 'Mercy' (*rahamim*) is a divine attribute associated with the *sefirah* of Binah.

[16] Isaiah 53 depicts 'God's suffering servant'—a figuration of the messiah. On this, see below.

[Prov. 5: 16] . . . The Faithful Shepherd then blessed the Holy Luminary, saying: 'Indeed, it is you who will shine with my light, at that hour when the sun sets and its brightness goes dim. May the Merciful One illuminate you with the brilliance of His Name.'[17]

In these passages, suffused with light and its many cognates, the Zohar celebrates its self-given title and evokes lyrical intimations of its mystical essence. 'The enlightened'—a general, undefined entity in Daniel's vision—here are named in no uncertain terms as the very heroes whose experiences fill many pages of the Zohar. Rabbi Shimon and his companions have been illuminated, or will be illuminated, with an influx of esoteric wisdom. It flows unmediated into them from some mysterious, transcendent source of abundance. Once contained, that radiance emanates from within their souls and shines through their teachings. The record of all this becomes a literary work.

The author of the Zohar is particularly intent in these passages on evoking the intangible, dynamic moment of encounter between giver and receiver. Vibrant nature metaphors arouse a sense of organic, deeply moving connectedness to a source that is far too great to be fully contained. That source—the 'hidden spring' in the earth's depths, the 'glowing sun' beyond the horizon—is presented as an agent that has withdrawn from sight. Only the trace of its presence—reflected, welling up, refracted, re-formed elsewhere—bears testimony to the immanent connection that still endures between receiver and giver.

It is 'the enlightened', here called 'masters of kabbalah'—literally, 'masters of receiving'—who embody that moment. Moses, the paradigmatic receiver of the Torah at Sinai, the symbolic sun, names Rabbi Shimon bar Yohai as his successor. With daring elan, the Zohar's central hero is portrayed in these passages as the chosen, even as the exclusive next link in the traditionally conceived chain of reception and transmission.[18] Now, 'the brilliance of His Name'—encrypted in Scripture, known as the 'Torah of Moses'—will be passed on and entrusted to Rabbi Shimon alone. While Daniel the prophet was ordered to 'obscure these matters and seal your book until the end of days',

---

[17] Zohar iii. 280a, *Ra'aya mehemna*. This part of the Zohar, Tishby noted, 'exists in manuscripts as a separate work, copied independently. The central figure here is Moses himself, who received the commandments at Sinai, and the title, "The Faithful Shepherd [*Ra'aya mehemna*]", refers to him' (*The Wisdom of the Zohar*, i. 5). The dramatic setting of the passage cited is a dialogue between Moses and Rabbi Shimon, whom the Zohar often names as 'holy luminary' (*butsina kadisha*). 'At that hour when the sun sets' alludes to Gen. 24: 11.

[18] On the use and connotations of the words *kabalah* and *maskilim* in kabbalistic literature see Hallamish, *An Introduction to the Kabbalah*, 87–93.

that unimaginable future has suddenly arrived. 'Your book', now unsealed and disclosed, is re-identified as Rabbi Shimon's composition: 'the book' of the Zohar. The esoteric wisdom shimmering in its leaves promises understanding and healing. Ultimately, it is the 'deep, long-concealed mysteries' that Rabbi Shimon has been permitted to reveal at last and record in the Zohar that will lead the world to redemption by restoring its primordial connection to the source of Life.[19] The unresolved paradox in all this, of course, is that although the Zohar refers to itself as a written text, normatively defined and publicly accessible, nonetheless the world carries on, centuries later, still unredeemed.

R. Moses Hayim Ephraim's reading here addresses that paradox. It points out a crucial link joining the redemptive potential inherent in the Zohar as a mystical, literary composition and the redemptive potential of hasidic teaching. That link is the moment called revelation. 'When the book of the Zohar is revealed', 'when your [the Ba'al Shem Tov's] teaching will be revealed'— then exile will end. These phrases, borrowed, adapted, and recombined together in R. Moses Hayim Ephraim's *derashah*, suggest that, most fundamentally, true acquisition of what has been 'revealed' can take place only through a complex, historically contingent dialectical process. After an illuminated moment of bestowal, darkness inevitably sets in. The master, present for a time, shares his wisdom and passes on; what was given will always, tragically, lose its wholeness and disintegrate. Only afterwards, in the void of absence, does the real task of understanding begin. It can be won through innovative acts of reconstruction, a transformative remembering of what was once revealed. "'Your wellsprings will flow forth"' . . . "'Indeed, it is you who will shine with my light."' In the Zohar passages that R. Moses Hayim Ephraim cites, with these parting words Moses bequeaths the secret heart of the Torah, given to him at Sinai, to Rabbi Shimon bar Yohai and names him as emissary. As a literary persona, Rabbi Shimon is to repair and heal the world, to awaken human consciousness for the advent of the messiah. The means to that end is engagement with the Torah and other sacred Jewish works. 'Your book'—the

[19] The 'healing' power ascribed here to the book of the Zohar is drawn through the 'creative philology' its author suggests, linking the biblical description of 'God's suffering servant' (Isa. 53) and 'his wounds'—*ḥaburato*—to other words sharing the same root: *ḥibura* (composition) and *ḥibur* (bond or connection). Here, Moses fills the role of past (and future) redeemer. Hebrew Scripture is known in Jewish collective consciousness as 'the Torah of Moses'—figuratively, Moses' composition. The eternal bond forged at Sinai between God and the Jewish people that the Torah embodies is conceived as the ultimate source of healing. The Torah, then, is the binding force that sustains the Jewish nation through the millennia of its exile. These motifs figure significantly in hasidic thought, as we will see.

Zohar, with the breathtaking reflexivity so central to its *ars poetica*—shows, testifies to, and enacts a profound mystical-religious-emotional experience, one that is rooted in exegesis.

Although not named explicitly, it seems that a second very important text also underlies the vision of hasidic teaching and the figure of the Ba'al Shem Tov that R. Moses Hayim Ephraim presents.[20] It reflects a highly similar self-understanding, articulated at length some 200 years earlier by R. Hayim Vital regarding the kabbalistic teachings of his own master, R. Isaac Luria Ash-kenazi (the Ari), and their connection to the secrets encoded in the Zohar.[21]

In the transparently programmatic introduction to his monumental work *Ets hayim* (*Tree of Life*), R. Hayim sets out his perception of Lurianic teaching and its role in cosmic history. With the death of Rabbi Shimon bar Yohai, he explains, the entire body of esoteric wisdom was hidden away from the world. Although lone mystics continued to transmit it partially, in whispers, from one generation to the next, the arcane truths hinted at in the Zohar remained concealed and largely inaccessible for centuries, up until his own time. Yet premonitions of the Ari's advent and the master's revolutionary insights, he claims, are covertly disclosed in its very pages. He notes that they may be detected in passages such as this one, spoken by the prophet Elijah himself to Rabbi Shimon bar Yohai: 'Multitudes in the lower realm will be sustained by your composition when it is revealed below in the last generation, at the end of days.'[22] Or, more pointedly, as God avers: 'You, Elijah, will reveal yourself

[20] Here, it seems, is a prime instance of what Rachel Elior describes as 'the polyphony of the hasidic spiritual renaissance and its dialectical ties to the kabbalistic tradition'; *The Mystical Origins of Hasidism*, 24.

[21] R. Hayim Vital was the most outspoken and prolific among the Ari's close circle of disciples. His writings combine kabbalistic teachings that he recorded in the name of his master, as well as biographical and autobiographical reflections. The huge and labyrinthine corpus of Lurianic material was recorded by various disciples, and redacted and edited by many later hands. While scholars may doubt the objectivity of R. Hayim Vital's biographical disclosures, their influence on less critical readers has been unquestionable. For an extensive study of the Ari's life and his relationship to his circle of disciples, see Fine, *Physician of the Soul*. Fine points out that it was versions of Lurianic teachings based on manuscripts by R. Hayim Vital (published in 1630–60 by Jacob Zemach and his student Meir Poppers) that served to disseminate Lurianic kabbalah in Germany, Poland, and eastern Europe in general (pp. 16–17). Hagiographic sources show an impressive kinship between the figure of R. Isaac Luria portrayed in the collection *In Praise of the Ari* (*Shivhei ha'ari*) and the Ba'al Shem Tov as portrayed in *In Praise of the Baal Shem Tov* (*Shivhei habesht*). My discussion here touches on only one aspect of this kinship. On R. Hayim Vital's introduction see Elior, 'Messianic Expectations and Spiritualization of Religious Life'.

[22] Introduction to *Ets hayim*, 15, citing *Tikunei zohar* 23*b*–24*a*.

at the end of days, and there is one to whom you will appear face to face.'[23] Indeed, R. Hayim declares, 'the interpretations [*derushim*] and the very words of this composition [*Ets ḥayim*] bear witness: no human intellect could possibly have invented such profound and wondrous things—they can only have been divinely inspired, and indeed, they were conveyed to my master by Elijah, of blessed memory.'[24] In other words, in R. Hayim Vital's personal historiography of kabbalistic tradition, the Ari's appearance marks the onset of the 'last generation' preceding the messianic era to which the Zohar alludes. Lurianic teaching, by means of creative exegesis of the Zohar along with myriad innovative expansions, will finally bring to light what had been 'obscured and sealed until the time of the End'.[25]

R. Moses Hayim Ephraim does not mention this seminal text in his *derashah*, but he does distinctly articulate the same acute time consciousness and rhetorical stance that is voiced in it. Whereas R. Hayim Vital juxtaposed the persona of Rabbi Shimon bar Yohai with his master the Ari, R. Moses Hayim Ephraim draws the same essential connection between Rabbi Shimon and his own grandfather, the Ba'al Shem Tov. In doing so, he places these monumental figures together on the same eschatological horizon. Now, it is the Ba'al Shem Tov who has been ordained to take up the role of his illustrious forebears. Hasidic teaching, embedded in the sacred canon of Jewish tradition, which has been augmented in the meantime by the Zohar, Lurianic teaching, and other esoteric and exoteric works, has been invested, in turn, with the power to engender a powerful spiritual awakening, through exegetical engagement with all those texts. That awakening is 'the secret of redemption'.

Returning, finally, to the 'Holy Epistle', it is now clear that the Ba'al Shem Tov himself engages, whether consciously or unconsciously, with the experiential dimensions that the Zohar and other mystical accounts portray so vividly.[26] In his testimonial to that otherworldly encounter, he responds with

---

[23] Introduction to *Ets ḥayim*, 19. He cites 'a manuscript of the introduction to the *tikunim* [*Tikunei zohar*]'.

[24] Ibid. For a biographical sketch of R. Hayim Vital and a study of his motivations, see Faierstein, 'Charisma and Anti-Charisma in Safed'.

[25] An allusion to Dan. 12: 2–10, cited above.

[26] It is doubtless more than coincidence that the dialogue this letter reconstructs directly cites the promise of the Shekhinah-*magid* to R. Joseph Karo. His diary entry dated 28 Kislev (the *sidrah* 'Mikets') reads: 'Soon it will come to pass . . . that you will gain recognition in the world, your wellsprings will flow forth, and I will grant you numerous students . . . and your students shall shine, radiant as the heavens'; Karo, *Magid meisharim*, 37. On him see Werblowsky, *Joseph Karo*.

acute awareness of just how complex his mission will be. This point deserves our attention. Not, I think, as an autobiographical gesture of disclosure or hint towards a defined ideological or theurgic plan of action. Rather, I would suggest that his response should be read as a deeply self-reflexive moment. Like the protagonists of the Zohar (and other notable real-life mystics), the Ba'al Shem Tov portrays himself here as having crossed over the threshold between worlds. His 'soul ascent' took him to a mysterious realm of meaning concealed from ordinary human sensibilities. The understanding he was granted there is too enormous, essential, or recondite to be told. Back on this side, the recounting of that experience is far more than a rare moment of personal confession. It is a gesture of constructing a self-identity, and it marks a turning point in transforming what has been bequeathed into '*your* teaching'. In his 'Holy Epistle', the Ba'al Shem Tov—as disciple and master, as healer and mystic, as a spiritual guide able to cross the threshold between realms of being—thus intimates a founding ethos and a mode of experience, one that is deeply hermeneutical in nature.[27] Communicating that ethos—causing the wellsprings to flow forth—will then be the crucial historical stage leading to the messianic era and, ultimately, to the world's redemption.

'When Your Wellsprings Will Flow Forth'

To evaluate the self-understanding of hasidic masters in subsequent generations and their perception of hasidism and its exegetical project, it would make sense to examine texts in which they address those subjects directly. The main problem, though, is that hasidism had existed for more than a century and a quarter before anyone composed a systematic discussion of that nature. The first figures who treated these issues in historical perspective were from the dynasties of Habad and Izbica, in the last decades of the nineteenth century. Central representatives of those groups did formulate explicit self-reflexive statements and framed them in a historiosophical perspective. In both cases, however, their focus was on articulating a strong claim of exclu-

---

[27] In light of the original or quasi-etymological meaning of hermeneutics, drawn from the mythical figure of Hermes. Richard Palmer's insights on the connection between hermeneutical methods and the figure of Hermes are instructive here: 'As guide and interpreter, Hermes is a liminal figure, a facilitator. . . . And it would seem to be the essence of hermeneutics to be liminal, to mediate between realms of being, whether between god and human beings, wakefulness and sleep, the conscious and unconscious, life and afterlife, visible and invisible, day and night'. See Palmer's enlightening discussion: 'The Liminality of Hermes and the Meaning of Hermeneutics', 12–14.

sivity. The version of the 'chain of reception' that those dynasties constructed, although inarguably an important aspect of each one's unique self-understanding, emphasizes particularistic rather than general features of hasidic teaching. Moreover, valuable academic studies have already been devoted to the complex ideological, historical, and political contexts in which the self-image of Habad and Izbica developed, and so I've chosen not to review them again here.[28] Expressions of self-understanding in the early generations of hasidism, then, must be sought elsewhere.

Academic enquiry has pursued other important directions in the attempt to understand how the early hasidic masters perceived their own activity. With a predominantly historical-critical approach, scholars have mapped the development of hasidism from its origins through stages of evolution to becoming a mass movement. Major studies have utilized both the polemical literature and hasidic homiletical works to analyse the figure of the *tsadik* as concept and social reality. They have highlighted the role of *tsadikim* as public figures and spiritual leaders and their influence in determining the social ethics of the hasidic court. Scholars have examined the doctrine of tsadikism and its use as a propaganda technique, and studied the movement's evolution 'as hasidic groups rallied around a *tsadik* and used a grassroots network to preach the hasidic gospel'.[29] A second significant research avenue has been individual hasidic figures. With the aid of discursive (and frequently programmatic) statements made by hasidic masters about themselves, by disciples about their master, or by followers about their *rebbe*, scholars have speculated on various aspects of these figures' self-perception. Research in all these areas has included the serious critical re-evaluation of primary sources, their authenticity, and their value in reconstructing historical truth. All this scholarship has contributed greatly to my own work.

Now, however, what interests me above all is the ways in which ideas are brought to the fore through exegesis. A deeply authentic dimension of self-understanding finds expression, I believe, in the motifs and images that the hasidic authors develop reflectively. In the next sections of this chapter I will consider some central elements of that kind that appear in a wide range of hasidic homiletical works, specifically *derashot* dating from the first, formative

[28] On Habad see Elior, *The Paradoxical Ascent to God*; Etkes, *Ba'al Hatanya*; and Loewenthal, *Communicating the Infinite*. On Izbica see Faierstein, *All Is in the Hands of Heaven*; Magid, *Hasidism on the Margin*; Wiskind-Elper, *Wisdom of the Heart*.

[29] Piekarz discusses the 'doctrine of *tsadikism*' in *The Hasidic Leadership* (Heb.); on propaganda techniques see Dynner, *Men of Silk*. The final citation is from Petrovsky-Shtern, "*Hasidei de'ar'a* and *Hasidei dekokhvaya*'", 54.

years, what is known as the first three 'generations' of hasidism.[30] In terms of methodology, the focus will be on primary motifs developed by some early hasidic masters. The passages that I have selected are representative of larger and shared concerns. I will not compare or contrast ideological approaches taken by other hasidic schools of thought or by non-hasidic trends on any issue that may arise in the course of my discussion. The originality of these *derashot* lies not in the invention of the motifs and thematic images that I will name as self-reflexive, because all of them can be found in earlier Jewish sources. What is innovative is the hasidic masters' reconception of those elements, along with the emotional attitudes that accompany and inform them. Through a close reading, I will try to understand how their re-presentation gives voice to the ethos and sensibility that the Ba'al Shem Tov developed in his teachings and bequeathed to those who saw themselves as his followers. As hasidic authors engaged with the sacred works of Jewish tradition, they showed an awareness of the power of hasidic teaching to bring the world closer to redemption.

To Create New Worlds with Words: R. Jacob Joseph of Polonnoye, *Toledot ya'akov yosef*

R. Jacob Joseph of Polonnoye (1710–*c*.1782) was one of the Ba'al Shem Tov's earliest and most devoted disciples and author of the first published book of hasidic thought.[31] Drawing freely on a varied store of kabbalistic terms and concepts, his writings present, albeit unsystematically, central and founding tools of hasidic exegesis. In many cases, the Ba'al Shem Tov is credited as their originator, and the disciple both records and illustrates them as tools he has learned. Other hermeneutical techniques are of R. Jacob Joseph's invention; these often come to the fore as his own expansions on received traditions. The following passage from his commentary on Genesis, *Ben porat yosef*, presents a remarkable exegetical move. The principle it illustrates is a guiding force in hasidic hermeneutics as a whole. In subsequent generations, other hasidic masters would take up the basic exegetical tools he sets out and adapt them to various ends, as we will see throughout my discussion. For now, as he

---

[30] Moshe Rosman reviews (and critiques) the 'conventional periodization of the Hasidic movement in both academic and Hasidic circles', which identifies 'three generations of the classic movement, founded by the Ba'al Shem Tov (Besht), beginning around 1740, stabilized and spread by the Maggid of Mezerich from circa 1760 until his death in 1772, and conducted thereafter as an institutionally mature enterprise by the Maggid's students'; 'Hasidism as a Modern Phenomenon', 2.   [31] *Toledot ya'akov yosef* (1780).

reflects on the opening verse of Scripture, R. Jacob Joseph considers the elusive, mysterious moment of divine Creation and explores its deeper meaning.

To explain the midrash, 'Rabbi Oshaya said: the Torah was as a tool in the Artist's hand' [*Gen. Rab.* 1: 1]; and to understand the meaning of the verse, 'In the beginning God created the heavens and the earth' [Gen. 1: 1] . . . we will examine the saying 'Know what is above you' [*da mah lema'alah mimekha*; Mishnah *Avot* 2: 1]. As I have written elsewhere, this implies that what is above can be perceived by means of what is below—that is, through self-reflection [*mimekha*—lit. 'from yourself'].[32] Now, it seems to me that the Bible starts out by disproving the infamous contention that the cosmos was pre-existent. Here we see clearly that there is a Creator, and He brought the world from nothingness into being. . . . Indeed, human beings—in their own innovative interpretations of the Torah—are the ultimate proof of creation *ex nihilo*. For us, too, in the beginning there is always nothingness. Then suddenly, from within that void, the mind conceives something new. As my master [the Ba'al Shem Tov] taught, the human psyche contains the ten *sefirot*. 'Father' and 'mother' [Hokhmah and Binah]—they engender a new interpretation. It first comes into being in a moment of mercy [Hesed] and expands endlessly. Then there must be a controlling force [Gevurah] that can contract the idea, enabling one to grasp it, to communicate it to others. All this has to happen in balance [Tiferet]. After that, what is needed is faith [*emunah*] . . . standing solidly on the aspects of Netsah and Hod. Then, the gratification that comes from having innovated something—this is Yesod, which senses pleasure. Finally, the idea can be revealed through speech, or Malkhut.[33] Now, the same process, just as it unfolds here below, within our consciousness, takes place in God's creation of the world out of nothingness. And thus the Rabbis said: 'You can know what is above—by means of introspection [*da mah lema'alah—mimekha*].' Understand this.[34]

We will pause here for a moment before moving on to the second part of the *derashah*. R. Jacob Joseph's starting point is, quite unoriginally, the incomprehensible secret of beginnings that is stated with uncanny directness in the opening verse of Scripture. As his readers well know, kabbalists over the centuries have striven to unlock the enigma of Creation. Peering beyond that first verse, back to the primordial eras before the revealed world came into being, Jewish mystics developed various theosophical models of the ten *sefirot*, their

---

[32] The double meaning of the word *mimekha* stems from two meanings of the Hebrew preposition *mi*. It can signify a comparative state—'above or higher than you'—or a derivative relationship: 'from, on the basis of, yourself'. Below I will discuss the teaching to which he refers.

[33] R. Jacob Joseph signals that the Ba'al Shem Tov's teaching ends here using the traditional code for 'end-quote' דפח"ח, derived from the verse 'the words of a wise man win favour' (Eccl. 10: 12).   [34] *Ben porat yosef*, 12*b*.

emanation or gradual emergence 'from naught' until finally becoming immanent, in one form or another, in the material world. R. Jacob Joseph gestures towards that vast and varied body of esoteric wisdom. His main point, however, is that for such enquiry—'knowing what is above'—really to make any sense, one must first become cognizant of a crucial dimension of human experience—what he elliptically calls 'knowing what is below'. The 'proof-text' he introduces to ground that central argument, perhaps unexpectedly, is a familiar rabbinical statement from the mishnaic tractate *Pirkei avot* (*Ethics of the Fathers*) that seems to be saying something rather different. In its original context, that statement is normative moral guidance, intoned with a distinct measure of paternal censure: 'Contemplate three things and you will not sin; know what is above you: a seeing eye, a listening ear, and all your deeds being inscribed in a book' (*Avot* 2: 1). This, indeed, is the straightforward meaning that we hear the first time R. Jacob Joseph cites the saying. But by the end of the passage, when he cites it for the second time, the words have reconfigured. Decontextualized, syntactically adjusted, they come to bespeak a radically new mode of awareness. On the alternative reading that emerges, warning ('contemplate . . . and you will not sin') has become promise: 'Thus the Rabbis said: "You can know what is above—by means of introspection."' In other words, attentiveness to the dynamics taking place in one's internal universe can provide a vital epistemological key, one that will potentially open the way to a 'knowing' of the highest order: perception of the metaphysical dimensions of being.

After presenting this thesis, R. Jacob Joseph unfolds the Ba'al Shem Tov's seminal insight that 'the human psyche contains the ten *sefirot*' with an extended analogy.[35] Its focal point is the phenomenon of newness and the way people experience it. Fundamentally, he suggests, anything 'new'—be it an infant, an idea, a world—manifests itself in our consciousness as the sudden, wholly unexplainable presence of 'something' where 'nothing' was before. Summoning the core vocabulary of esotericism, the names and attributes of the *sefirot*, R. Jacob Joseph draws out some of the more subtle, evocative connotations of those terms to speak of what is, after all, an intimately familiar dimension of life. As he reintegrates that nomenclature in a more accessible psychological context, the same terms now describe the stages of cognition, or how thoughts develop, stage by stage, from preconscious embodiment to some final, communicable form. These kabbalistic concepts, we realize, bear heavy

---

[35] As noted above, the entire teaching, including the stages it outlines, is attributed in this *derashah* to the Ba'al Shem Tov.

emotional weight: mother, father, between them the secret miracle of conception, an always unmerited bestowal of kindness. Then, the long struggle to define and delineate inchoate matter. Uncertainty, hope. Finally, gratification, an opening outwards with new fullness to share. At bottom, what R. Jacob Joseph describes is primary aspects of being human. Presented in this manner, ideas that once sounded esoteric, abstract, and disconnected from day-to-day life now give voice to the experience of beginnings familiar to everyone.

We would be mistaken, however, to assume that the Ba'al Shem Tov's objective was to refashion basic elements of Jewish mysticism as mere allegories, or to reduce the *sefirot* to metaphors of psychological processes.[36] Rather, in integrating this analogy in his *derashah*, R. Jacob Joseph alerts his reader to the complex interrelationship that exists between the realms of the human and the Divine. Introspection is conceived here as a crucial moment of looking inwards to gain greater awareness of the workings of the human psyche. It is not the final goal, but a vitally important part of a larger trajectory. To become cognizant of the 'world within', in this context in particular, means to take note of the dynamics at the core of thought processes. Naming those intimately recognizable aspects of mental life with the attributes of the *sefirot* enables an opening towards a new mode of attentiveness. From the 'world within' to 'worlds beyond'—the affinities between those two dimensions of reality can come into view.

But how do these dynamics (which I have presented here in abstract, analytical terms) play themselves out? Notably, in the first lines of the *derashah*, R. Jacob Joseph refers to one of his earlier works, in which he sets out the same idea with two important additions. A brief look at that passage is in order, as his insights there are an important subtext in the present *derashah*. On the same saying from *Avot*, there he remarked, "'Know what is above you": through yourself [*mimekha*] you can know what is above. For every individual is a microcosm, a "mirror of the legions" [*hu marot hatsovot*].'[37] This, to be

[36] Scholem famously held that a central innovation of hasidism was its imbuing of kabbalistic concepts and metaphysical ideas with psychological meaning. Idel, on the basis of a fragmentary version of this teaching in *Ben porat yosef* in another work (*Toledot ya'akov yosef*, fo. 86*a*), contends that 'it is nevertheless obvious that the founder of Hasidism interpreted the entire sefirotic scheme as referring to mystical states on the human level . . . the sefirotic entities stood for a sequence of experiences'; *Kabbalah: New Perspectives*, 150.

[37] *Toledot ya'akov yosef*, 'Vayikra', 2: *ki ha'adam nikra olam katan vehu marot hatsovot*. The notion of the human microcosm (*olam katan*) appears in midrashic sources (e.g. *Avot derabi natan* A 31). It was developed further in medieval Jewish thought and greatly elaborated in the mystical tradition. On the latter see Idel, *Kabbalah: New Perspectives*, 146–53. This hasidic

sure, is a terse and cryptic statement. What R. Jacob Joseph is positing, it seems, is an essential correspondence between the 'inner universe' of the psyche ('a microcosm') and the sefirotic structure of the (macro-) cosmos. This correspondence is expressed through the powerful and fascinating metonymy of the self as mirror. With due circumspection, we should keep in mind that premodern Jewish texts, for lack of a simpler term, sometimes used the phrase *marot hatsovot* to denote a mirror in the regular sense.[38] But as a literary allusion, this mirror image bears much richer connotations. It is those overtones of meaning, I think, that are the guiding force in the passage at hand. Let me give them some attention now in the hope of understanding them better.

The 'mirrors of the legions' are mentioned very briefly in the biblical narrative, and are greatly embellished in midrashic tradition. They refer to the burnished copper hand-mirrors that legions of righteous Jewish women, newly redeemed from bondage in Egypt, had donated towards the construction of the Tabernacle. The reflective inner surface of the laver that stood in the courtyard of the Tabernacle, near its entrance, was composed of their gifts.[39] With acute interest in the peculiarities of optical physics, the Rabbis and biblical commentators after them considered the effects those myriad inlaid mirrors may have produced. Many note the moment of oblique seeing they provided, which enabled the *kohanim* to perform their priestly duties without looking directly into the faces of the women who had brought offerings. One exceptionally imaginative source posits that the reflective interior of the laver enabled a surreal extension of normal vision.[40] In her commentary on Exodus, Avivah Gottlieb Zornberg considers just how this came about. As she puts it, the polished, curved inner surface of the laver 'served as a kind

teaching won scathing critique from the *mitnaged* R. David of Makov: *Shever poshim*, 67*b* in Wilensky, *Hasidim and Mitnagedim* (Heb.), ii. 163–4.

[38] The invention of plate glass in eighteenth-century Vienna was a significant technological achievement, enabling the mass production of mirrors for personal use. In the history of ideas, the effects of this development—psychological as well as social—were revolutionary. See Lionel Trilling's comments, *Sincerity and Authenticity*, 25. The term *marot hatsovot* appears in the responsa literature concerning the question of whether or not men are permitted to use mirrors for aesthetic reasons.

[39] Exod. 38: 8; *Tanhuma*, 'Pekudei', 9. On a second midrashic interpretation, the phrase refers to 'the mirrors of those who created or begot the hosts' (*tseva'ot*)—i.e. the collective 'children of Israel', as in the verse 'All the hosts of God went out of the land of Egypt' (Exod. 12: 41).

[40] In his late seventeenth-century, rather eclectic anthology of midrashic readings of Scripture, R. David ben Naftali Posner cites this as an anonymous source ('And there are those who interpret . . .'); *Yalkut david* (Dyhernfurth, 1691), fo. 54*b*.

of mirror-system, like a periscope or a telescope'. Visitors, who were permitted to come no closer than the outer courtyard of that holy space, were able to gaze into the laver; through the mirrors inlaid in it, they caught a refracted glimpse all the way into the sacred, banned inner recesses of the Tabernacle. As a whole, we could say that the rabbinic and medieval commentaries on the 'mirrors of the legions' explore the phenomenon of reflection to suggest a variety of real and symbolic meanings. Most basically, Zornberg notes, mirrors 'allow vision at oblique angles, around corners, at a distance . . . they function as revealers of the inaccessible'—whether that be one's own countenance or holy ground.[41]

'For every individual is a microcosm, a "mirror of the legions".' R. Jacob Joseph does not cite these images directly in his *derashah* on the first verse of Genesis. Nonetheless, the notion of the self (or the imagination) as a mirror is clearly the axis of his contention there. It makes it evident that the concept of the 'ten *sefirot* in the human psyche' does much more than translate a kabbalistic model into psychological terms. The extended analogy he offers in fact outlines an inherent correspondence between the human 'inner world' and the metaphysical counter-world beyond. Moreover it hints, by the implicit trope of self as mirror, that introspection enables a vital moment of deflected, augmented vision. That double-vectored seeing, moving from 'inward' to 'upward', is what allows one to perceive and comprehend corresponding dimensions of divine reality hidden from the human eye.

With these insights in hand, we will read on. In the second section of this *derashah*, R. Jacob Joseph returns to the opening verse of Genesis and to the midrashic image with which he began. The figure of the Creator as artist, wielding the Torah as a 'tool in His hand', now brings him to seek its corresponding human figure. His answer, it seems to me, discloses a highly important facet of R. Jacob Joseph's self-perception. Moreover, seen within the cultural context of late eighteenth-century Jewish eastern Europe, this passage gives voice to a revolutionary aspect of the ethos that hasidic teaching sought to forward.

Now, then, we can understand that 'In the beginning' refers to two 'beginnings'—that is, to two dimensions of creating: one above and the other here below, in our world.[42] For God created the universe with Wisdom, that is, through the Torah;[43] and human beings, made in God's image, likewise create heaven and earth with the wisdom of

[41] *The Particulars of Rapture*, 61–2.

[42] *Be-reshit*—the first letter of the word, *beit*, signifies the number two; *reshit* = beginning.

[43] That is, not in the sense of 'wisely'; 'wisdom' here is a proper noun, a cognate of 'the Torah'. See *Targum yerushalmi* (Gen. 1:1).

the Torah. So it says in the Zohar [i. *4b–5a*]: 'Rabbi Shimon began, "And I will place My words in your mouth" [Isa. 51: 16]. At the moment when a new interpretation—impenetrable, secret wisdom—is there, in one's mouth, a new firmament comes into being. And other innovative interpretations of Torah engender the lands of the living, new worlds on earth. "Then say to Zion, You are My people" [ibid.]. Do not read *ami* [My people], but *imi* [with Me]. Be a partner with Me! Just as I create heaven and earth with My words, as it is written, "By the word of the Lord were the heavens made" [Ps. 33: 6], so too can you.'[44] Clearly, then: just as in the supernal realm it was with the Torah, like a tool in the artist's hand, that God created the heavens and the earth, so too, here below, humans—through their own novel Torah interpretations —bring into being 'new heaven and earth'.[45]

At the risk of anachronism, I'll venture to say that what R. Jacob Joseph is proposing here is a strikingly modern perception of creativity, innovation, and what could be called 'the genesis of the poetic'. Anachronism—not only because such terms themselves were of course wholly absent from the lexicon of mid-eighteenth-century rabbinical discourse. More basically, because both the terms and the ideas they embody—ideas that are now so deeply rooted in the modern consciousness that we might assume they have always been there—in fact emerged in west European intellectual tradition only some decades later, in the course of the nineteenth century with the rise of romanticism.[46] Nonetheless, it does seem that in this part of his *derashah* R. Jacob Joseph introduces these important key concepts as he sets out three more crucial points of correspondence between the divine and human realms. Firstly, he speaks of creativity as an essential human faculty, analogous to, yet separate from, the divine agent. Human creative acts, here, are generative in a literal sense. They are invested with a real power to bring into being new 'worlds' (of meaning, perception, experience, understanding), and these 'worlds' will bear the mark of their individual creator. Secondly, the human mind is capable of

[44] My translation of the Zohar is based on Tishby, *Wisdom of the Zohar*, iii. 1127–30, but it reflects R. Jacob Joseph's partial citations, paraphrases, and omissions of many elements in the original Zohar passage. In this innovative reading of Isaiah 51: 16, the author of the Zohar adopts the midrashic technique known as *al tikrei* and applies it to a new verse; no similar reading of this verse appears in rabbinic literature. I have filled in this line so that the Zohar passage make sense exegetically. Although he does not cite it in full, R. Jacob Joseph's understanding is actually founded on this instance of *al tikrei*.   [45] *Ben porat yosef*, 12b.

[46] On the 'topology of the self' as possessing inner and outer dimensions (as portrayed in this *derashah*), within a consideration of the historical context in which it developed, see Taylor, *Sources of the Self*, pt. 2, 'Inwardness'. On R. Jacob Joseph's interest in the dynamics of the creative process, compare Rob Pope's discussion in *Creativity: Theory, History, Practice*, 70–137. On changing metaphors of mind and the notion of 'creativity' from the eighteenth to the nineteenth centuries, see Abrams, *The Mirror and the Lamp*; Clark, *The Theory of Inspiration*.

radical innovation—that is, of inventing or discovering or unveiling something original, new, unique, unexpected, formerly unknown.[47] Thirdly, the
ultimate instance of human creative and innovative activity is bound up with
the Torah. Invested with infinite potentialities of interpretation and limitless
cosmic power, that sacred text offers itself as a tool. By its means, human
beings can engender something that is uniquely their own. Innovative rereadings of Scripture are thus 'poetic' in a primary etymological sense: they fabri-
cate or produce new 'worlds of meaning' through language, in the mode of
exegetical activity envisioned here.[48] We should note, finally, the subtly self-
referential aspect of these reflections. As he contemplates the metaphysics of
interpreting the Torah and explores the dynamics of the creative process,
innovative thinking, and the poetics of exegesis, R. Jacob Joseph in effect
masterfully performs each of them in the course of his own discussion.

To conclude, this *derashah* offers a rare window onto the inner dynamics of
hasidic hermeneutics, its means and its ends. Moreover, it seems to give voice
to an ethics of reading and writing, teaching and learning, well worth our
notice. In effect, the passage from the Zohar (i. 5*a*) that R. Jacob Joseph cites—
an important statement of mystical doctrine, voiced there by Rabbi Shimon
bar Yohai himself—does highlight the ontological function and creative
power of language and the Torah, and their nexus with various other dimensions of reality.[49] But in recalling that passage, R. Jacob Joseph shifts the focus
from the mystical or magical meanings implicit in the kabbalistic notion of
creating esoteric 'new worlds' through words. His interest in this *derashah* is
not in abstract linguistic codes or virtual, theurgic potencies that may be
unleashed by deconstructing the sacred text, nor in performing a mystical
event or a 'ritualistic reading'.[50] Rather, the hermeneutic that he envisages uses

[47] Pope (*Creativity: Theory, History, Practice*, 57, citing Boden, *Dimensions of Creativity*)
notes that 'novelty may be defined with reference either to the individual concerned or to the
whole of human history. This allows for the fact that someone may make a discovery or experience a personal break-through (what Boden calls 'P-creativity', new to the person) but that it
may be already known or at some time have been known (what she calls 'H-creativity', new in
history).'

[48] The English term 'poetics' comes from the Greek *poiesis*, which in turn comes from *poiein*,
'to make, to do'. On this sense see Arendt, *The Human Condition*, 169–70: 'Thus Democritus
praised the divine genius of Homer, who "framed a cosmos out of all kinds of words" . . . from
thought's original home in the heart or head of man [to] its eventual destination in the world . . .
written down and transformed into a tangible thing among things.'

[49] The passage from the Zohar is frequently cited, both by kabbalists and hasidic masters.

[50] My reading here parts ways with the approach that has dominated academic interest in
hasidic hermeneutics to date. See pp. 18–21 of the Introduction above.

language in an immediate, communicative way. Its purpose is to create or enact or offer an experience of reading that moves beyond the notions of 'text' and 'interpretation' current in postmodern discourse. Ultimately, this mode of 'novel Torah interpretations' seeks to illuminate new horizons of meaning: to uncover the deepest mysteries of human existence, to sense the presence of God in history, to perceive the affinities that secretly bind together all the scattered fragments of reality. Here, I think, is the root source of its transformative, redemptive potential and creative vitality. R. Jacob Joseph's *derashah* on Genesis, with its implicit new reading of a central passage from the Zohar, thus sets out a fundamentally important aspect of hasidic hermeneutics, its power and its promise.

'They Made Their Souls Anew': R. Menahem Nahum Twersky of Chernobyl, *Me'or einayim*

As metaphor and as mystical reality, the term 'worlds' bears richly evocative associations in traditional Jewish sources. I'd like to read the following *derashah* as another hasidic master's perspective on what it means to create new worlds, the urgency of the task, and the crucial role of hermeneutical engagement with the Torah in order to carry it out. The author of this teaching is R. Menahem Nahum Twersky (1730–97). He began his path as a follower of the Ba'al Shem Tov and then joined the circle of R. Dov Baer, the Magid of Mezhirech. In the latter part of the eighteenth century he served as town preacher of Chernobyl. The *derashot* collected in his two works, *Me'or einayim* (*Light of the Eyes*) and *Hanhagot yeshirot* (*Upright Practices*), record his discourses from those years.[51]

'God appeared [*vayera*] to him while he sat at the opening of the tent' [Gen. 18: 1]. The Torah, as we know, is called *torah* because it shows the way [*hora'at derekh*].[52] This means that from all the stories, from the hints concealed in each word of the Torah, we must try to seek counsel, to learn the ways of serving God.[53] And although the fullness of its mystery will be revealed only when the Messiah comes, when 'the whole earth will be filled with knowledge of the Lord' [Isa. 11: 9], even now the Torah is read

[51] On the figure of R. Nahum, as he was called, and for an introduction to his teachings, see Green, *Upright Practices*, 18, 20–4. In the following decades, his eight grandsons would become the founders of powerful hasidic dynasties throughout Ukraine.

[52] The three words emphasized in this opening sentence are conceived as sharing a common root: *vayera*, *torah*, *hora'ah*.

[53] Alluding to Rashi on this verse (Gen. 18: 1): 'God appeared to counsel him regarding circumcision', cited in other *derashot*. See *Me'or einayim*, 38, 40.

on multiple levels, called PARDES.[54] And so it is up to us to detect the signs in it that show us how to do His will. See: 'In the beginning' [*bereshit*]: it was for the Torah and for the people of Israel that God created the heavens and the earth.[55] And because this is so—that the world's existence depends on the Torah and on Israel, that they never separate from one another, but Israel must cleave to the Torah forever—if then a Jew, heaven forbid, should cut himself off from the Torah, the righteous of the generation must try to bring him back. They must pull his precious essence out from the mire into which he has sunken . . . And when the *tsadik* merits to help such Jews return, of him it is written, 'If you bring forth an honourable person from depravity, then you will be like My own mouth' [Jer. 15: 19]. This means that just as I created the heavens and the earth with the words of My mouth [Ps. 33: 6], so too must you. Create new heavens and earth with your words, now, continually . . . as the Zohar teaches. Such a thing can come about when, united in partnership, as it were, with God, the *tsadik*—through his innovative, new interpretations of the Torah—manages to draw precious souls out from the husks of impurity.[56]

As R. Nahum contemplates the beginning of the weekly portion of 'Vayera', its first verse signals a mode of reading and living that he recognizes as essential. To clarify the semantic connection between the two words he juxtaposes—*vayera* and *torah*—he takes a closer look at the scenario with which the *parashah* opens. Its details lead him to propose that certain hints of meaning concealed in the verses of Scripture may suddenly appear in the landscape of one's consciousness—in much the same way that God 'made Himself visible' to Abraham here, first of all, before any direct act of speech.[57] And although neither he nor his life's story is referred to explicitly in the rest of this teaching, the figure of Abraham and the idea of his larger mission are a formative presence in it. To appreciate what R. Nahum is doing in this *derashah*, we need first to recall some of its subtexts—the essential features attributed to Abraham in the midrashic imagination and in kabbalistic tradition.

[54] On the four levels of scriptural meaning in Jewish tradition known as *pardes* see Katz, 'Mysticism and the Interpretation of Sacred Scripture'; Idel, *Absorbing Perfections*, 429–48; Fishbane, *Sacred Attunement*, ch. 2.

[55] Cf. Rashi on Gen. 1: 1, after the midrash in *Gen. Rab.* 1: 4.

[56] *Me'or einayim*, 'Vayera', 40.

[57] R. Nahum devotes much attention to this narrative and the notion of the covenant. Most directly, it is a covenant of flesh, represented in the act of circumcision (*berit milah*); metaphorically, what is at issue is a covenant of the heart. One who can risk the vulnerability of an 'exposed' heart, he suggests, can merit a revelation of the Torah's concealed meaning (30, 32, 37). In another *derashah* he offers an alternative reading of this story. 'As we know, what the holy Torah recounts takes place in every individual, eternally. And so, in truth, the Creator is there with each Jew, even the most notorious of sinners. The proof: there isn't an evildoer who doesn't

A few chapters earlier in the biblical narrative, Abraham (with Sarah) is noted as having won renown for 'the souls that they made' in Haran (Gen. 12: 5). These souls, the Rabbis taught, were converts: Abraham had liberated them from pagan superstitions and initiated them into monotheistic belief. Or, put less philosophically, through concern for their creaturely needs, he aroused in them a new awareness of their Creator and the desire to live in accordance with God's will.[58] A second midrashic reading transplants Abraham's valiant soul-making efforts from the quasi-historical setting of the biblical narrative to a more supernatural plane. It is this second reading most of all, along with its thematic images and emotional charge, that R. Nahum takes up and integrates into his own conception. In a characteristic exegetical move, the Rabbis conflate Abraham's 'making of souls' and the scenario with which 'Vayera' begins. Here are two variants of that reading:

'At the opening of the tent' [Gen. 18: 1]. You, Abraham, made an 'opening' for wayfarers, you opened the way for converts; if not for you, I would not have created heaven and earth . . . Rabbi Levi said: In time to come, Abraham will sit at the opening to Gehenna and he will rescue every circumcised Jew from having to pass through it.[59]

Rabbi Shimon ben Lakish explained the verse 'Wayfarers journeying through the vale of tears' [Ps. 84: 7]: These are transgressors who deserve to be punished in Gehenna. But Abraham meets them on their way. He pulls them up and brings them back—all of them, that is, except for Jews who took idolatresses and those who disguise their circumcision. Them he does not recognize.[60]

'At the opening'. Beckoning inwards into the home, leading out towards the road, caverning downwards into hell, offered metaphorically to a stranger in a quiet gesture of kindness—'the opening' is a powerful trope. The Rabbis combine these connotations of 'opening' to depict a manner of presence that, in their eyes, Abraham embodies. As mentor or teacher or saviour, as guardian of the original divine covenant, the indelible fleshly mark of Jewish identity, Abraham exerts a transformative influence. Significantly, on this particularistic midrashic reading 'the souls that they made' refers less to converts than to renegades-become-penitents: those wayward children of Israel who are drifting towards the abyss yet are longing, perhaps, to be found along the way, somehow to return to the Jewish community before they're lost.

have pangs of conscience from time to time—this is God revealing Himself to those wayward Jews as they go on their way' (*Me'or einayim*, 36).

---

[58] *Gen. Rab.* 39: 14; BT *Sot.* 10*b*.   [59] *Gen. Rab.* 48: 8.

[60] Citing the scenario that appears in BT *Eruv.* 19*a*; my translation follows Rashi's commentary there.

These midrashic associations resonate clearly in R. Nahum's *derashah*. Adding a second concept, drawn from kabbalistic teaching, he reconceives Abraham's mode of being in the world on the model of the hasidic *tsadik*.[61] As social reality and as symbol, that righteous individual is charged with the responsibility to restore unity in places of disconnection and estrangement. To do so, Abraham as *tsadik* must go out into the world, 'lower himself' from his spiritual heights in order to meet the other, and care about worldly needs. His holy task is 'to draw precious souls out from the husks of impurity' and aid them in recovering spiritual wholeness and their connection with God: as R. Nahum puts it simply in another *derashah*—to help them 'recognize that they are Jews'.[62] These encounters are personal, emotional, and charged with ethical urgency. Abraham as *tsadik* lives out the fecundity at the heart of the teacher–student relationship. The mandate set out in the Zohar, transplanted into the context of R. Nahum's *derashah*, now alludes to Abraham's primary, generative mission: 'Just as I created the heavens and the earth with the words of My mouth [Ps. 33: 6], so too must you. Create new worlds with your words, now, continually.' Abraham, as R. Nahum noted in the opening lines of the *derashah*, knows how to attend to the signs that reveal themselves to him, to 'take counsel' both from God's clear directives and from what remains unsaid, between the lines. 'Your words', then, give voice to the *tsadik*'s own renewed, renewing awareness of the Divine concealed-revealed in the Torah and in the world. Communicated to others, his words have a transformative, even redeeming, effect. 'Innovative interpretations of Torah', associated in this

---

[61] Conceived already in rabbinical sources, the figure of the perfectly righteous individual was further developed in medieval ethical literature, Lurianic kabbalah, and of course Shabatean writings. In effect, almost none of the thematic elements associated with the *tsadik* in hasidic teaching are original, while pre-hasidic sources develop them in abundance. R. Elijah ben Abraham Hakohen Itamari's *Shevet musar* (Constantinople, 1712) is an illuminating example. A highly influential book of popular kabbalah widely circulated in Hebrew and Yiddish, and drawing heavily on earlier sources, this work contains a long list of attributes associated with the *tsadik*. Some of them are clearly echoed in the hasidic sermon that we are discussing and others we'll read soon, such as: *boneh olam* (builder of worlds), *mevatel gezerot, mehapekh gezerah* (annuls and reverses divine decrees); *makhtir torah* (interprets the Torah's mysteries with honour); *mesame'aḥ elyonim* (brings joy to heaven through his teachings); *matsil nefashot* (saves souls); *madrikh shavim* (guides penitents); *podeh nefashot* (redeems souls from hell, pulls 'sparks of holiness out of the husks of impurity'). Cf. *Shevet musar*, ch. 39. Already in midrashic sources, central biblical figures are associated with the image of the righteous person (*tsadik*). On the hasidic concept of the *tsadik*, see Rapoport-Albert, 'God and the Zaddik'; Green, 'The Zaddik as *Axis Mundi*'; Elior, *The Mystical Origins of Hasidism*, 126–51.

[62] *Me'or einayim*, 'Vayera', 39. On the figure of Abraham as *tsadik*, directed to 'go out into the world', see *Me'or einayim*, 'Lekh lekha', 23.

derashah with Abraham as hasidic *tsadik*, can 'open' those he meets to new dimensions of experience and understanding, perhaps even inspire them to change their lives. In this sense, what R. Nahum depicts is a mode of hermeneutical engagement that is profoundly creative—in a literal as well as figurative sense. Hasidic teaching, embodied here in the figure of Abraham, has thus been invested with the power to 'make souls', or make them anew. And, as the Rabbis said, to save a Jewish soul is commensurate with saving 'a whole world'.[63]

To See and To Be Seen: R. Levi Isaac of Berdichev, *Kedushat levi*

We should recall, however, that in late eighteenth-century eastern Europe this 'making of souls' for hasidism was, in the eyes of many, an insidious tactic and one that portended the ruin of the entire Jewish world. Research on the history of the conflict between hasidism and its opponents, the *mitnagedim*, has brought to light the central issues of contention. Among them were struggles for political power, with severe economic and social repercussions, separatist religious and halakhic practices, and perceived heretical beliefs —all of which threatened to undermine traditional hegemony. Adversaries accused the hasidim of subverting Jewish religious and social values and condemned their teachings as perversions of Jewish sacred texts. As the *mitnagedim* saw it, hasidic leaders were 'hunting down throngs of young Jewish souls with the help of their emissaries, whom they send to every Jewish town to incite them and lead them astray, telling them: This is our new path—our forefathers never even imagined it'.[64]

The *derashah* that concerns us next might profitably be read against the background of this conflict. Its author is R. Levi Isaac of Berdichev (1740–1809), one of the Magid of Mezhirech's closest disciples and follower of the Magid of Zlochow (Żelechów). In the course of his lifetime R. Levi Isaac served in the rabbinate in four east European cities: Ryczywół, Żelechów, Pinsk, and Berdichev. He was one of the most distinctive community leaders

---

[63] Mishnah *San.* 4: 5; Tos. *Hor.* 2; BT *BB* 85a; *Avot derabi natan* A 26. The phrase 'We make our souls anew' is Arnold Schoenberg's, appearing at the end of the introduction he wrote to his *Kol Nidre* (1938). It gives voice to the composer's own dramatic awakening and return, after some thirty-five years of alienation, to Judaism, to community, and to God. As Andre Neher put it, 'Here Schoenberg was the representative of *teshuva* as such' (*They Made Their Souls Anew*, 168).

[64] R. David of Makov, *Shever poshim*, 64b–65a, in Wilensky, *Hasidim and Mitnagedim* (Heb.), ii. 160; 'our forefathers never even imagined it' alludes to Deut. 32: 17.

of the time, and his activism is unusually well documented in both hasidic and anti-hasidic sources. As contemporary historical documents, they offer important insight into the issues of contention. One telling event involving R. Levi Isaac took place sometime before 1781: R. Abraham Katzenellenbogen, the rabbi of Brest-Litovsk, challenged him to a public debate, which was held in Praga, near Warsaw. At its end, the *mitnagedim* claimed victory. But as the hasidim showed no sign of having been defeated, three years later R. Katzenellenbogen initiated a second round of dispute. This time it took place in written form, at R. Levi Isaac's request. In a public letter dated 1784, R. Katzenellenbogen presented a list of accusations condemning hasidic practices in general and calumniating R. Levi Isaac in particular. The latter apparently made no response.[65] A second zealous *mitnaged* who did not conceal his personal antagonism towards R. Levi Isaac was R. David of Makov. His twenty-four-page anti-hasidic essay, *Zamir aritsim*, published in 1798, levels a scathing attack on sixteen major hasidic figures, from the Ba'al Shem Tov (d.1760) and to the author's own day, R. Levi Isaac among them. Citing the Ba'al Shem's 'Holy Epistle', the famed letter to his brother-in-law recounting his soul ascent, R. David derides that account as a hallucinatory dream of grandeur or, worse, an outright lie. The Ba'al Shem Tov's teachings, along with those of his followers, he declares, are incomprehensible—not for the esoteric reasons they pretend to (their depth and complexity), but because the hasidim, in their boorish ignorance of grammar and syntax, hideously distort the purity of the Holy Tongue. What can be made out from their teachings is condemnatory and so, R. David repeatedly concludes, their writings must be burnt.[66]

[65] See Wilensky, *Hasidim and Mitnagedim* (Heb.), i. 122. In his essay *Zamir aritsim* (1798), R. David of Makov cites R. Katzenellenbogen's letter to R. Levi Isaac, and remarks that the latter did not respond to him. He contrasts the audacity and overweening pride evident, as he sees it, in R. Levi Isaac's silence to R. Jonathan Eybeshuetz's effusive and humble expressions of self-defense in response to R. Jacob Emden's accusations against him. See Wilensky, *Hasidim and Mitnagedim* (Heb.), ii. 218. The comparison is pointedly suggestive, apparently with the intent of underlining just how heinous hasidism was in R. David's eyes. Notably, at the synod held in Mir in 1752, R. Katzenellebogen, as rabbi of Slutsk, had signed a proposition to excommunicate R. Jonathan Eybeschuetz as a Shabatean.

[66] See Wilensky, *Hasidim and Mitnagedim* (Heb.), ii. 27–8. In this essay, R. David phrases his accusations only in general terms. But in a second collection of anti-hasidic documents published anonymously, entitled *Shever poshim*, he attacks R. Isaac Levi personally (Wilensky, ii. 196–7), cites specific teachings that he has read in hasidic homiletical works, such as *Toledot ya'akov yosef*, *Tsofenat pa'ane'aḥ*, *Magid devarav leya'akov*, *No'am elimelekh*, and the *Tanya*, and condemns them as heretical in content. See Wilensky, ii. 194–201.

Without doubt, R. Levi Isaac was aware that the exegetical approach developed in hasidism—specifically, the radical autonomy claimed by hasidic authors in their rereading of canonical works—was controversial. The following *derashah* offers an oblique, perhaps even ironic response, tinged with humour, to some of the larger issues at hand. Implicitly, R. Levi Isaac touches here on two crucial questions: What value (personal, existential, metaphysical) could there be in hasidic modes of engagement with Jewish textual tradition? And, most acutely: How does the original Author regard the hasidic masters' (mis)readings of His sacred text? His statements regarding hasidic hermeneutics are, I would suggest, an important instance of self-definition. Here, that self-definition is attained rhetorically 'from the outside': from the perspective of opposing others (the *mitnagedim*) and of the absolute Other.

Formally this *derashah* relates to the opening of chapter 6 of the mishnaic tractate *Avot*. The unusual redaction history of that final chapter is reflected in the words with which the Rabbis chose to preface it. These words alert R. Levi Isaac to a larger statement concealed within them, one with far-reaching implications.[67] He reads them as emblematic of the entire hermeneutical project called the Oral Torah:

'The Sages taught [this chapter] in the language of the Mishnah. Blessed be He who chose them and their teaching. R. Meir said: One who learns Torah for its own sake will merit many things. He is called friend, beloved, etc., rejoicer of God, etc.' [*Avot* 6: 1] To explain: it is known that we have two Torahs, one written and one oral—the Written Torah given to us at Sinai, and the Oral Torah, called 'our Torah' [*toratenu*]. As Rashi interpreted the verse, '[His desire is in God's Torah] and in his Torah [*torato*] he meditates day and night' [Ps. 1: 2]: once he has meditated on it, it becomes his own. Now, the Oral Torah is called 'ours' because the Jewish people—that is, our *tana'im* and *amora'im* [the sages of the Mishnah and Talmud] and the wise in the generations after them—have the power to explicate and interpret the Written Torah as they will, according to their own understanding, even if such was not the original intent of Heaven. So the Sages averred [BT *BM* 59b] in the incident concerning Rabbi Eliezer and Rabbi Joshua, when the latter got to his feet and declared, 'We'll take no notice of that voice from heaven claiming that Rabbi Eliezer is right.' The

---

[67] This section of the mishnaic tractate *Avot* originated as a separate *baraita* (a body of teachings by sages of the mishnaic era, but not included in the Mishnah). It is formulated in Hebrew, 'the language of the Mishnah' (rather than Aramaic), and was added to *Avot* as a final chapter. See Maimonides, *Perush hamishnayot, Avot* 5: 23. My translation reflects the partial citation of the Mishnah as it appears in R. Levi Isaac's *derashah*, as these are the components of the text that he develops. Compare a teaching associated with the Ba'al Shem Tov on the same mishnaic text in *Keter shem tov*, par. 320, p. 86.

very same is true of the *tsadikim* in our own times: they too have the power to explicate the Torah as they wish. And even if the original intent of Heaven was otherwise, they overturn divine will, so to speak, to conform with their will and their own reading of the Torah. And so it is in other domains as well—the power is theirs to reverse divine will and change decrees from evil to good, for '"the *tsadik* rules through the fear of God" [2 Sam. 23: 3]; who rules Me?—the *tsadik*! The Holy One blessed be He makes a decree and the righteous annul it' [BT *MK* 16*b*]. They make divine will conform, as it were, to their own.[68] . . .

Now, the individual who attains such a level is like the king's second [*mishneh*], his viceroy, for he can overturn and alter God's intent as he wishes—in interpreting the Torah and in everything else too. Indeed, the *tana'im* and Rabbi [Judah the Prince], who compiled the Oral Tradition—their learning enabled them to affect reality, to change divine will, to repair worlds . . . and thus their teaching is called Mishnah.[69]

Let me take a moment to consider the exegetical techniques at play here in the first part of the *derashah*. In effect, this passage is a mosaic of citations. R. Levi Isaac extends the immediate meaning of each of them, metaphorically or associatively. He links the various textual allusions to one another through logical or causal connections. Thematically, this passage brings together well-known hermeneutical rules and precedents set out in rabbinical literature. Adopting the Rabbis' rhetorical stance as his own, R. Levi Isaac presents hasidism as the organic continuation of Jewish exegetical tradition. Implicitly, all this frames a fundamental, controversial issue: the legitimacy of originating new, unexpected meanings from canonical texts, meanings that even seem blatantly to contradict 'the original intent of Heaven'.

R. Levi Isaac's defence of the *tsadikim* and their actions (theurgic and exegetical) is founded on a re-evaluation of some central concepts. One of them, provocatively named 'two Torahs' by the Rabbis, concerns the primary distinction between written and oral tradition.[70] Unarguably, the Written Torah records the 'original intent of Heaven'—what we might want to call the objective meaning of the text, while the Oral Torah would be various

---

[68] 'As it were'—*kiveyekhol*.

[69] *Kedushat levi*, *Likutim*, 306. These lines indicate third variant vocalizations of the same consonant cluster: *mishneh* ('second' to the King); *mishnah* (rabbinic teaching); *meshaneh* (change, alter). The etymological root of *mishnah* is sh-n-h, meaning to learn or study.

[70] The term 'two Torahs' appears in many midrashic sources, e.g. *Num. Rab.* 14: 9; it is provocative because the term 'two Torahs' also bears a second, negative connotation of divisiveness within the Jewish world brought on by stubborn and destructive disputes. Shaul Magid discusses a teaching of the Ba'al Shem Tov on the same passage from *Avot* in 'The Intolerance of Tolerance', 362.

imperfect, 'subjective' understandings reached by the Rabbis, and now equally by 'the wise in the generations after them'. But R. Levi Isaac rejects the false antithesis of the interpreter's subjectivity and some single, superior, objective, absolute meaning-in-itself. Instead, he perceives Oral Torah as an event, a vital instance of appropriation and assimilation: 'once he has meditated on it, it becomes his own'.[71] The opening lines of *Avot* 6: 1 indeed affirm that, from a divine perspective, this is the 'chosen', most desirable mode of engagement with the Written Torah.

Turning now to the next lines of the Mishnah that he cites—'He is called friend, beloved, etc., rejoicer of God'—R. Levi Isaac explores the dynamics of that intimacy. The crucial sense of belonging to tradition, signalled in the phrases 'our Torah' / 'his Torah', enables and also justifies personal interpretation of it. To highlight the emotional, counter-rational modalities involved here, R. Levi Isaac offers a parable (not cited in the passage above). Heard from his master R. Dov Baer, the Magid of Mezhirech, the parable tells of a father and his beloved only son. So great is the father's affection for his son that he will gladly yield to his wishes. Effectively this means that the son can cause the father to want something new, different from what he willed at first. Moreover, the father rejoices in the son's ability to 'change his mind'.

This father–beloved son relationship, with the reversal in hierarchy it will potentially tolerate, models the connection that people called *tsadikim* have with God. In the next lines of his *derashah* R. Levi Isaac alludes, through the prism of the midrashic imagination, to an array of people whom the Rabbis describe as *tsadikim* in light of their power to reverse natural law and overturn divine decrees. Among the figures mentioned in that role in midrashic and kabbalistic tradition are Abraham, Jacob, Moses, Joshua, Samuel, Elijah, Elisha, and Rabbi Shimon bar Yohai.[72] The deeds of these righteous individuals, cast or recast in post-biblical tradition in the role of God's 'beloved son', show how each of them made divine will conform to his own intent. Significantly, their stories emphasize that in each case their annulment of divine decrees actually fulfilled God's ultimate will. Admittedly, though, in all of this the image of the *tsadik* has little about it that is truly novel. As the proof-texts attest, these elements already appear in earlier sources.

---

[71] Gadamer uses these terms to speak of the 'new creation of understanding' that comes about by listening intently to what the tradition has 'to say to me'; *Truth and Method*, 468, 355.

[72] See e.g. Abraham's story (Gen. 18: 17–33) retold by the Rabbis in *Deut. Rab.* 10: 3. Further examples include BT *MK* 16*b* concerning miracles enacted by the prophets Elijah, Elisha, and Samuel; Zohar i. 10*a* in reference to Moses as *tsadik*; Zohar iii. 15*a* concerning Rabbi Shimon bar Yohai.

And yet R. Levi Isaac's *derashah* also displays a number of radically innovative exegetical moves. For one, he abstracts the concept of Oral Torah;
in doing so he extends the Rabbis' unbounded creative licence to 'the wise of
all the generations'—including, of course, the hasidic ones among them.
Secondly, he states that 'the *tsadikim* in our own times' enjoy the very same
intimate and indulgent father–beloved son relationship with God that was
modelled by their most illustrious forebears. Thirdly, now the theurgic power
that has been entrusted to the *tsadikim*, enabling them to overturn divine will
and reverse heavenly decrees, is manifest above all in their exegetical activity:
the *tsadik* 'can overturn and alter God's intent as he wishes—in interpreting
the Torah and in everything else too'. Notably, what all this means is that
these metaphysical powers charge the hasidic *tsadik* with a heavy burden of
incumbency. In his role as 'second to the King', his crucial task is to sweeten
harsh judgements that threaten suffering and destruction, and so to change
the face of reality. That is to be accomplished, above all, through a transformative reading of the Torah, by understanding its verses in a way that can 'save
the world'.

Shifting perspective, R. Levi Isaac concludes his *derashah* with a glance at
this immense project from the rhetorical vantage point of the absolute Other.
To put it bluntly: what does God have to say about the hasidic masters' daring
revisions of His sacred text? The answer, R. Levi Isaac proposes, may be
detected in a well-known passage in the Talmud (BT *Shab.* 105*a*). On his reading, here in fact is one of the most self-revealing statements found in rabbinical teaching, voiced by the original Author himself, as it were, regarding his
greatest masterpiece and its readership:

This is what the Rabbis hinted in their interpretation of the verse 'I am the Lord your
God' [Exod. 20: 2]. The letters spelling 'I' [*anokhi*] open to mean, 'My will, recorded in
the Written Torah, is given over to you'—it is My will that you should overturn My
will as you wish. Now, lest you think I'll be displeased when humans do such a thing,
'I' [can be decoded a second way]. The Rabbis continued: *anokhi* also means, 'I will
reveal to you what great pleasure it gives Me when you overpower Me'. And so they
said: 'The Holy One, blessed be He—[His children] defeat Him and He rejoices'
[BT *Pes.* 119*a*].[73]

---

[73] *Kedushat levi, Likutim,* 306. In the Talmud, the Rabbis 'decode' the word designating
God's 'self' (*anokhi*) with three different acrostics. The first phrase, offered by Rabbi Yohanan in
Aramaic, translated more literally (following Rashi), would be: 'I Myself write and give'. On the
traditional interpretation, this statement avers the unmediated, divine origin of the Written
Torah as the authentic record of divine will, and God's wilful surrender of that document into
human hands, enabling them to engender the Oral Torah from it themselves. The Rabbis then

This, undeniably, is a revisionary reading that well serves R. Levi Isaac's ends. Applying the principles he set out in the first part of the *derashah*, the talmudic passage addresses, equally, every Jew. His reading avers that in delivering the Written Torah into human hands, God's profoundest desire is for them to generate from it something of their own. Creative, personal understandings of scriptural meaning—the 'Oral Torah' that every individual can engender—are thus original in two paradoxically opposed yet intertwined senses. They can originate (that is, bring into existence) new dimensions of reality, while their power to do so necessarily stems from their connection to the pre-existing origin, the root source of authority—the Written Torah. In effect, as Harold Bloom puts it, the originality of 'strong readings' such as these comes about by their 'completing the precursor' through a deliberate act of misreading or misprision—retaining its terms but making them mean in a different and novel way.[74] Most striking, of course, is R. Levi Isaac's contention that the perverse necessity of misinterpretation is written into the Torah itself and enciphered in, of all places, its Author's very 'self' (*anokhi*). On his deciphering of that essential selfhood: 'it is My will that you should overturn My will as you wish.'

You must admit that no one but a 'beloved son' could make such a claim. In an admirable show of confidence, R. Levi Isaac has situated hasidic modes of reading squarely in the midst of traditional Jewish exegetical practices. This means, by implication, that contemporary *tsadikim* would assuredly be 'called friend, beloved, rejoicer of God'. Their teachings, even as they overturn the original intent of Heaven, must truly merit being called 'Torah for its own sake'.

We can only speculate on the self-referential dimensions of all this regarding R. Levi Isaac himself. But perhaps some intimation of them may be

offer two more acrostics for *anokhi* that similarly concern the primordial connection between the Written and Oral Torah, and affirm that both of them preserve and communicate God's original intent with absolute loyalty. See *Dikdukei soferim* on *Shab.* 105*a*; Edels (Maharsha), *Ḥidushei agadot* ad loc.; Horowitz, *Shenei luḥot haberit*, ii. 291–2.

[74] See Bloom, *The Anxiety of Influence*, 11–16; *The Necessity of Misreading*, 101–8; *A Map of Misreading*, 3. Rob Pope explores the ongoing history of the two senses of 'original': it means both 'from the origins' (the oldest) and 'innovative' (the newest). That is, it can mean 'from the beginning, former, ancient', and it can mean 'fresh, new, novel, unexpected'. The first meaning of 'original' was dominant until the middle of the eighteenth century; the second meaning became dominant thereafter. As Pope (p. 58) notes: 'Grasping the distinctions *and* connections between these two senses is crucial if there is to be an understanding of creativity that is itself both "old" and "new": historically informed and theoretically aware, sensitive to ancient precedent as well as modern preference.' *Creativity: Theory, History, Practice*, 59–60.

found elsewhere in his homiletical writings. In effect, in a second *derashah* R. Levi Isaac integrates this same reading of the talmudic passage (*Shab.* 105*a*). There he gives a name to the creative elan that may well have enabled it.[75] Re-examining the larger biblical context to which the Rabbis refer, he notes there that the giving of the Torah—with God's concomitant 'giving up' on absolute authorial control over its contents, thereby 'giving over' divine will to human whim—can take place only in an existential state of absolute freedom. That, indeed, is what the complete verse in question asserts: 'I [*anokhi*] am the Lord your God, who brought you out of the land of Egypt, out of the house of bondage' (Exod. 20: 2). To hear the overtones of meaning in this revelation of God's 'self' (*anokhi*) as the Rabbis did (and as R. Levi Isaac does even more intensely)—such a level of perception can be attained only in the spiritual mode that the kabbalists called *moḥin degadlut*. This elevated state of 'large-mindedness' is free of all manner of constriction, threatened by no one, without apologetics. And so, R. Levi Isaac continues:

'He who serves God in expanded consciousness [*moḥin degadlut*] feels no fear; nothing that happens to him will make him tremble, and the Other Side [the powers of evil] cannot subjugate him; rather, it is he who will emerge victorious. . . . When God makes a decree, he has the power to annul it and sweeten harsh judgments, to transform them from distress [**tsarah**] to favour [**retseh**].'[76]

The *tsadik* portrayed here has much in common with the image, in popular memory, of R. Levi Isaac himself—fearless protector of the Jewish people, compassionate and beloved *rebbe*.[77] His actions speak cogently of the many ways of serving God—as spiritual leader and as reader and interpreter of sacred texts. His *derashot* clearly offer new perspectives on hasidic hermeneutics. The spiritual stance that they give voice to is an important gesture of self-definition, an implicit response to opponents and naysayers. R. Levi Isaac of Berdichev, after all, was known by the sobriquet Defender of Israel. In these *derashot* he advocates on behalf of the hermeneutical project of hasidism and of the *tsadikim*, himself among them, who carry it out.

[75] *Kedushat levi*, 'Yitro', 134. This discourse is longer and more developed.

[76] Ibid. The words *tsarah* and *retseh* contain the same letters. Their permutation yields two radically different meanings; this symbolizes the possibility of transforming reality through similar gestures of 'reordering'.

[77] Ariel Evan Mayse discusses the influence of historical, hagiographical, polemical, and fictional sources that have contributed to the multi-faceted image of R. Levi Isaac in 'Of Letters and Leadership'. His essay includes an extensive survey of relevant primary and secondary sources.

'Well Said, Moses!': R. Gedaliah Rabinowitz of Linits, *Teshuot ḥen*

Of all the motifs and images that hasidic authors used self-reflexively, perhaps the most self-evident one is the biblical figure of Moses. The archetypal charismatic leader, Moses is impressive in his spiritual stature. A paragon of tireless aspiration, he is unparalleled in his devotion to the Jewish people, God, and the Torah. Moses is an intensely engaged receiver, intermediary, and translator; the ultimate Hermes figure, he crosses freely over the threshold between heaven and earth. Although his is the most intimate connection with God ever granted to a human being, he personifies humility and ego-annulment. All in all, a more obvious leadership model and exemplary illustration of hasidic ideology could not be found. At the beginning of this chapter, I noted Moses' part in the claim put forward by the hasidic masters for the legitimacy of the Ba'al Shem Tov's new path. Hasidism, as a link in the unbroken chain of reception and transmission of Jewish tradition, continues Moses' mission of bringing the world to its final redemption: 'Your light endures in all masters of law and received wisdom . . . as it is written, "Your wellsprings will flow forth"' (Zohar iii. 280*a*). Now I'd like to take a closer look at some more aspects of this evocative figure.

In the biblical narrative itself, and even more so in midrashic tradition, Moses' emotional world is made fully transparent and accessible to readers. One of the most remarkable dimensions of his inner experience is a nearly irremediable sense of insufficiency, marginality, and of his own contingency. This seems counterintuitive: after all, he is God's chosen prophet. Yet time and again, up to the last chapters of his life's story, the Bible recounts how Moses finds the role that has been imposed on him as leader to be overwhelming, stifling, even perilous. Are these aspects of his experience also meant to offer some kind of a role model for future generations? What useful insights could the hasidic masters possibly draw from them?

The following *derashah* touches on these questions. Its author is R. Gedaliah Rabinowitz of Linits (d.1803), an important but little-known figure who was active in the early period of hasidism.[78] R. Gedaliah's first encounter with

---

[78] To date there has been no academic study of his teachings. His discourses, collected in the book *Teshuot ḥen* (1816), were recorded by R. Gedaliah Rabinowitz's disciple, R. Leib Dayan of Linits—himself the son of R. Dov Baer of Linits, the author and redactor of *Shivḥei habesht* (In Praise of the Ba'al Shem Tov). In the introduction he wrote to *Teshuot ḥen*, R. Leib Dayan attests that his teacher R. Gedaliah read and approved his transcription (*Teshuot ḥen*, 27). A unique and important resource for early hasidic traditions, *Teshuot ḥen* preserves teachings in the name of

the Ba'al Shem Tov was in his childhood years, most probably in the late 1730s or early 1740s: on his visits to Polonnoye, the Ba'al Shem Tov would stay at the home of his father, R. Isaac Dayan. As a young man R. Gedaliah travelled from time to time to Międzybóż. The *derashot* recorded in his book entitled *Teshuot ḥen* include teachings that he heard from the Ba'al Shem Tov on those occasions. His main teacher and mentor, however, was R. Aryeh Leib, known as the Mokhiaḥ of Polonnoye, who numbered among the Ba'al Shem Tov's inner circle. From the age of 18 R. Gedaliah served as rabbi in the town of Ostropol, later becoming a preacher and rabbi in Myropil as well, and he eventually settled in Linits (Ilintsy) in southern Ukraine. Some of the more well-known hasidic figures who were his contemporaries and friends include R. Pinhas of Korets, R. Levi Isaac of Berdichev, R. Aryeh Leib, known as the Shpoler Zeyde, and R. Menahem Nahum Twersky of Chernobyl. Through his teachings, R. Gedaliah draws a nuanced psychological portrait of Moses that may offer a response of sorts to the questions posed above. In this *derashah* his image unfolds in a three-part exposition. The first part reads:

'And you shall command the Children of Israel that they take for you pure olive oil' [Exod. 27: 10]. To explain this verse: It is said that Moses embodied the essence of knowledge [*da'at*].[79] This means that by sharing his own knowing with the Jewish people—who are as branches stemming from his root—they were able to understand how to serve God and to rescue their own souls from evil desires. Now, 'what has been is what will be' [Eccl. 1: 9]—as then, so is it still: in each and every generation, the righteous of the generation have that same essence called 'Moses'.[80] They, too, must bestow their knowledge upon the world in abundance, so that every Jew can find succour and healing of the soul, to save themselves as best they can from the inner drives that tempt them ceaselessly. And each individual *tsadik*—he nourishes those

other little-known hasidic thinkers of the first and second generations who were contemporaries of the Ba'al Shem Tov. See Index of Figures, *Teshuot ḥen*, 368–9. The most recent edition of *Teshuot ḥen* was published in 2012 in Jerusalem by R. Gedaliah's descendant, himself a hasidic *rebbe* by the same name, R. Gedaliah Rabinowitz. For biographical information on the original author see Rabinowitz's introduction in this critical edition, 11–12. All references to this work are to the 2012 edition.

[79] See Zohar ii. 221*a*; R. Nathan Neta Shapira, *Megaleh amukot*, 'Shemot'. In translating this passage, I've chosen to use two words for the Hebrew *da'at*—knowledge and knowing. While 'knowledge' is more literally precise, it also denotes factual information that has been definitively acquired, and that meaning is at odds with the message here. 'Knowing' fits less idiomatically into the sentences, but it better evokes the intuitive and intimate aspects of understanding gained through personal experience that R. Gedaliah seems to be talking about.

[80] Alluding to the kabbalistic reading of the first three words of Eccl. 1: 9 (e.g. Vital, *Sha'ar hapesukim*, 'Yitro'), whose beginning letters conceal Moses' name: מה שהיה הוא שיהיה.

branches that stem from his own soul-root in accordance with the spiritual resources deep within himself. But even the insights a Torah scholar has on some halakhic matter—those, too, are the 'aspect of Moses' that he has been granted, the gift of knowing just bestowed upon him. And so the holy R. Isaac Luria explained the compliment the Rabbis sometimes gave—'Well said, Moses!' In using those words to praise a *tana* or an *amora* for his perceptive understanding of the law, what the Rabbis really meant was: Don't suppose you have won that insight by the power of your own intellect! —really, it comes from the 'aspect of Moses' that sparkles inside you.[81]

The imagery that R. Gedaliah evokes to portray this essential 'aspect of Moses' is drawn from the menorah, alluded to in the opening verse of the *derashah* by the 'pure olive oil' used to light it. In the Bible's description, the six branches of the candelabrum that stood in the Tabernacle stemmed from a central shaft, yet all its composite parts were interconnected to form one integral, organic unit. In rabbinic tradition, the menorah symbolizes illumination; the oil is a metaphor for wisdom, Torah, knowledge flowing in abundance, understanding given and received, drawn into wicks renewed and relit evening by evening. In setting out the metonymy of Moses and the menorah, R. Gedaliah emphasizes the ethical responsibility the 'root-source' has towards the 'branches' that stem from it. That is, the knowledge Moses has attained is not for him alone; it must be shared with others, as those others are in truth an inseparable component of himself. The same type of relation— signalled by the phrase 'the aspect of Moses'—is what most fundamentally defines the existence of 'the righteous of the generation', of each individual *tsadik*, and even of the solitary Torah scholar. Ironically, though, they themselves may not be fully aware of it. And so the last lines of this section introduce a necessary refocusing meant for them. On R. Gedaliah's counterreading, 'Well said, Moses!' is not praise but rather a call to conscience. To use Levinas's terms, these words are meant to disrupt the narcissistic enclosure of being and self to which they may have fallen victim. Interpreted this way, then, 'Well said, Moses!' aims at neutralizing the scholar's (and here equally the *tsadik*'s) ego, in two important senses. First, when he is addressed as 'Moses', his given name is erased, to remind him that the knowledge or spirit-

[81] *Teshuot ḥen*, 'Tetsaveh', 88 and n. 254: although the author attributes this explanation to R. Isaac Luria, its source is most probably R. Isaiah Horowitz's *Shenei luḥot haberit* (ii. 254); the rhetorical turn of phrase there is nearly identical to the formulation in our *derashah*. The basic concept of the soul-presence of Moses 'in every generation and in each and every *tsadik* [*itpashtuta demosheh bekhol dara vedara uvekhol tsadik vetsadik*] appears in earlier sources, e.g. *Tikunei zohar* 69 (112*a*, 114*b*). More on this in Chapters 2 and 3. On the original meaning of the concept see Liebes, *Sections of the Zohar Lexicon* (Heb.), 303–4.

ual prowess he would claim as his own attainment really comes from somewhere else: from 'the aspect of Moses that sparkles inside you'. Second, it breaks open the totality closing him in and compels him to recognize his ethical obligation to the world. Whatever insights he has won were not granted for his solitary enjoyment. Only when shared with others in need of them does his knowing truly become something of lasting value, as belonging to tradition received and transmitted.

But just how is this complex role to be lived out? Looking more closely, the ostensibly harmonious relationship being described actually seems asymmetrical in the extreme. If the righteous are obliged to bear endless, unconditional responsibility for their generation, that would essentially hold them hostage to it, as Levinas would say. Such a position surely does violence to the self by forcing it into a position of domination by the other. And Moses' life story does in effect testify to his arduous, recurrent struggle with that very problem. In the second section of the *derashah* R. Gedaliah turns his attention to this troubling dissonance between ideal and real life.

Yet in a number of places Moses seems to complain bitterly about his lot,[82] that he's been given the burden of being shepherd and leader of Israel—as he says, 'Did I conceive this entire people?!' [Num. 11: 12]. For the obligations of leadership mandate that the leader will always be somehow diminished, his level lowered. As the head, he cannot but feel the ache of every limb. If any member of the people turns from the straight path and commits a misdeed, the leader himself is affected, as it says, 'He was pained because of our rebellious sins' [Isa. 53: 5].[83] But in truth he loses nothing from all that—rather, the opposite. When he arouses people to realize what they have done, their heart will repent; in the end, the merit of the community will be to his merit as well, and then his recompense will be inestimably greater.[84] . . . And, moreover, when the leader is in need of wisdom to guide the people, even though that wisdom might really be beyond his own ability to grasp, it is given to him solely for their sake. The Rabbis spoke of all that when they interpreted the verse, 'Go, descend—for your people has become corrupt' [Exod. 32: 7]: '[The Holy One said to Moses, Down you go!] All the greatness I granted you—it was only for the sake of Israel. [Now that

---

[82] He adapts the phrase in BT *Meg.* 6a: 'Zevulun complained [*hayah mitra'em*] about his lot'—referring to the share of territory he had been given in the Land of Israel; similarly, in the *Mekhilta* cited at the end of this passage, the same expression appears regarding Barukh ben Neriah—'he complained to God' that prophecy had been denied him.

[83] Cf. the image of God's 'suffering servant', Isa. 52: 13–53: 12.

[84] After *Avot* 5: 18. In the following lines of the *derashah* he cites Ibn Pakuda, *Duties of the Heart*, 10: 6 to the effect that gain (economic and spiritual) is always proportional to the amount or principle invested.

they've sinned, what need do I have of you?].'[85] Or, as Jeremiah responded to Barukh ben Neriah when he grieved, 'I've found no rest'—for Barukh was complaining that he had not been granted prophecy like all the others—and so Jeremiah reproved him, 'You're seeking greatness for yourself?! Don't seek it!' [Jer. 45: 3–5]. Meaning, as Rashi explains after the midrash *Mekhilta*: 'The Holy One said to him, If there's no vineyard, no need for a fence; if there isn't a flock, no need for a shepherd. I reveal Myself to the prophets only for the sake of Israel.'[86]

The focus in this part of the *derashah* is on Moses' darkest moment of diminution, the nadir in his career as divinely inspired head of the nation.[87] The sin of the Golden Calf sends him abruptly, literally down to earth: 'Go, descend—for your people has become corrupt'. The midrash that R. Gedaliah cites underlines the interdependence between shepherd and flock, yet the consequences it carries are now dire: 'All the greatness I granted you—it was only for the sake of Israel.' Should his role become extraneous, Moses would be left without any reason or justification for his own existence—'if there isn't a flock, no need for a shepherd'. To be forced utterly beyond the margins would amount to a total, irreversible annulment not only of his ego but of his very being.

Moses' impassioned efforts to avert the people's destruction climax in an ultimate gesture of self-effacement: 'And now if You would but forgive their sin! But if not, erase me now from Your book that You have written' (Exod. 32: 32). On the basis of a midrashic tradition, R. Gedaliah recognizes that oath, conditionally phrased though it is, as the subtext implicit in the opening verse of 'Tetsaveh'. The third section of his *derashah* brings that subtext to light. To appreciate R. Gedaliah's intent in this final section, we must first take note of the causal connection that, on his reading, covertly links the scenes that the Bible presents out of chronological order. Here no proof-text is cited, but in another *derashah* he brings that midrashic perspective clearly to the fore. 'As the Rabbis said, from Moses' birth until the end of the Torah, there isn't a *sidrah* without mention of his name except for this one. But because he said "erase me now from Your book", Moses' name does not appear in the portion "Tetsaveh".'[88] On R. Gedaliah's reading, then, the next chapter in Moses'

---

85 BT *Ber.* 32a.

86 *Teshuot ḥen*, 88–9. Cf. Rashi, citing *Mekhilta derabi yishma'el*, 'Bo, masekhta depasḥa', 1.

87 This despite the positive lines in the middle, from 'But in truth' until 'for their sake'.

88 *Teshuot ḥen, Likutim*, 190. This so-called midrash actually seems to have first emerged in the late thirteenth or early fourteenth century. The earliest indications of it appear in the Zohar corpus (Zohar iii. 246a; *Zohar ḥadash* 2, *Shir hashirim* 1a) and in the Torah commentaries of R. Bahya ben Asher (Exod. 32: 32) and R. Asher ben Jehiel (Rosh) (Exod. 27: 20), who notes that

story reflects his dismay as he realizes that his oath has become a painful reality: his name has de facto been erased from this part of 'the book that You have written'. How is he to contend with this distressing turn of events?

This, then, is the meaning of the verse, 'Now you shall command the Children of Israel'. These are words of comfort that God spoke to console Moses' heart and encourage him. He will continue to lead the Jewish people; his worries should grieve him no longer. Surely his reward will be doubled. For the connection between Israel and their Father in Heaven will, in the end, be attained by his merit. Thus He said, 'You shall command [*tetsaveh*] the Children of Israel': you shall bind them to Me. Even the sinners of Israel, you can draw them up from the lowest of places—for *tetsaveh* signifies connectedness, joining together, unification.[89] And then in recompense, and in response to your travails for their sake, 'they will take for you pure olive oil' [Exod. 27: 10]. . . . Through them, you will be granted an influx of wisdom—far greater than anything you have attained before. Because you share your own knowing with them, you can pull them up from the dregs—the forgetting and loss that olives symbolize—and all that will be transformed to oil, which means wisdom.[90]

Recontextualized in this manner, the opening verses of the Torah portion 'Tetsaveh' now read as a crucial resolution: God is effectively reframing Moses' trials with his burdensome, violative people into a larger picture. The spectre of violence and domination gives way, and Moses can finally catch sight of a possible relation of reciprocity between himself and the nation. It is what R. Léon Ashkenazi (Manitou) calls an 'equation of fraternity'—'an equilibrium, a balance, a particular way of giving and receiving that maintains the dignity of each'.[91] R. Gedaliah sets the tone of this exchange rhetorically by using direct address (echoing, of course, the biblical verses, formulated as they are in the second person: 'You shall command') to convey a sense of closeness and solicitude. This, now, is a significant pedagogical event. God's

he heard it from a Rabbi Dan Ashkenazi. R. Gedaliah's source seems, in fact, to be Rabbenu Asher, as he cites him nearly verbatim. The rabbinical saying integrated in these sources, 'The curse of the wise, even if said conditionally, becomes reality', appears in BT *Mak.* 10a. In that context, however, it does not refer to Moses; the connection between 'the curse of the wise' and the compositional aspects of the book of Exodus first appears in the medieval sources I've noted.

[89] *Tetsaveh*, in its literal meaning, is 'to command', from the root *tsav*. R. Gedaliah draws here on a kabbalistic reading that links *tetsaveh* to an Aramaic root signifying joining or connection, as in the word *tsavta*. See R. Elazar Azikri, *Sefer ḥaredim*, ch. 70 (268–9).

[90] *Teshuot ḥen*, 'Tetsaveh', 89. On olives and olive oil, forgetting and remembrance, see BT *Hor.* 13b; *Shulḥan arukh*, 'Oraḥ ḥayim', 170; *Magen avraham*, 100: 19; *Likutei torah, ta'amei hamitsvot*, 'Ekev'. Compare *Teshuot ḥen, Hashmatot*, 228.

[91] Handelman, 'The Philosopher, the Rabbi, and the Rhetorician', 593.

words, drawing on a metaphorical sense of the injunction *tetsaveh*, are meant to recall to Moses his own essence—the aspect called Da'at. Both words—*tetsaveh*, recalling the idea of connectedness, and *da'at*, alluding to the most intimate kind of 'knowing'—connote a joining together to form a unity. Within the larger context of Moses' life story those words urge him to realize that his perspective must change fundamentally. The opposition of self and other that has weighed on him so heavily must be dispelled. In its place, Moses—and by implication the righteous of every generation, and each individual Torah scholar—is challenged continually to live out the dynamic relationship of mutuality and responsiveness that R. Gedaliah described in the first part of the *derashah*. What it enables is surely a difficult, paradoxical kind of greatness. But that, it seems, is the only hope there is for knowing anything of true and lasting value.

I would like to reflect, in conclusion, on some of the formal aspects of this *derashah* and their role in constructing its meaning. In terms of literary style, R. Gedaliah portrays his subject with striking realism. Moses, rather than modelling ideal, schematically conceived qualities or patently admirable traits, is a psychologically complex character who struggles audibly with conflicting, even negative, emotions. His actual and symbolic identities are formed here using the compositional technique that Paul Ricoeur calls emplotment. Drawing on a variety of traditional sources, R. Gedaliah gathers disparate happenings, personages, motivations, and causes and links them together to form Moses' life story into a concordant narrative unity.[92] But, embroiled as he is in the confusing, dramatic events of his nation's current history, the hero himself is unable to envision that overarching unity. If he is to understand his destiny as emissary and intermediary, along with the complex relation with others implicit in it, Moses needs a teacher. God fills that role by rhetorical means: through dialogue with Moses, God communicates something to him about his 'essence' and the meaning of his trials, and in doing so empowers him to understand them in a new light. This configuring act, performed in R. Gedaliah's *derashah*, constructs Moses as a dynamic personality capable of change and personal growth. His story can then teach that vital mode of being to others.

Returning to the larger question with which we began: What aspects of self-understanding—representative of the hasidic masters in general, or relating to R. Gedaliah of Linits in particular—might this *derashah* reveal? Find-

---

[92] Ricoeur developed the notion of emplotment in *Time and Narrative* (vol. ii); on the role of emplotment in creating narrative unity, see *Oneself as Another*, 141–68.

ing an answer here is no easy matter, first of all because in the traditional Jewish society of mid-eighteenth-century eastern Europe, autobiographical writing was virtually non-existent. Moreover, almost no first-hand impressions that R. Gedaliah's disciples or family members may have recorded about him are extant. It is thus impossible to draw a reliable correlation between his homiletical works and the personal side of his experience as religious leader and Torah scholar. We can only surmise that he addressed certain themes because they mattered to him in one way or other; his manner of treating them might also shed light on their value in his eyes. And so, rather than speculate on the strictly biographical aspects of this *derashah*, my comments focus on what he seems to be saying about being a solitary Torah scholar, and about experiences that hasidic preachers, teachers, spiritual mentors, and community leaders of his time most likely shared.

Moses, as R. Gedaliah portrays him in this *derashah*, combines these two dimensions of identity—the private and the public. Both are perpetuated, symbolically, beyond him in time: "'what has been is what will be"—as then, so is it still: in each and every generation, the righteous of the generation have that same essence called "Moses". This, however, is not a theoretical statement defining the role of the *tsadik* or a programmatic formulation of hasidic ideology. Rather, through hermeneutical engagement with the figure of Moses and his life's story, R. Gedaliah seeks to prescribe an attitude towards learning and teaching within the framework of the Jewish community. Moses's soul-presence in each generation, then, speaks of the responsibility to continue the process of receiving the sacred works of Jewish tradition, and of transmitting the 'knowing' one has gained to others.

Modes of Reading

Earth's crammed with heaven,
And every common bush afire with God;
But only he who sees, takes off his shoes,
The rest sit round it and pluck blackberries

ELIZABETH BARRETT BROWNING
'Aurora Leigh'

CHAPTER 1 opened with a look at some self-referential elements in writings by and about the Ba'al Shem Tov. In that context, I noted the motivating force that came to inform hasidic teaching: to engender a spiritual awakening with profound redemptive power. I then turned to consider how other early hasidic masters conceived of that mission, and of themselves as agents carrying it out. The subject that will concern us now is the means that were developed in hasidic tradition towards that end—to cause 'the wellsprings to flow forth'. In the Introduction I reviewed the methods that historians have delineated—the social stratagem and realpolitik tactics that proved highly effective in disseminating hasidism throughout the nineteenth century. Scholars have also examined hasidic leaders' public activism, from the last third of the eighteenth century to the present, and have studied their cultural influence in the formation of distinct hasidic groups and the recruitment of new members. I will be going in a very different direction here. The methods I want to discover are of another nature. What is it that grants homiletical activity the power to engender a spiritual awakening—one so far-reaching that hasidic authors consider it to be 'the secret of redemption'? But first there are some even more primary questions that require our attention: What is the connection between exegesis and redemption? When the hasidic masters engage with holy texts, what is it that they are really trying to interpret?

These issues are so elementary that, before going any further, our subject itself demands reframing. I think the following insights voiced by literary critic Frank Kermode can set us in that direction. Concluding his book *The Uses of Error*, Kermode writes:

The history of interpretation, the skills by which we keep alive in our minds the light and the dark of past literature and past humanity, is to an incalculable extent a history of error. Or perhaps it would be better to say, of ambiguity, of antithetical senses. The history of biblical interpretation will provide many instances of fruitful misunderstanding. It arises because we want to have more of the story than was originally offered, or we want to see into the depths of that story . . . the mysteries of such stories, and perhaps of language itself, are familiar to us from our interpretations of our own lives. [The work of a later poet, reusing and transforming earlier works,] was, if you like, an act of genius; but it is what, in our more humdrum way, we all habitually do— make new combinations of disparate experience, settle for ambiguity, confront the antithetical senses. . . . We bring ourselves and our conflicts to words, to poems and pictures, as we bring them to the world; and thus we change the poems and the pictures, or perhaps it is ourselves we change.[1]

Kermode's reflections here, the fruit of a long and creative life spent with literature, can offer an alternative, perhaps less common way of thinking about hasidic exegetical modes. Most fundamentally, he insists that it is impossible to read anything while keeping oneself out of the picture. Text, life, and self are hopelessly entangled. All together, they form the fabric of human experience. While most of us can probably accept that Kermode's view may well be valid in the case of interpreting just any text, things get more uncomfortable when it comes to sacred works of a religious legacy. This is especially so for conservative souls who suppose they know very well what the simple and straightforward meaning of those works 'really' is. To such a mindset, informed by predefined categories and clear rules, hasidic readings appear to have little to do with commentary in any normative sense. Rather, it would seem, as Moshe Idel puts it, that 'the hasidic masters either project their thoughts into the divine text as if interpreting it, or they receive some form of revelation'. Be that as it may, Idel contends, their 'exegetical enterprise is much less a matter of listening attentively to the specificity of the message found in a certain given text'.[2] In light of Kermode's insights, however, we should recall that the canonical works of Jewish tradition are sacred and eternally relevant because they are open to multiple readings. Their meaning is not specific or predetermined, but rather something that appears while 'listening attentively' —reading, reflecting, and exchanging impressions with others in search of understanding.

In the first part of this chapter I will look at some of the ways in which the hasidic masters portray the relationship between text and reader from their

---

[1] *The Uses of Error*, 431–2.   [2] Idel, 'Hermeneutics in Hasidism', 15.

own perspective. My sense is that the modes of exegesis they developed, radical as they might appear in comparison to rationalist approaches, don't necessarily mandate an 'anthropology of the righteous person as a semi-divine being', as Idel holds. More reasonably, it seems to me, the hasidic masters caught sight of the basic truth that Kermode sets out, and made it into a guiding principle of reading. There is a rich and tangled web of connections between text and world—or, more particularly here, between one's inner, spiritual universe, the world outside, and the holy works of Jewish tradition —and it is these interrelationships that many hasidic *derashot* bring to light. Put simply, the assumption that underlies this interpretative approach is that when you 'take the text wrong' (what Harold Bloom calls *misprision*), it may 'take you' somewhere new. Or, as Kermode has it, 'we bring ourselves and our conflicts to words, to poems and pictures, as we bring them to the world; and thus we change the poems and the pictures, or perhaps it is our-selves we change.' In the pages that follow I will explore some of the ways in which hasidic masters relate to the task of explicating that tangle of text, self, and world, and consider some of the places they reached by reading otherwise.

Metaphors We Live By: R. Gedaliah Rabinowitz of Linits, *Teshuot ḥen*

Hasidism developed a new sensibility, a way of 'being in the world'. It is informed by a deeply rooted awareness that everything visible contains other, concealed facets of meaning. Contemplating even the most prosaic details of everyday life thus becomes a means of opening one's consciousness to a higher order of understanding. Such a spiritual modality, and the religious devotion it might awaken, are fundamentals of the hasidic ethos. The dynamic element that enables this kind of contemplation is metaphorical thinking—that is, perceiving what it is that secretly connects disparate elements and, in doing so, freeing them from the mundane confines of the 'real' world and translating them to mean something more. Rather than elaborating on the theoretical aspects of metaphors just now, let us first consider a *derashah* that sets out this idea by means of exegesis. The following passage by R. Gedaliah of Linits (a contemporary of the Ba'al Shem Tov, introduced in Chapter 1) presents the biblical figure of Abraham and his initiation, so to speak, into the mode of being that hasidism sought to bring to the fore.[3]

[3] 'Mode of being' is a central term in hermeneutics. As Heidegger contended, understand-

'God said to Abram: Go, yourself from your land . . . to the land [*ha'arets*] that I will show you' [Gen. 12: 1]. To explain, first, a related verse: [God promised Abraham:] 'All the land that you can see—I will give it to you and your seed forever' [Gen. 13: 15]. 'All that you can see'—only that and no more? But the human eye is so weak, its vision so poor and limited! Yet the verse seems to imply that this is a tremendous gift. What, then, could it mean? Well, the Rabbis taught that Abraham won his perception of the Divine through his own 'landedness' [*artsiyut*]. He gazed at the vault of heaven and its stars, and this enabled him to recognize the source from which they had emanated and the force that guided them.[4] Now, the Zohar [i. 78*a*] also says that Abraham was able to perceive the specific power that rules each earthly realm. Only that of the Land of Israel remained beyond his comprehension. And so God said to him, 'Go, your-self': go to yourself, to your unique essence. Supernal perception is yours to attain, through your own being—that is, 'from your land'. When you have done so, although on your own you are unable fully to comprehend the Land of Israel, 'I will show you'—I will enable you to attain it. Now we can understand that God really does award him a tremendous gift. 'All of the land that you see—I will give it to you.' For 'seeing' here refers not to physical vision but to cognitive insight. This is what the Rabbis meant in saying that God 'folded all of the Land of Israel underneath him'[5]— He 'folded' Abraham's understanding up together with Abraham's self, and gave him the Land to become his own.[6]

On this reading, Abraham's calling is tightly bound up with his 'being in the world'. His journey towards realizing the mission he has been given passes through a place of non-understanding, a moment of standing face to face with a stark inability to comprehend either the Land or his own unique essence. God's sudden adjuration to him here: "'Go, yourself"—go to yourself' thus

---

ing is 'neither a method of reading nor the outcome of a willed and carefully conducted proce-dure of critical reflection. It is not something we consciously do or fail to do, but something we are. Understanding is a mode of being, and as such it is characteristic of human being, of *Dasein*.' See Ramberg and Gjesdal, 'Hermeneutics'.

   [4] R. Gedaliah refers here to Zohar i. 86*a*; the reading of the Zohar is based on a talmudic passage that interprets the verse 'Who aroused the one from the East' (Isa. 41: 2) as referring to Abraham, who journeyed from the east (Aram) to Canaan (BT *BB* 15*a*). In the Zohar the con-nection is more than associative; there, the verse from Isaiah speaks of a formative moment of intellectual and emotional arousal (*hitorerut*) that is profoundly metaphorical. Night, darkness, stars give way: as Abraham watches the sun rise in the east, it suddenly 'dawns' on him that a Higher Power rules the world. R. Gedaliah alludes, in effect, to this figurative reading.

   [5] BT *Ḥul.* 91*b*.

   [6] *Teshuot ḥen*, 'Lekh lekha', 11–12. Although R. Gedaliah cites the Zohar as his proof-text, he clearly expands its meaning. The Zohar reads 'Go, yourself' more simply, as an injunction for Abraham to restore his integrity by distancing himself from the heathen fatherland.

marks a turning point on his path. To accomplish his weighty mission, Abraham must learn how to see on a different plane, beyond the patently physical. Reaching that plane of perception will ultimately bring him to a new and important kind of understanding. The task, then, first of all, is to discern the hidden ontological correspondences between things. What enables one to gain a perceptual capacity of that order—on R. Gedaliah's reading of the biblical verses—is the embodied self. 'Your self', with its manifold psychological, existential, and spatial dimensions, contains a wealth of resources for creative metaphorical thinking.

The essence of metaphor, as literary critics, philosophers, linguists, and psychologists have remarked, is the understanding of one thing in terms of another. Pervasively present and not only in language, metaphor defines our everyday reality. It structures our perceptions, informs the ways we think, what we experience, and how we act. The Greek word *metapherein* means 'to carry across'—as does its equivalent 'transfer', from the Latin *transferre*, whose past participle (*translatum*, 'something carried across') underlies the notion of translation. A metaphorical line of thinking, then, involves combining a concrete element with an abstract sense and carrying the meaning of one across to the other.[7] While we may never be fully aware of their influence, metaphors (alive or dead) nonetheless remain an inseparable part of our conceptions and discourse. As a case in point: my sense just now is that we've 'reached a crossroads' in this chapter. I must confess that it's been hard enough until now to 'capture my ideas in words' and am wondering how I'll ever 'get my full meaning across' to you, worried as I am about 'burying good thoughts' in inexcusably dense paragraphs. 'Standing up for myself', though, I reaffirm that a candid look at metaphors 'leads us' to realize that language really has no strictly literal meanings—if we take 'literal' to mean completely disconnected from the resources of imagery and comparison. Here, then, are some of our most basic metaphorical concepts: writing and reading as a journey, with forking paths and, we hope, a final destination; communication as an exchange of

---

[7] After setting out these etymological basics, Rob Pope notes that historically, 'the view that language is essentially metaphorical can be found as far back as Bacon's *Novum Organum* (1620), where it is perceived as a major problem, and Vico's *The New Science* (1725), where it is perceived as a major potential . . . And nowadays it is virtually axiomatic among philosophers of language that, for better and worse, metaphor plays a central and quite routine role in processes of symbolisation and signification' (*Creativity: Theory, History, Practice*, 157). Among the earliest literary critics to stress the central role of metaphors in cognition were Richards, *The Philosophy of Rhetoric*; Abrams, *The Mirror and the Lamp*; more recently, Gadamer, Ricoeur, and Eco.

containers into which meaning is put and from which it is extracted; values defined in terms of spatial orientation, where 'up', 'beyond', and 'in' usually seem better than 'low', 'down', and 'out'.[8]

Recognizing the metaphorical nature of language and human experience thus brings basic issues of knowledge and perception to the fore. Unanticipated facets of meaning, truth, and understanding may then come into view. This intuition, it seems, is what guides R. Gedaliah's retelling of the biblical dialogue between God and Abraham: 'Supernal perception is yours to attain, through your own being—that is, "from your land". When you have done so, although on your own you are unable fully to comprehend the Land of Israel, "I will show you"—I will enable you to attain it.' In other words: what you must do first of all is attend, with utmost seriousness, to the natural world, to human existence, and to life in all its complexity. Then, after that, go beyond the verse: try to describe the world anew using metaphor as a vehicle for insight. You may then find yourself on a bridge that leads you from the concrete, visible plane of existence to concealed, metaphysical dimensions and other possible worlds.

All this suggests a very different perspective to be kept in mind as we evaluate hasidic modes of reading. To put it negatively, a middle ground is needed between two prejudices. Firstly, the poetic lines of thinking in hasidic exegesis shouldn't be discounted as ornamental, rhetorical, or didactic—handy tools but extraneous, really, as if the same thing could have been said plain and simple, without all the flourish. Secondly, from the opposite perspective, the figurative language and rhetorical style of hasidic teaching must not be 'explained away' as abstract allegorical rereadings using kabbalistic ideas or as allusions to private mystical experiences. In the next few pages, I will try to map out the middle ground between these two views and demonstrate the alternative approach to hasidic texts of this genre that I'm proposing, with a focus on the ways in which their message is formed. This, I hope, will forward some of the larger aims of this book.

Many hasidic teachings could serve to illustrate the premises that I have outlined above; the *derashot* in the following pages give particularly cogent expression to a number of them. I will present the teachings in this section in historical order from earlier to later, covering nearly a century of hasidic homiletical activity.

---

[8] Lakoff and Johnson's study *The Metaphors We Live By* reconceived the notion of metaphor using semiotics and psychology. It has guided my thoughts here.

A Parable in Waiting: R. Elimelekh of Lizhensk, *No'am elimelekh*

The author of the first passage is R. Elimelekh of Lizhensk (1717–87). He was a central figure in the circle of disciples that gathered around R. Dov Baer, the Magid of Mezhirech. After the death of his master, R. Elimelekh became a highly influential figure in the rapid expansion of hasidism throughout Poland and Galicia in the late eighteenth and early nineteenth centuries, as his own students and contemporaries branched out to found hasidic courts of their own. The following sermon gives voice to an interpretative dynamic whose implications are far-reaching.

In the Gemara, 'A harp was hung over David's bed'.[9] 'Bed' signifies conjoining, for the righteous one connects and unifies worlds through his holy acts. But King David could do even more—so great was his devotion that songs of praise emerged from him as if of their own accord. And so the harp that was suspended over his bed: 'when midnight came'—for the holy Zohar calls the Shekhinah 'midnight'[10] . . . 'a northern breeze [*ruaḥ tsefonit*] would sweep through it [or him]'. This means that the spirit of holiness concealed within him [*ruaḥ . . . tsafun imo*] would animate him with passionate devotion and he would play, beyond his own willing it. . . . Thus King David said, 'I will incline my ear to the parable' [Ps. 49: 5]—that is, to the Torah.[11] . . . Indeed, one must listen closely to understand what the Torah is really saying, and never imagine, heaven forbid, that it is just telling stories, as the Zohar warns.[12] [He continued,] 'with a harp I will resolve my secret' [Ps. 49: 5]—this, too, comes about through my divine service: with my songs of praise I open up another whole vast world, far beyond this one, a world called 'my secret'. For a secret is something more profound than what the ear can hear.[13]

R. Elimelekh draws his central metaphor of the wind harp from the Talmud —undeniably an ancient source. At the same time, the poetic image that takes shape in this passage strongly resembles one that became emblematic of the nineteenth-century Romantic canon: the Aeolian lyre. As a metaphorical figure, the wind harp was used to evoke the mind in perception and the poetic mind in composition. So Wordsworth, for instance, described the 'Aeolian

---

[9] BT *Ber.* 3*b*: 'A harp hung over David's bed and when midnight came a north wind would blow through it and it would play by itself. Then he would rise and learn Torah until dawn.'

[10] Zohar i. 92*b*.

[11] After Rashi, whose reading of this verse in Psalms follows his interpretation of 1 Sam. 24: 14. There the Torah, as Rashi understands it, is called a parable (*mashal*) belonging to the Ancient One (God). See also Rashi on BT *Mak.* 10*b*.   [12] Zohar iii. 149*b*.

[13] *No'am elimelekh*, *Likutei shoshanah*, 108*a*–*b*. 'I will incline my ear to the parable [*mashal*]; with a harp I will resolve my secret [*ḥidati*].'

visitations' of poetry: 'In a kindred sense | Of passion [I] was obedient as a lute | That waits upon the touches of the wind. . . . I had a world about me—'twas my own, | I made it.'[14] Or, in Shelley's 'Ode to the West Wind', the Aeolian harp is metonymic, embodying the most intimate facets of the poet's being: 'Make me thy lyre, even as the forest is: | What if my leaves are falling like its own! . . . Be thou, Spirit fierce, | My spirit! Be thou me, impetuous one!'[15]

R. Elimelekh's overtly named subject is King David, and his literary source is a midrashic image associated with the stringed instrument the Bible calls *kinor* (which I've translated, admittedly anachronistically, as 'harp'). All the same, the human experience that interests him here is clearly a universal one. As an extended metaphor the wind harp offers him, as it does the Romantics, a model of consciousness and artistic creativity. It represents what happens when inspired souls—the hasidic *tsadik* among them—are roused to speak 'words of Torah'. In the first part of the sermon R. Elimelekh portrays such a moment of heightened perception in the classic sense used in the Western literary tradition, in which the poet feels he is animated by some super-conscious spiritual source that is somehow indwelling as well.[16]

A more unexpected exegetical move comes in the second part of the *derashah*, where R. Elimelekh rereads the biblical verses spoken by King David that give voice to the experience 'from the inside'. In their broader context: 'My mouth will speak wisdom; my heart's thoughts will murmur knowledge. I will incline my ear to the parable; with a harp I will resolve my secret. Why should I fear in days of evil?' (Ps. 49: 4–6) On R. Elimelekh's reading, what these verses describe is much less a moment of passively receiving divine revelation or some kind of mystical inspiration than of attentive, active listening turned inwards. Text (here, the Torah) and the world itself are parables waiting for their interpreter. Whatever of them can be 'resolved' —literally, opened (*eftaḥ*)—will be somehow connected to the interpreter's own search for understanding, to the questions and troubles propelling that search. R. Elimelekh describes this encounter, in which meaning unfolds through interpretation, as a transformative event. 'With my songs of praise

---

[14] *The Prelude* (1855), III. 136–42. Similarly, Coleridge uses the image of the wind harp to portray the thinking mind: 'And what if all of animated nature | Be but organic Harps diversely framed, | That tremble into thought, as o'er them sweeps | Plastic and vast, one intellectual breeze, | At once the Soul of each, and God of all?' ('The Eolian Harp' (1795)). See Abrams, *The Mirror and the Lamp*, 61, 346 n. 63.   [15] 'Ode to the West Wind', ll. 57–62.

[16] Rob Pope notes that classic appeals to inspiration are typically made 'in terms of "breath", "breeze", "wind", "spirit" or "fire"; and they draw on the rich ambiguity of literal and metaphoric senses'; *Creativity: Theory, History, Practice*, 111.

I open up another whole vast world, far beyond this one, a world called "my secret". For a secret is something more profound than what the ear can hear.' Significantly, he calls the event in question 'divine service'. This implies that he conceives of it as a deeply spiritual and religious experience.

But if, as I suggest, R. Elimelekh is portraying King David not simply as a (stereotyped) *tsadik* or 'righteous one' but as a model of consciousness and artistic creativity, this reading makes an important statement. To appreciate his meaning, we might recall a seminal insight in Hans-Georg Gadamer's conception of the hermeneutical enterprise as a whole. Understanding, Gadamer stressed, always comes about through a 'fusion of horizons' between the interpreter's own present experience and background and his or her object. Here, such a moment of merging or fusion takes place between the horizon of 'another whole vast world . . . called "my secret"' and that of the parable still resounding from some illimitable past. What this means is that interpretation, whether it concerns the Torah, world history, or a lonely hour of private suffering, does not simply reproduce some single, unchanging, verifiable meaning. Nor, from the other side, is it a wholly subjective or relativistic imposing of meaning upon some external object. Rather, through the figure of King David, R. Elimelekh depicts an 'event of meaning', as Gadamer might put it.[17] It is an experience that he himself knows intimately—not, primarily, in his celebrated social role as *tsadik*, religious leader, or preacher, but as a Jew simply trying to read the sacred works of tradition in a way that matters.

We turn now to a series of *derashot* that develop this subject in a number of interrelated directions. Their authors belong to three generations of the Przysucha school, a particularly innovative trend in Polish hasidism that was fathered in a sense by R. Elimelekh. Near the end of his life (in 1785) one of his closest disciples, R. Jacob Isaac Horowitz, originally of Lantset (Łańcut, c.1745–1815), left Lizhensk to establish a hasidic court of his own. R. Jacob Isaac's visionary powers soon won him renown as the Seer, or Hozeh, of

---

[17] It was Martin Heidegger who first rejected the traditional account of cultural activity as a search for universally valid foundations for human action and knowledge. His main work, *Sein und Zeit* (1927), is a powerful critique of the Cartesian ideal of objectivity. Gadamer furthered Heidegger's hermeneutical reflections. To counter the concept of personal subject and the ideal of objective truth, and yet avoid a radical relativism, Gadamer proposed to describe cultural activity as a continual, free, and unpredictable process of 'fusions of horizons'; *Truth and Method*, 300–11. And it was Edmund Husserl, the originator of phenomenology, who first placed the notion of the horizon (*Horizont*) at the centre of philosophical enquiry. On the deep influence of Husserl's conception of 'horizon' on Gadamer's thought, see Moran, 'Gadamer and Husserl on Horizon, Intersubjectivity, and the Lifeworld'. On the terms 'event of meaning' and 'experience' in Gadamer's thought, see Translators' Preface, *Truth and Method*, pp. xiii–xiv.

Lublin. His spiritual stature, charismatic leadership, and aura as a miracle-worker were crucial factors in the rapid spread of hasidism. During the years of his leadership, hasidism was transformed from a small circle of elite scholars and mystics to a religious movement with enormous popular appeal. Jews from all walks of life were drawn to his court. The study house that he founded in Lublin was, for his followers, the centre of the world—the Jerusalem of Poland. Nearly all the major hasidic figures in Poland and Galicia in his generation and the next considered themselves his disciples and him their mentor.

In 1812 one of the Seer's most brilliant and closest disciples, R. Jacob Isaac Rabinowitz (1766–1814), later to be known as 'the Holy Jew' (Hayehudi Hakadosh), parted ways with his own master. He left Lublin and moved to the nearby town of Przysucha, where he established his court and forged a radically novel direction for hasidism. The Przysucha school revisited and recovered a large set of conceptual categories from early hasidic teaching. At the same time, a new vocabulary evolved, one that could address the fundamental concerns of contemporary religious life and speak in new ways of how human beings go about understanding themselves and the world.

Within a decade, the Przysucha school had become (in)famous, drawing both adherents and fierce opposition from other hasidic factions—first under the leadership of the Holy Jew, and even more so in the days of his successor, R. Simhah Bunim (1765–1827). Throughout the nineteenth century, Przysucha hasidism continued to develop incisive and sophisticated hermeneutical tools. In the following pages I present four *derashot* that form a thematic unit of sorts. The first two passages are teachings by R. Simhah Bunim; the third belongs to one of his pre-eminent disciples, R. Mordecai Joseph Leiner of Izbica; the last *derashah* is by R. Jacob Leiner of Izbica-Radzyn, R. Mordecai Joseph's son and successor.

But first of all we need to give some attention to the surroundings that would have fostered these lines of thinking. The vibrant economic and cultural climate of central Poland was fertile ground for innovative activity. The first decades of the nineteenth century saw dramatic political developments, demographic changes, and shifting social structures. The incipient industrial revolution, acculturation, and assimilation also began to make inroads into the Jewish world and marked hasidic community life.[18] R. Simhah Bunim's unusual personal profile and world-view reflect the influence of modernity in

---

[18] Glenn Dynner examines the impact of these factors on hasidism in central Poland and cites R. Simhah Bunim as a case in point: 'Oral traditions and eyewitness accounts repeatedly

a number of intriguing ways, as we will see. Przysucha hasidism was known, moreover, for its revival of interest in medieval Jewish philosophy and the works of R. Judah Loew (Maharal) of Prague; these factors, too, shaped its teachings.[19]

One more important cultural force at work needs to be mentioned. Romanticism, which Isaiah Berlin famously termed 'the largest recent movement to transform the lives and the thought of the Western world . . . the greatest single shift in the consciousness of the West', gained force in those years.[20] Poets, artists, and philosophers challenged the central ideals of the Enlightenment. The eighteenth-century discourse of reason, which had championed rationality over spirituality, the scientist over the poet, was forcefully undermined. Romantics turned instead to explore the 'inscape' of humanness, to discover the intuitive working of the mind. Imagination now became the ultimate source of metaphysical truth, imbued with the power to transform and transcend reality. And so the poet-prophet, in William Blake's radical vision, is charged to perceive the world by 'melting apparent surfaces away, and displaying the infinite which was hid'.[21] The *derashot* that will concern us now seem to accord in a number of striking ways with this new sensibility. What interests me above all in the following pages is the hermeneutical aspects of these teachings: the various ways in which hasidic masters read the Torah through the prisms of self and world and other metaphorical 'texts'.

acclaim [his] success as a lumber and grain merchant and, eventually, a pharmacist. . . . That a merchant became the most popular Polish zaddik of his day bespeaks the spirit of the region.' He, along with other tsadikim, through 'their worldliness and intimate contacts with wealthy elites produced a more urban, cosmopolitan, and politically savvy Hasidism' (*Men of Silk*, 36).

[19] See Rabinowicz, *From Przysucha to Lublin* (Heb.), 308. On Maharal's influence on the Przysucha-Kotsk school see Sherwin, *Mystical Theology and Social Dissent*, 51–5. On the Przysucha school see Brill, 'Grandeur and Humility in the Writings of R. Simhah Bunim of Przysucha'; Dynner, *Men of Silk*; Rosen, *The Quest for Authenticity*, 338–48.

[20] Berlin, *The Roots of Romanticism*, 1–2. For a general overview of intellectual and cultural features of Romanticism and a bibliography of major studies, see Faflak and Wright, 'Introduction', *A Handbook of Romanticism Studies*. Needless to say, 'Romantic' here does not refer to the neo-Romanticism of early twentieth-century scholars of hasidism such as Samuel Abba Horodetsky and Martin Buber.

[21] Gerard Manley Hopkins used 'inscape' to speak of the unified complex of elements that makes each thing unique and differentiated from other things. Although it is a characteristically Romantic and post-Romantic idea, Hopkins's notion of inscape is also deeply religious, as it intimates the true reasons 'each mortal thing' was created: see *The Letters of Gerard Manley Hopkins to Robert Bridges*, 263. See 'The Marriage of Heaven and Hell', in *The Complete Poetry and Prose of William Blake*, ed. Erdman, 32.

Imagining the World: R. Simhah Bunim of Przysucha, *Torat simḥah*

The first two *derashot* are R. Simhah Bunim's, as recorded by two of his disciples. Like other prominent figures before and after him in the Przysucha tradition, R. Simhah Bunim did not write down his own homilies and so the transcriptions, questions of authenticity aside, are the only records we have of his teaching.[22] Translating the first of these passages to English has been especially challenging—not least of all due to its laconic, allusive language and faintly ironic tone.

'And God said, Let us make humans in Our image, after Our likeness' [Gen. 1: 26]. 'Humans' [*adam*] derives from *adamah* ['earth'] / *edameh* ['I will imagine'].[23] Once all of His handiwork had been brought to glorious perfection, the Creator wished to show it off. But nothing else in existence, no one but human beings, can conceive the reality of something other than itself. So God created humans, and composed them of powers from the upper and lower realms. That enables them to comprehend everything—by discerning resemblances. Indeed, this is the essence of being human: the ability to see and understand and imagine—this and this alone. And so the verse says that they were created 'in Our image, after Our likeness' [*kidemutenu*]—that is, 'with the letter of resemblance/the ability to imagine' [*kaf hadimayon*]. For only when there is resemblance is imagining possible.[24]

A strange, not to say unorthodox, scene. Artist in search of someone to admire

---

[22] Other figures in that tradition who did not record their teachings include R. Jacob Isaac, the 'Holy Jew', and R. Menahem Mendel of Kotsk. Both of the passages we will read appear in early works containing material received firsthand. Both have textual parallels in a second early source preserving R. Simhah Bunim's teachings, recorded by a different disciple. These factors indicate a good measure of authenticity. The singular importance of orality in the Przysucha tradition has been discussed by a number of scholars, most perceptively by Avi'ezer Hacohen in "'I Wanted to Write a Book...'" (Heb.).

[23] The first of these 'etymologies' is, of course, contextually evident (Gen. 2: 7); the second alludes to Isa. 14: 14 or perhaps to Hos. 12: 11 (*edameh/adameh*—'I will liken'). R. Simhah Bunim's *derashot* were published without vocalization, making it unclear which word was intended. These various connotations and the part of each in understanding the 'human condition' are a central theme in R. Simhah Bunim's second *derashah*, as we will see shortly. There, he cites the verse from Isaiah. Because both sermons concern the ambivalent double meaning of *adam*—i.e. the inherent duality of human nature, combining 'upper' (abstract cognitive faculties) and 'lower' (physical, material, earth-bound) worlds—it made most sense to offer both transliterations (*adamah/edameh*) here.

[24] *Kol simḥah*, 'Bereshit'. Compare the commentary of R. Bahya ben Asher on Gen. 1: 26 (citing Nahmanides and his own sources), which may have influenced R. Simhah Bunim's reading.

His latest creation, but no one's to be found. Each thing is imprisoned in its own monadic existence. All of them, as Kant put it, 'are confined within the world of their sense perceptions . . . they can form no idea of "possible" things'.[25] God gets beyond this impasse, as it were, by creating a hybrid entity, one that will not be so immured in its separate, incommunicable reality. The unique ability of humans to conceive of an Other outside the self, R. Simhah Bunim notes, is thus bound up with their composite nature. Humans contain both 'upper' and 'lower' and that is what enables them to sense the resemblance between disparate aspects of reality, to imagine 'possible' things. This capacity above all, R. Simhah Bunim declares with uncommon certainty, is the very 'essence of being human'.

It is rapidly becoming clear that this *derashah* addresses some very weighty questions. They concern epistemology, theology, ethics, and metaphysics—issues at the epicentre of some of the most dramatic revolutions in Western intellectual history. R. Simhah Bunim's choice of proof-text as a platform for engaging with such questions really should come as no surprise. Throughout history, philosophers and exegetes, believers and unbelievers have scrutinized the biblical accounts of creation as a primary resource. R. Simhah Bunim's reading showcases his own dialogue with some of the conflicting views and changing attitudes that have shaped the Jewish history of ideas, ranging from midrashic sources to medieval philosophy to early modern countertrends. As in the case of R. Elimelekh's *derashah*, my intuition here, too, is that this renewed attention to the 'inscape' of humanness resonates with the spirit of the times—more on that near the end of this section. For now, to telescope many centuries of thought into a few brief sentences, I will note the following points.

R. Simhah Bunim's statement that God invested humans with 'powers from the upper and lower realms' echoes a fundamental of rabbinic anthropology: *imago dei* comprises spiritual capacities—a divine soul, the 'soul of life' —as well as physical features—a material body, fashioned from 'the dust of the earth'.[26] A significant revision of this duality took place in medieval Jewish philosophy. Its major trend, represented most prominently by Maimonides, redefined the spiritual capacity in question as intellectual essence. That human beings were created 'in God's image, after His likeness', now meant

---

[25] I draw here on Cassirer's *An Essay on Man*. His insights on Kant's *Critique of Judgement* (sects. 76, 77) appear on p. 79. Cassirer remarks on the biologist Uexküll's description of the reality experienced by lower organisms: 'Every organism is, so to speak, a monadic being. It has a world of its own because it has an experience of its own' (*An Essay on Man*, 41).

[26] See *Gen. Rab.* 8: 11, 14: 3, to which R. Simhah Bunim elliptically refers here.

that the aspect of the Divine instilled in them is the rational soul. A strict hierarchy of values accompanied this premise, one that opposed 'soul' to 'body', 'form' to 'matter', intellectual perception to all other, non-rational human faculties in irresolvable tension. The medieval philosophical terms that designate these non-rational elements are *ko'aḥ hamedameh*, *dimayon*, *dimyonot*; they refer to imagining, fantasy, intuition, and the like.[27] Significantly for our purposes, in Maimonides' philosophical interpretation of Genesis this dialectic, with all its composite factors, takes centre stage. In eating of the tree, Maimonides contended, Adam and Eve allowed themselves to be distracted from pure intellectual activity, and sought satisfaction in inferior, imagined venues. Human sense perceptions, along with all the non-rational modes of experience implicit in them, are thus recast in this scenario as the primeval source of ruinous error. For all generations to come, 'imagination' would pose a ceaseless, ever-present threat to the life of holiness won through pure intellectual effort, in quest of ultimate spiritual perfection.

It is this binary scheme—with its implicit depreciation of corporeity, earthly pleasures, the non-rational, and all that has to do with the 'second' side of humanness—that R. Simhah Bunim proceeds to dismantle. Re-examining the key phrase in which 'the essence of being human' is encrypted, he catches sight of a radically different meaning. To have been created 'in Our image, after Our likeness' now means something fundamental about image-ining and about seeing like-ness. That is to say: the aspect of the Divine that has been instilled in human beings, on his reading, is the ability to imagine other possible realities, to perceive resemblances—in spite of and through all the differences—and in so doing, to restore the world's wholeness. '"After Our likeness"—for only when there is like-ness is imagining possible.'

Call it, if you wish, a carefree, even defiant, show of creative philology.[28] Be it as it may, R. Simhah Bunim truly takes the Bible 'at its word' to affirm an alternative, primordial connection between the human and the Divine. It is

---

[27] *The Guide of the Perplexed*, ii. 36. For scholarship concerning the imaginative faculty in Maimonides' thought, see *Moreh nevukhim*, trans. Schwartz (Heb.), i. 384 n. 4.

[28] Yitshak Heinemann coined the term 'creative philology' in his classic study *Darkhei ha'agadah* (The Methods of the Agadah; Jerusalem, 1970) to describe the exegetical method that the Rabbis often used to convey meaning. To unpack the creative philology at hand: the core concept of our *derashah* is the essence of the human (*adam*). R. Simhah Bunim suggests an associative connection (with no proper grammatical basis) between the root *a-d-m* and another root with two letters in common: *d-m-h*. Among the words that derive from that second root are image (*demut*), imagination (*dimayon*), and similarity (also *dimayon*). Grammarians termed the letter *kaf* 'the letter of comparison'—*kaf hadimayon*—because of its role of designating similarity (X is like Y = *ke* . . .). The term *kaf hadimayon*, however, bears a double meaning;

above all in their creative acts—imagining what could be or is not yet, discovering the hidden connections between things, 'conceiving the reality of something other than themselves'—that human beings most resemble the Creator. To put it another way: bringing them into being 'with the letter of resemblance' (*kaf hadimayon*) means that God endowed humans with the gift of thinking metaphorically. It is this poetic capacity that enables them to 'make new combinations of disparate experience, settle for ambiguity, confront the antithetical senses', as Kermode has it. Imagination, then, is the power to redescribe reality in a way that can give form and meaning to human experience.[29] That creative ability stems, above all, from our very dual nature as physical and spiritual creatures.

The Essence of Being Human: R. Simhah Bunim of Przysucha, *Kol simḥah*, and R. Samuel of Shinova, *Ramatayim tsofim*

The innovative perspective that we saw in the *derashah* above seems to be a guiding force in R. Simhah Bunim's reading of the next episodes of the Genesis narrative as well. I propose this with some caution because, you will recall, these texts were not written by R. Simhah Bunim himself. They are transcriptions of teachings heard and recorded from memory by others. Could a consistent exegetical approach really inform texts of that nature? Can hasidic teachings scattered in the books of different disciples possibly combine into a coherent, integrated conception? The sceptics do have a case. Nonetheless I will try to argue convincingly that a clear ideological substructure indeed underlies R. Simhah Bunim's teachings on this central question.[30] In a second *derashah* he continues to reflect on the emergent role of imagination in defining the 'essence of the human'. That role crystallizes as the biblical narrative

metaphorically, the same phrase refers to the imagination. Finally, in conjugated form, 'I will liken/I will resemble' (*adameh/edameh*) shares the letters that signify the base material origins of humanity, formed from 'the dust of the earth' (*adamah*).

[29] See p. 65 above. These insights, in my reading of the *derashah* at least, recall some of Ricoeur's explorations of metaphor. See his 'The Metaphorical Process as Cognition, Imagination, and Feeling', 143–52; 'The Bible and the Imagination', 144; see also Mark Wallace's perceptive introduction to Ricoeur's thought, *Figuring the Sacred*, 1–32.

[30] I maintain that an ideological substructure can be discerned, not only in this biblical narrative but in a variety of contexts, throughout R. Simhah Bunim's teachings and those of his followers. See my discussions in *Wisdom of the Heart*, 85–9; and 'Hermeneutics and Hasidic Thought' (Heb.).

unfolds—in the moments just after the sin, and more so in the aftermath, already out of Eden.

R. Samuel of Shinova was a hasid and scholar who enjoyed close personal contact with the most renowned hasidic masters of his day—among them the Seer of Lublin, the Holy Jew of Przysucha, R. Simhah Bunim, R. Menahem Mendel of Kotsk, and R. Isaac Meir of Ger. The work he compiled, *Ramatayim tsofim*, is an anthology of original materials, homiletical as well as hagiographic, that he gathered over many years. It is a rare and valuable collection of primary sources, which R. Samuel took care to attribute to their respective authors and subjects. The first section of *Ramatayim tsofim* is organized loosely and associatively as a commentary on the midrash entitled *Tana devei eliyahu*.[31] It is the opening lines of that midrash that provide the starting point for R. Simhah Bunim's teaching. This is the biblical scene to which the midrash relates, followed by the *derashah*:

Then the Lord God said, Behold, humans have become like the Unique One among us, knowing good and evil. And now, lest they put forth their hand and take also of the Tree of Life and eat and live forever. So the Lord God banished them from the Garden of Eden, to work the soil from which man had been taken. (Gen. 3: 22–3)

"'So He banished [*vayegaresh*] them"—this teaches that the Holy One gave them a bill of divorce [*gerushin*]' [*Eliyahu rabah* 1: 1]. The midrash explains what 'human' means. As I heard from my saintly master, Rebbe Simhah Bunim of Przysucha, its intent is to say that even after having sinned they were called 'human' [*adam*], just as a woman, after divorce, is no less a woman.[32] . . . In truth, in Eden humankind had been caught up in an unending moment of divine revelation. It nullified all consciousness

---

[31] The Talmud (*Ket.* 105*b*) does refer to teachings that Elijah the prophet transmitted personally to the third-century *amora* Rabbi Anan. Historians, however, date this collection of aggadic material to the tenth century. *Tana devei eliyahu* consists of two parts of unequal length called *Eliyahu rabah* and *Eliyahu zuta*. The sermons it contains were most likely delivered to Jewish communities in Babylonia by a travelling preacher. Hasidim, probably from the days of the Ba'al Shem Tov himself, would customarily study midrash (*Tanḥuma* especially) alongside the weekly Torah reading. It was quite plausibly within such a framework of weekly study that R. Samuel of Shinova heard these teachings; the structure of *Tana devei eliyahu* would then be the natural order in which to arrange them for publication. The second part of *Ramatayim tsofim* is composed of tales recounted by and about a wide variety of hasidic masters, as well as short homilies attributed by name to one or another of them. That section uses no meta-text as an organizing principle.

[32] R. Simhah Bunim's point here (based on the sections of the *derashah* that I've not included in this translation) seems to be that while the term 'woman' [*ishah*] is related in both an etymological and an experiential sense to an entity called *ish* (man/husband), nonetheless divorce cannot change the woman ontologically. In other words, although her connection to a

of their separate, autonomous existence; they attained the supernal level of nothingness [*ayin*]. But then—so I heard in my master's name—[once they had sinned, the
verse says:] 'Humankind has become like the Unique One.'That is, they had suddenly
become cognizant, with the complete and total mindfulness that is God's alone, of
their own lofty spiritual selves. Before the sin, humanity had been called *adam* in the
sense of boundless 'pure thought' [after Isa. 14: 14: *edameh le'elyon*]. Then, they had
been oblivious to their own existence; all their senses, their vitality, their entire souls
were immersed in abstract being. . . . With the sin they lost that all-encompassing
state of unity [*devekut*]: they had become self-conscious. That is what the verse
means, as certain holy books teach us.[33] And so they could remain in the Garden of
Eden no longer. There, their divine service had been wholly spiritual. . . . But now,
having become fleshy, embodied creatures, separated from God, their task would be to
repair themselves and the world through physicality—this would be their essential
rectification, the path that could bring them back to regain their former glory. . . .
Clearly, then, their leaving Eden was the first, vital stage towards reaching the
ultimate and complete restoration [*tikun*].[34]

We should note that R. Simhah Bunim's main interest in this *derashah* is in
exploring the existential and ontological dimensions of 'leaving Eden'. That is
to say, conspicuously absent here is any mention of paramount theological
and philosophical issues related to free choice, moral failing, and divine retri-
bution—those age-old questions that commentators have confronted in dealing with these biblical verses. I suspect there's an intentional irony in this
deflected focus. In effect, it is sustained by the alternative approach that the
Przysucha school developed towards sin, guilt, and human failure as part of a
comprehensive world-view. Here, however, our interest will be in matters at
hand.

R. Simhah Bunim's homily opens with three vaguely incongruent statements. The biblical verse 'So He banished [*vayegaresh*] them', read through

male has been severed, that does not diminish the woman in the most basic human sense. This is
a very empowering bit of exegesis, as close study of the entire *derashah* makes clear. But to keep
to the subject at hand, my discussion here focuses on the sections that concern humanity in
general.

[33] The reference here is not named. An educated guess might be R. Isaiah Horowitz's reading in *Shenei luḥot haberit*, iii. 128. He evokes the same double etymology and states that the
essence of humanness (*adam*) comprehends two opposing valences, each of them a potential
path. Specifically, one may either 'adhere to the Most High and resemble His ways' (*edameh*) in a
life of holiness, or 'separate oneself' from that spiritual intimacy and disintegrate, ultimately,
back into the earth (*adamah*).

[34] *Ramatayim tsofim*, 1–2. Another version of part of this *derashah* appears in a second collection of homilies by R. Simhah Bunim: *Kol simḥah*, 'Bereshit', par. 14.

the prism of the midrash, 'this teaches that the Holy One gave them a bill of divorce [*gerushin*]', leads him to comment: 'The midrash explains what "human" means.' Listening closely through that disjointedness, it seems that R. Simhah Bunim is once again taking the biblical text 'at its word'—this time taking his cue from the midrashic reading he cites. The central metaphor of 'banishment' as divorce proves to contain a set of richly evocative meanings. As he sorts out those meanings, he presents these fateful moments of human history in a new light. In the process, he forwards the radical contention that 'the essence of being human' is fully realized only out of Eden, after the sin. This, of course, is a provocative challenge to conventional religious views. But what, then, *is* the connection between leaving the Garden of Eden as 'divorce' and the emergent human condition? What deeper meaning is that metaphor supposed to convey?

Using midrashic and mystical associations, R. Simhah Bunim frames 'divorce' within its wider experiential context. What preceded the moment of rupture, as he points out in the next lines of the *derashah*, was an interrelationship of unspeakable intimacy. Humanity, from its engendering in the Garden of Eden, existed in a state he describes in philosophical terms as 'boundless pure thought' and, in kabbalistic terms, as the ultimate level of mystical union called *devekut*. Engulfed in infinite divine Being, humans were suspended in a state of selflessness, an undifferentiated totality of experience. That oneness splintered with the Fall. On R. Simhah Bunim's innovative reading, here is the primary intent of the biblical verse 'Humankind has become *like* the Unique One [*ke'eḥad*]'. No longer 'one with' God, human beings suddenly became aware of themselves as separate, distinct entities, knowingly engaged in contemplating the Other.[35] In the wake of sin, a schism thus formed between the human and the Divine, between knower and the object of knowledge.

---

[35] This striking argument is articulated even more clearly in the textual parallel of this *derashah* recorded in *Kol simḥah*, 'Bereshit', par. 14. After the sin, 'Man became aware of his own cognitive powers; now he knew he was engaged in the act of contemplating. That is the meaning of the verse "Humankind has become like the Unique One"—that is, a unique and separate entity, consciously involved in contemplation.' The categories named here seem to echo medieval philosophical terms; recall Maimonides' statement that in God knower, knowledge, and the known are all one (*Mishneh torah*, 'Yesodei hatorah', 2: 10; *The Guide of the Perplexed*, trans. Schwartz (Heb.), i. 68). This view, of course, reflects Aristotelian epistemology, in which knowledge is the union of knower with the object known. Another avenue to Maimonides' stance, perhaps more immediate for nineteenth-century hasidic thinkers like R. Simhah Bunim, would have been R. Shneur Zalman of Lyady, *Tanya*, chs. 7, 48.

Divorce, then, signals the final dissolution of an already fractured connection. The heavy reality of separation, having been banished from the Garden, indeed tolls finality. But from that point the future also begins.[36] In the first *derashah*, we recall, R. Simhah Bunim stated that 'no one but humankind can conceive the reality of something other than itself'. This unique dimension of self-consciousness can be realized only once Paradise has been lost. Separate, on their own, human beings now set out to make sense of things: to search actively for traces of resemblance, to connect fragments of reality together again in some meaningful way. That task is what hasidic teaching calls *avodah begashmiyut*—divine service performed through the mundane details of the world. On this reading of the biblical narrative, then, it is through the embodied self, the capacity of imagination, and poetic modes of being most of all that humanity might hope to restore something of that lost wholeness, to bring themselves and the world closer to redemption.

Bread-Eaters and Dreamers: R. Mordecai Joseph Leiner of Izbica, *Mei hashilo'ah*

R. Mordecai Joseph Leiner of Izbica reached the hasidic court in Przysucha in his late teens, and remained there as part of R. Simhah Bunim's close circle of disciples until the master's death in 1827. Those years deeply affected his thought. His teachings, published in two volumes entitled *Mei hashilo'ah*, integrate and reflect further on many of R. Simhah Bunim's insights. The following *derashah* introduces a powerful metaphor to speak of the task of understanding. At the same time it effectively models the interpretative mode of being 'out of Eden' that the master described. The narrative context here is the biblical story of Joseph; its much broader theme—the art of discerning meaning by way of various and sundry things.

'You can hear a dream and interpret it' [Gen. 41: 15]. For everything in this world is like a dream to be interpreted. And whatever interpretation one gives, so will it be for that person.[37] Thus one who understands, through everything in the world, that God

---

[36] It is difficult to overlook the resonance here with Emmanuel Levinas's thought. Levinas held that 'the idea of infinity requires the separation of the same from the Other. This separation is a fall of the same and Other from totality. The level of separation is a level of fallenness. But this fall from totality produces infinity' (*Totality and Infinity*, 104).

[37] In its phrasing, this line seems to refer obliquely to BT *Ber.* 55*b*, concerning the anecdote recounted by Rabbi Banai: twenty-four interpreters told him the meaning(s) of his dream; all their explanations 'came to be' for him (*kulam nitkayamu bi*). The Rabbis conclude the passage with a popular saying to the effect that dreams themselves are indeterminate, and that it is the

is the source of all, and that what emanates from His mouth sustains all being—such an individual can grasp the meaning of each thing and attain a life of truth. And so it is with bread: its life-giving essence emanates from the mouth of God. Whoever eats it dully, like an animal, all it gives that person is mundane, physical being. But one who realizes that the true source of vitality is what emanates from God's mouth—such an individual wins eternal life. For bread [*leḥem*] and dream [*ḥalom*] have the same letters; bread, too, needs to be interpreted. The same is true of the pleasures and the good of this world—all that is called the 'bread' of life.[38]

Bread and dreams, linked in this *derashah* in unlikely fraternity, are evocative metaphors of the hermeneutical task. Both equally present 'texts' to be deciphered: just as dream images might reveal long-hidden, unimagined secrets, so might bread—along with other everyday needs—mean in some way beyond itself. The meaning they convey is neither wholly sealed away nor just plain there. It may emerge, but only through the labour of mediation between signs and symbols and letters reconfigured.

R. Mordecai Joseph's intuition here seems to echo certain Romantic notions of his age: the awareness of hidden, unconscious elements in human nature and their power over the conscious intellect, and the interest in how that dynamic plays out in dreams and in metaphor. These notions evolved further in psychoanalytic theory, taking shape as representations of reality in symbolic language and as models of dream analysis. Indeed, Lionel Trilling notes that 'the whole notion of rich ambiguity in literature, of the interplay between the apparent meaning and the latent—not "hidden"—meaning, has been reinforced by the Freudian concepts, perhaps even received its first impetus from them'.[39]

That being said, however, the most interesting and original aspect of this *derashah* is not its recognition of dreams and bread as texts in a metaphorical

interpretation (lit. 'the mouth') that fixes their meaning. Commentators are divided over what the contention of this anecdote might be. In the broader context, the Talmud presents multiple and contradictory stances on the intrinsic value of dreams as well as their interpretation. All that, however, lies beyond the bounds of our discussion. What concerns us here is R. Mordecai Joseph's creative reconception of the subject as a whole.

[38] *Mei hashilo'aḥ*, 'Mikets', i. 53.

[39] 'Freud and Literature', 183–4, 195; see Freud, *The Interpretation of Dreams*, ch. 6, 'The Dream Work'. Trilling here is interested in what he calls *Zeitgeist*. He places Freud at the end of the Romantic era and suggests he was influenced by Romanticism; at the same time, Freud's work has deeply affected the way we read literature. Trilling writes: 'Yet the relationship is reciprocal, and the effect of Freud upon literature has been no greater than the effect of literature upon Freud.'

sense but rather the mode of hermeneutical engagement with them that it proposes. In this R. Mordecai Joseph's reading surely accords with postmodern sensibilities. Most evident, of course, is the theoretical assumption that literary texts are indeterminate, that they have no self-contained, definitive message, and so interpreting them does not entail a prying out or reconstruction of some 'real' meaning their author intended. Instead, New Critics contend, the interaction between reader and text is what creates literary meaning and value. An actively engaged agent, the reader responds to the work, participates in, realizes, and completes its meaning through interpretation.[40] Phenomenologists stress the personal element in the communication of meaning at large. We read with the expectation that the text has something to say to us; inevitably, then, the meaning that emerges from it will respond to our questions and our history of experience, to the particular consciousness that shapes our perspective on everything. As Gadamer put it, 'a person reading a text is himself part of the meaning he apprehends'. R. Mordecai Joseph expresses the same idea regarding his metaphorical texts: 'whatever interpretation one gives, so will it be for that person'. And so, to discount this fundamental reciprocity between reader and 'text' as subjective and relativistic is to miss the point of what the 'experience of meaning' is all about.[41]

Yet I believe that this *derashah* does more than reread the traditional sources, biblical and rabbinic, with a hasidic 'hermeneutical twist'. As he develops the metaphor of dreams, bread, and the stuff of our lives as texts, R. Mordecai Joseph stresses the ethical dimension at stake in the act of interpreting them. He comments that it is possible, only too easy, really, to ignore the task—to eat one's bread 'dully, like an animal' and dream for nothing. Countering the inertia of that way of living, however, is the promise of real gains: 'One who understands, through everything in the world, that God is the source of all, and that what emanates from His mouth sustains all being— such an individual can grasp the meaning [*ta'am*] of each thing and attain a life of truth.' That promise, we realize in a flash of intuition, is encoded in the bread metaphor itself. The biblical verse that resonates here is this: 'He fed you the manna . . . to make you know that not by bread alone do people live, but by everything that emanates from the mouth of God do they live.'[42] In other words, the meaning of my 'bread'—its taste [*ta'am*] in my mouth and

---

[40] Important reader-response theorists whose views are relevant here include Iser (*The Implied Reader*) and Fish (*Is There a Text in This Class?*).

[41] See Gadamer, *Truth and Method*, 118, 390. On these aspects of hermeneutical philosophy and phenomenology see Grondin, 'Hermeneutics', 982–7.   [42] Deut. 8: 3.

its power to nurture me towards a 'life of truth'—will be commensurate with my efforts to know its ultimate source. Knowing, in the vital sense that R. Mordecai Joseph refers to here, can be attained through metaphorical acts of reading. That requires one to see past the 'plain sense' of things, to let one's dreams make sense of one's life. Quite strikingly, R. Mordecai Joseph performs the very activity that he describes. In other words, his *derashah* is not only *about* imagining and interpreting; in the course of it he enacts an experience of understanding through those very actions.[43]

I conclude this part of my discussion with a final *derashah* from the Przysucha school. R. Jacob of Izbica-Radzyn, son of R. Mordecai Joseph, takes up a number of the themes that have occupied us in this chapter, while introducing one more important element. Reading this passage, I would like to pay close attention both to what R. Jacob says and to what he does. This will help me tie together two central concerns: the self-image of the hasidic master as reader-interpreter and the understanding of hasidic hermeneutics that I am trying to develop.

Know Me in Translation: R. Jacob Leiner of Izbica-Radzyn, *Beit ya'akov*

'The clever should not glory in their wisdom, nor warriors in their strength, nor the wealthy in their riches. No, this alone wins one glory: Translate [*haskel*] and know Me' [Jer. 9: 23]. . . . As the Talmud says: '[Those psalms that King David prefaced with the word] *maskil*—they were given over by an intermediary [*meturgeman*; BT *Pes.* 117a].'[44]

---

[43] In the words 'enact' and 'perform', I draw in a general sense on insights from performance theory, a major theoretical concern in contemporary literary studies, pedagogy, and postmodern thought. More immediately, I am guided by Susan Handelman's work on rabbinic tales. Handelman reflects: 'They are not only *about* teachers and students; they also enact a *way of teaching* through their dramatic literary and rhetorical structures, their images, metaphors, allusions, enigmas. They have no simple moral, nor can they be reduced to any concise expository statements about pedagogy. In that sense, they are not didactic, but they are deep and self-conscious teachings. They beckon and seduce us to enter their world, to sit among the Sages and be their students, to argue with them, to feel their exaltation and pain, to judge, and to question our judgments.' *Make Yourself a Teacher*, 21; for references to performance theory, see ibid. 109 n. 23.

[44] A more literal translation of *haskel* would be 'contemplate' or 'realize'. R. Jacob draws attention to the common root of these two words, *maskil* and *haskel*. As we saw in Chapter 1, *maskil* designates an individual who, through contemplation, has become 'enlightened'. Notably, in biblical Hebrew the word *maskil* appears both as a noun and as a transitive verb (see Neh. 8: 13). Underlying R. Jacob's reading here is the latter sense: the task of the translator-interpreter or *meturgeman* is pedagogical in the most primary sense: he enlightens others by

Now, any middleman knows less completely than the source itself, and so some of the original wisdom becomes concealed. As it is being translated, that wisdom gets clothed in different garments and other words so that common people can understand it somehow. This must happen, for wisdom, when it emerges from the source, its light is too brilliant to bear. To be received it must be partly obscured. The midrash [*Exod. Rab.* 41: 3] compares this to one who wants to convey to another the taste of the food in his mouth—such a thing can be done only by saying it otherwise.[45]

The core questions that R. Jacob addresses in this *derashah* are: How is meaning communicated? How can knowledge be attained? Implicated as we are just now in those very acts, the figure of the *meturgeman* seems to offer a key to understanding them. Historically the *meturgeman* filled a variety of roles: he was a spokesman who projected a speaker's words to make them audible to a large audience; he translated Scripture from Hebrew to Aramaic on behalf of the unlearned; he was the expositor of tradition, in dialogue with the wider Jewish community.[46] In the more abstract sense that R. Jacob implies, we could say that the *meturgeman*'s role is to mediate as best he can between the (divine) source of wisdom and a community of receivers. The gulf that separates the two is both linguistic and ontological. And so his task as translator and as interpreter, in the sense R. Jacob describes here, is to labour between two disparate, truly estranged 'worlds' of words and of being. To bridge the

transmitting knowledge. My translation of the biblical verse attempts to comprehend the multiple connotations of these terms that come to the fore in the course of the *derashah*. Note the 'light' metaphor at work in the passage: to 'win glory' (*yithalel*) in the biblical verse stems from the root *h-l-l* (*h-l-h*), connoting light or illumination.

[45] R. Jacob Leiner of Izbica-Radzyn, *Sefer hazemanim, Rosh ḥodesh iyar*, 53b. This passage is part of a series of teachings whose temporal context is the Hebrew month of Iyar. Kabbalistic tradition connects this opening verse (Jer. 9: 23) with Iyar due to the particular permutation of the divine Name encoded in it. Already in rabbinic teaching, Iyar is identified as what the Bible calls *ḥodesh ziv*—'the month of brilliance'. The motif of light that informs this *derashah* stems from that association.

[46] R. Jacob's image of the *meturgeman* integrates these historical roles, yet the focus in this *derashah* is on the nature of his hermeneutical activity. On the *meturgeman* as spokesman see e.g. BT *MK* 21a; Rashi on Ps. 88: 1; Rashbam on BT *Pes.* 116b. In the centuries after the Temple's destruction, Hebrew as a spoken language generally fell into disuse, while Aramaic and other languages became the vernacular. A *meturgeman* was thus needed to translate as well as interpret Scripture for most of the Jewish community. In Babylonia the *meturgeman* also served as interpreter of the Mishnah; there he was also called *amora*—literally, an expounder and transmitter of tradition. Sectarian tensions within Jewish society impelled the rabbinical establishment to curtail the poetic licence that the *meturgeman* had enjoyed. Fixed translations, the *targumim*, came to replace them, while the *darshan* or preacher gradually took on the role of interpreter, mediating between Scripture and the wider Jewish community.

gap, to carry meaning across their boundaries, he must find a way of 'saying things otherwise'.

This *derashah* is emblematic of what hermeneutics is all about. I will try to explain. In a primary sense, hermeneutics is a reading and interpreting of sacred texts whose meaning is no longer fully present. If these texts are to remain a vital part of an ongoing tradition, mediation is needed. And so hermeneutical engagement with them has clear ethical implications: the meaning that the interpreter-translator-middleman imparts to the heirs of that tradition has to be one that can help people better understand the world, God, history, and themselves. All this suggests, in addition, that the hermeneutical task presents a crucial pedagogical moment. When R. Jacob cites the lines of the Talmud, he highlights this dimension by noting that the opaque biblical term *maskil* 'translates' to the image of the *meturgeman*. What he's indicating is that the role of the intermediary is most essentially to teach or instruct his audience. Whether in the person of translator, interpreter, or hasidic master, his task is to guide his listeners towards 'enlightenment'—to share with them some intimation of the brilliance, taste, and meaning of the Source. R. Jacob seeks to do just that, it seems, through his own transformative engagement with the sacred texts of Jewish tradition.

But I think this *derashah* is valuable in a second important sense as well: it sets out a hermeneutical model of existence.[47] The *meturgeman* embodies the dynamic of mediation at the heart of human experience. To make sense of our lives, to convey 'the taste of the food in my mouth' to others, to teach and to learn—all these efforts draw us endlessly into acts of mediation. We translate ourselves and our inner worlds to others; we make new combinations of disparate experience. We labour to communicate what words will not contain, to comprehend the unknowable. To bring this point home, R. Jacob concludes the *derashah* with a fragmentary parable. It sends the attentive reader back with uncommon rhetorical force to the verse with which he began. 'The midrash compares this to one who wants to convey to another the taste of the food in his mouth.' Within the wider exegetical context of that midrash, 'the taste of the food in His mouth' alludes to the recondite, innermost reaches of the Torah known to God alone. Inarguably, the Rabbis

---

[47] Ricoeur points out that one of the earliest words for a translator in Greek was *hermeneus* and in Latin *interpres*. Both terms suggest an intermediary labouring between two distinct languages or speakers to transfer meaning from one to the other. See Kearney, 'Paul Ricoeur and the Hermeneutics of Translation'. Ricoeur's hermeneutical project has informed my own understanding of many aspects of hasidic teaching. My discussion here is particularly indebted to Kearney's and Jean Grondin's insights on Ricoeur's thought.

counter, that 'original' Text in all of its plenitude of meaning can never be conveyed. But the biblical verse (Jer. 9: 23) hints at an alternative possible mode of understanding. 'Know Me'—it will always, incommensurably, be only in translation. But 'know Me'—by translating, interpreting, concealing, and revealing a taste of divine wisdom, a relationship takes shape; something of infinity may be shared. That event is called 'knowing'.

Conclusions So Far

The *derashot* that we have been looking at in this chapter offer some sense of the hermeneutical awareness that the hasidic masters developed. Their approach to reading sacred texts is unquestionably radical. By radical, though, I don't mean subversive or deconstructive. It is radical in a literal sense, in that they strike down to the root of what exegesis is really all about. The word 'exegesis', the Oxford English Dictionary notes, stems from the Greek *exegeisthai*, 'explain, interpret'—composed of *ex* (out) + *hegeisthai* (to lead, guide); it relates to the proto-Indo-European root **sag*, 'to track down, seek out'. Not accidentally, the Hebrew root *d-r-sh* at the heart of the words *midrash* and *derashah* has the very same meaning. What this implies is that hasidic modes of reading are exegetical in the most primary sense of the term.[48] Their object, in many instances at least, is to discover and decode meaning latent in the sacred texts of Jewish tradition. Whatever flashes of truth these texts might reveal are then conveyed through innovative interpretative moves. Nehemia Polen aptly describes this as 'illuminated exegesis'.[49] And so the overarching goal of their enterprise is to preserve and strengthen the authority of tradition by showing the enduring relevance of its sacred works for every contemporary audience. To that end, hasidic commentary often draws attention to a crucial interface between the written tradition and

[48] Revising the definition of 'exegesis' in this way clarifies an important issue. In the Introduction to this book I noted that leading scholars see hasidic teaching as having little to do with exegesis. That judgement, it seems, implicitly adopts the formalist view of homiletics as an inferior form of textual engagement in contrast to the linguistic and textual rigour of (medieval) modes of biblical exegesis. Joseph Dan makes the distinction clearly: 'if [the author] is primarily concerned with the ancient text, the work will be regarded as exegetical; but if it is in the form of a sermon, it will be regarded as homiletic'. In arguing, for his part, that midrash is by no means 'exegesis', Dan's working definition incorporates the Christian concept of exegesis, which indeed is 'deeply connected with the endeavor to differentiate between right and wrong, and to seek the original, completely true text expressing the one supreme divine meaning'. Dan, 'Is Midrash Exegesis?', 81–99. My suggestion here is that 'exegesis' should be defined in a more basic (pre-Christian) sense.   [49] In his essay 'Hasidic *Derashah* as Illuminated Exegesis'.

the world outside—an interface that is not often addressed in conventional Jewish exegesis. A basic tenet of the hasidic ethos is manifest here: the conviction that every aspect of reality, including the human psyche, contains hidden significance. Metaphorical texts such as these offer themselves to be deciphered and explained. The meanings that their perceptive 'reader' might bring to light can transform lives.

In noting the performative aspect of certain *derashot* I've tried to highlight what the hasidic masters are doing as well as what they are saying. Their teachings model how the world itself might be contemplated and better understood through the lens of Jewish sacred works. As intermediaries, they grapple with sources of knowledge that, at first sight, might seem obscure, recondite, confusing, even threatening. If they manage to translate them into an idiom that speaks to the community of receivers, their efforts might aid others in dealing with life's complexity and ambiguity. Like all of us, the hasidic masters bring their own world to bear on their texts. Horizons merge; understanding, when it emerges, is inescapably personal, subjective, and relative. But for that very reason such acts of reading, figurative as well as literal, have the power to generate an essential dialogue. It takes place between text and outside world, teacher and learner, past and present.

*

Returning now to the question with which this chapter opened: What is it that gives hasidic teaching the power to engender a spiritual awakening—one so powerful that it can be called 'the secret of redemption'? How does the hermeneutic of the *derashah* create that potentially transformative effect in an audience—its own contemporary listeners and readers in generations to come?

How to Teach, How to Learn: R. Mordecai Joseph Leiner of Izbica, *Mei hashilo'ah*

'They shall make an ark of acacia wood: two and a half cubits its length, a cubit and a half its width, and a cubit and a half its height' [Exod. 25: 10]. All the dimensions of the ark were half-measures. To learn anything, one needs to realize that one is lacking, halfway, in the middle—and that without Torah, one remains incomplete. For God grants understanding of Torah only to those who know they are missing something, and who sense what it is they need to become whole. But if a person only craves words of Torah like foreign wisdom [*hokhmah aheret*]—well, the angels coveted the Torah too [but it was denied them—see BT *Shab.* 88*a*]. . . . That is what Elijah, of blessed memory, said [in the midrash *Tana devei eliyahu rabah*, 20: 'While I was standing there, along came a student who knew almost nothing about Torah law. He said to me, "Rabbi, I'm trying to learn, and I truly crave and lust for understanding of Torah to come to me. I'm waiting and pining away, but it's just not coming."] Elijah responded: 'My son, no one's ever been given understanding of words of Torah without committing his soul to them for the sake of Heaven.' Now, it can't be that the student's desire for Torah knowledge was unworthy—after all, if he merited having Elijah reveal himself to him, his intent must have been worthy. What was wrong, as he himself admitted, was that he wanted Torah like any other wisdom. And, similarly [in another midrash voiced by Elijah, *Tana devei eliyahu zuta*, 14: 'Once I came upon a scorner and I reproached him, "My son, what will you say to your Father in Heaven on the day of judgement?" He answered, "Oh, I have an answer for Him, Rabbi. I'll tell Him that I wasn't given knowledge or understanding from Above." I responded, "Son, what's your trade?" He said, "I'm a fisherman."'] Then Elijah asked him, 'My son, how did you understand that you need to take flax and weave it into nets and cast them onto the sea and draw out fish?' What Elijah was saying was: If only you know that you need Torah like bread to eat—*then* you'll be able to understand about fear of God.[50]

This *derashah*, most fundamentally, is about how learning takes place. Its author, R. Mordecai Joseph of Izbica, doesn't expound on the subject in theoretical or conceptual terms. Instead, he enacts an event of learning through the agency of the prophet Elijah. We should note that Elijah here is no longer the fiery, impassioned man of God that the Bible portrays. Midrash and Jewish folklore transformed him into a discerning teacher, miraculous healer, and beneficent saviour, who might suddenly appear to wise and simple people alike. Beyond death, Elijah visits each Jewish home on Passover night; his chair awaits him at every baby's circumcision. It is this Elijah who will lead estranged parents and children back to one another, resolve age-old mysteries, and ready the world for the coming messiah.

R. Mordecai Joseph draws on these weighty associations in forming his

---

[50] *Mei hashilo'aḥ*, 'Terumah', ii. 57–8. For Izbica-Radzyn commentary on this *derashah* see: *Beit ya'akov*, 'Terumah', ii. 345–6; *Sod yesharim*, 'Simḥat Torah', 38, 75–6; *Dover tsedek*, 24. Earlier Bible commentators had already noted that these dimensions are 'broken' units, half-measures; interpretations include the need to 'break' the ego in learning Torah, to abandon one's imagined sense of complete mastery, to study with humility. See R. Bahya ben Asher and *Keli yakar* on Exod. 25: 10. The half-measure as an existential motif appears in the Magid of Mezhirech's famous teaching on the verse: 'These are the two trumpets [*ḥatsotserot*] of silver' (Num. 10: 2) to mean that a human being is only a *ḥetsi tsurah*, a half-form—the other half being God. *Magid devarav leya'akov*, s. 24 (pp. 38–40) and parallels.

message. The two midrashic scenes that he integrates in his *derashah* tell of chance meetings on the road, a mundane exchange of words between strangely familiar strangers. But in those few moments Elijah, as an insightful healer of the soul, helps his interlocutor recognize the misconceptions that have led him sadly astray. His mild rebuke, tempered with solicitude, is meant to awaken the other in a basic existential sense. His words are not an explanatory lesson or the interpretation of a specific object. Their message is more open and subtle, directed inwards. 'To learn anything, one needs to realize that one is lacking, halfway, in the middle—and that without Torah, one remains incomplete.' This kind of learning begins from a place of not knowing. Hunger and desire drive it on, in search of something to fill the emptiness. It is this sense of immediacy and exigency—in relation to the Torah, to God, and to one's teacher—that R. Mordecai Joseph's *derashah* seeks to communicate.

This passage is emblematic of my subject here. In Chapter 1 we saw that the Ba'al Shem Tov was charged with the task, through his new path called hasidism, to awake others spiritually by means of the sacred texts of Jewish tradition. That awakening would be 'the secret of redemption'. The logic that holds together these two elements is the sense that understanding (of sacred texts, of human life, of history) must be part of a larger process of repair, or *tikun*—a process that takes place on many levels, from personal and national to universal. Kabbalistic tradition focused on the concept of *tikun* as a theosophical and cosmic restoration, and mystics sought to achieve it through solitary contemplation, mystical experiences, and theurgic techniques. Hasidism took these powerful ideas and rechannelled their esoteric valences. The project of repair would now be the responsibility of every individual, and would be connected, first of all, to the most immediate aspects of day-to-day life.

To reconstruct broken selves and worlds, to heal the soul and mend the cosmos—these are big ideas with untold existential force. Hasidism joined the notion of *tikun* with a second central innovation: a new mode of relationship between the spiritual master, the *tsadik* or *rebbe*, and his followers—his hasidim. Countless sources from within and outside the hasidic world—hagiographical, polemical, and homiletical—bear witness to the far-reaching influence of these leaders. From a *tsadik* or *rebbe*, ordinary folk as well as Torah scholars received the inspiration they needed and guidance on their path. Conversely as well, it was only through his relationship with them that the *tsadik* could fulfil his purpose as a leader of the Jewish nation. As hasidism developed into a movement of mass appeal, the *tsadik* came to be seen as the axis uniting heaven and earth, a conduit for divine blessings. In his righteousness, he was invested with the supernatural ability to annul evil decrees; some charismatic figures were renowned for their paranormal healing powers and penetrating vision into the souls of others.[51]

Academic scholarship has thoroughly mapped the vicissitudes of 'tsadik-ism' as an institution in the course of the nineteenth century, with attention to its positive and negative effects in Jewish society and culture. I would like to foreground another dimension of that relationship, so central to hasidic experience—one that bears directly on the themes of this book. The core element that concerns us here is the personal connection between *tsadik* or *rebbe* and those he teaches.[52] This dimension is modelled by Elijah and his interaction with others in the passage we have just read.

Returning to R. Mordecai Joseph's *derashah*, we see now that its subtext is this biblical verse: 'My son . . . if only you call out to understanding . . . if you seek it out like silver, if you search for it as hidden treasures—then you will understand the fear of God, and discover knowledge of the Lord' (Prov. 2: 3–5). The tone of paternal caring—'if only'—along with the promise of concealed riches is picked up rhetorically by the midrash. R. Mordecai Joseph preserves that emotional atmosphere in his own staging of the scene. The figure of Elijah, as he is portrayed in this *derashah*, illuminates a central element of hermeneutics. It is manifest in the relation between *tsadik* and hasid that I want to portray. A knower of roads (heavenly and earthly), Elijah is a liminal figure, a facilitator. He sees into the souls of those he meets on the way and hears their secret longing. From that point of intimacy, he is able to offer insightful counsel—to direct others towards a different perspective, perhaps even set them on the path to spiritual repair. In the same way, the *rebbe* or *tsadik* has deeper wisdom concerning the Torah and God's will expressed in it. He also knows about human suffering. All that empowers him to discern meaning, hidden in sacred texts and in life. When he manages to communicate something of what he knows to others, his words and his presence can heal. One final element of this literally hermeneutical activity: Elijah, a master teacher and guide, communicates by indirection. The same, notably, is said of

[51] See Idel, "'The Besht Passed His Hand over His Face'". On the use of the Ba'al Shem Tov's teachings in modern-day therapy, see Mordechai Rotenberg, *Dialogue with Deviance*; id., *Hasidic Psychology*; also, E. Frankel, *Sacred Therapy*, 130–1. Hasidic stories offer an important window onto the psychological elements of hasidism and their expression in everyday life.

[52] My discussion here has been enriched by important work on the pedagogical ethos by Parker Palmer and, in Jewish tradition, by Shalom Carmi, Susan Handelman, and Elie Holzer.

the figure of Hermes: 'his manner of giving treasure to people is that he permits them to find it'. And so, in a parallel way, the purpose of hermeneutical methods is to 'enable the text to yield its treasure, but the interpreter only leads the reader to the treasure and then retires'.[53] Here, those hidden treasures—'the fear of God . . . knowledge of the Lord'—are a deeply personal kind of understanding that will invest one's life with meaning. Elijah, in the role of *tsadik*, mediates the search and the finding. To encounter such a person, then, might engender a profound inner 'repair'.

The next sermons in this chapter touch on relationships between hasidic masters and those who seek them out. Each of the passages contains a paradigmatic story about the bond between the *rebbe* and his hasidim. These stories will help us see how the interpretative dynamic of the *derashah* enacts that bond as well. Sections of these texts could be (and have been) excavated profitably for information about the historical or social realities of the hasidic world. I won't be reading them in that light. What I am trying to catch sight of are the resources that are brought to bear in these commentaries to communicate ideas and religious experience, and the ways they suggest that understanding can be gained.

To Know or Not to Know: R. Solomon Hakohen Rabinowicz of Radomsk, *Tiferet shelomoh* on R. Hayim Haykl of Amdur

The spiritual journey of R. Hayim Haykl of Amdur (Indura, near Grodno) most probably began in the early 1760s. Some say he was then a loyalist to the Vilna Gaon, the illustrious rabbinic figure who was soon to lead the fierce opposition to the new 'sect' called hasidism. Hagiographical sources recount that it was R. Aaron the Great of Karlin (1736–72) who first happened upon him sitting solitary in a house of study during his travels through the northern lands of Lithuania. One of the Magid of Mezhirech's earliest disciples and already an important religious leader in his own right, R. Aaron was searching out promising young Torah scholars to join the ranks of his master's followers. He brought R. Hayim Haykl to Mezhirech for a sabbath that would change his life.[54] A second account, recorded by R. Solomon Hakohen Rabinowicz

---

[53] On the connection between hermeneutical methods and the figure of Hermes, see R. Palmer, 'The Liminality of Hermes and the Meaning of Hermeneutics', 12–14.

[54] This story is preserved in the tradition of the Karlin-Stolin dynasty. See Shor, 'Rabbi Aaron the Great', 152–3. On R. Hayim Haykl's court in Amdur, his persona in the polemical

of Radomsk (1803–66), offers a rare glimpse into the inner dimensions of his beginnings:

So we heard—the holy Rebbe of Radoshitz would often recall the story of the righteous R. Hayka Amdura, of blessed memory: how he fasted and afflicted himself severely for weeks on end, how he spent a thousand sleepless nights learning Torah. But still his soul was plagued with a feeling of incompleteness. Until he came to the sainted Rebbe, our master Dov Baer of Mezhirech. Then he attained his *tikun* [soul repair] and finally became whole. For the meaning that the *tsadik* gives to one's labour —that is essential like nothing else.[55]

This story of origins tells of a young man's initiation and transformation into a hasid. Its central motif is the sense of lack, which finds no fulfilment until he meets his spiritual mentor—here, the great Magid, who guides him to an intensely personal 'repair'.[56] The same author, R. Solomon of Radomsk, revisits R. Hayim Haykl's story in a number of his *derashot*. I'd like to take a close look at one passage from his commentary on the book of Genesis, with particular attention to the role that this fragmentary, emblematic human experience plays in conveying R. Solomon's larger message.

The biblical epic of Joseph and his brothers is a story charged with ambivalence, confusion, half-concealed intrigues, and uncertain motives. As its dramatic climax approaches, Jacob's sons try desperately to convince their father that they have no choice but to return to Egypt, together with his beloved youngest son Benjamin, to face the man who will decide their destiny.

---

literature, his role in the dispute between hasidim and *mitnagedim*, and his teachings, see Rabinowitsch, *Lithuanian Hasidism*, 121–49.

[55] *Tiferet shelomoh*, 'Simḥat Torah', ii. 145. He cites this story in the name of R. Yissachar Dov Ber of Radoshitz (1765–1843), whose father was also a disciple of the great Magid. See also *Tiferet shelomoh*, 'Tsav', i. 222; 'Beḥukotai', i. 260–1. R. Solomon Hakohen Rabinowicz founded the hasidic dynasty of Radomsk in 1843. He was a disciple of R. Meir of Apt, whose own master had been the Seer of Lublin.

[56] Caution is needed, however, in evaluating the nature of that transformation. The devotional behaviour this story describes is the old-style mystical-ascetic 'hasidism' that spread from sixteenth-century kabbalistic circles in Safed to eastern Europe. Prominent members of the Ba'al Shem Tov's circle are known to have adopted these stringent practices of self-purification aimed towards spiritual goals—among them Dov Baer, the Magid of Mezhirech, and R. Jacob Joseph of Polonnoye, as well as the Ba'al Shem Tov himself in his younger years. R. Aaron the Great of Karlin, along with many other hasidic leaders in that early period, was outspokenly opposed to frequent fasting and self-mortification. Yet it appears that R. Hayim Haykl continued his severe ascetic practices in his own court even after his 'conversion' to hasidism; see Shor, n. 64. This would suggest that the 'repair' he experienced in his encounter with the Magid was of another order.

R. Solomon opens his *derashah* with Judah's plea to Jacob to relent and let them go: 'Had we not delayed, by now we could have returned twice over' (Gen. 43: 10). Taking a step back from the biblical narrative, R. Solomon remarks that this verse touches on a central aspect of religious life: the spiritual dynamic called repentance, or *teshuvah*—literally 'return'. Recast in that broader context, Judah's words now refer to the difficult yet essential phase that precedes every instance of spiritual repair. To begin restoration one must first understand what went wrong and take measure of one's own accountability. Joseph's brothers, here, are at an impasse. The recent chapters of their lives have indeed been filled with 'delays', seemingly unexplainable complications, and unspoken suffering. Yet, as R. Solomon points out, throughout the twenty-two years that have passed since they sold Joseph into slavery, the brothers have sincerely believed they acted justly.[57] From such a static mental stance, no movement towards repair is at all conceivable. R. Solomon proposes an insightful reading of the biblical narrative through a creative synthesis of traditional sources. He gestures only briefly towards R. Hayim Haykl's personal story here;[58] nonetheless, I suggest that it is the unifying force in his reading. As the *derashah* unfolds its significance becomes clear:

'Had we not delayed, by now we could have returned twice over' [Gen. 43: 10]. Maybe this verse can be better understood through what we say in [the Amidah] prayer: 'Return us, our Father, to Your Torah'. Now, the Rabbis taught, [when one is beset by suffering and can't discover why,] one should attribute it to negligence in Torah study.[59] But if a person knows he hasn't been studying, what sense is there in saying one 'can't discover why'? In truth, though, even if one studies Torah relentlessly yet fails to guard oneself from misdeed—then all that studying is virtually null and void, as non-existent as neglected crumbs.[60] For the real purpose of learning is to teach a

---

[57] Jewish commentators struggle with the ambivalence of the biblical story and propose various understandings of the motives and actions that it recounts. Of particular interest here is the psychological complexity that our author highlights.

[58] Some of the *derashot* in R. Solomon's homiletical work, *Tiferet shelomoh*, were penned by the author himself; others were written down by his disciples on the basis of discourses that he delivered orally. It is reasonable to assume that for his listening audience R. Solomon retold R. Hayim Haykl's story in greater detail than the abbreviated version cited here.

[59] BT *Ber.* 5a.

[60] BT *Pes.* 4b. The irony in this contention evades my attempts at direct translation. A number of elements link these talmudic passages (*Ber.* 5a and *Pes.* 4b). Both relate to a situation in which something (the reason for suffering/leaven) is sought but not found (*pishpesh velo matsa*); the endpoint of the search is nullification (*bitul torah/bitul hamets*); in both contexts the Torah is involved (worthless Torah learning/concerning Pesach: 'the search for leaven is [required only] by rabbinical law, for by scriptural law mere nullification suffices'). R. Solomon links the same concepts in a second *derashah*: *Tiferet shelomoh*, 'Tazria', i. 233.

person the straight path of serving the Creator. If the Torah doesn't guide one closer to that goal, all one's study is as naught. The remedy for such a situation is set out in the Zohar: whoever rises at midnight to study Torah, reflects bitterly on his deeds, and regrets all those empty, wasted days—'the Torah itself will make that person's wrongs known to him'.[61] Once that has happened, with clear vision and in full cognizance of where one has erred, it is possible to return in complete repentance. Thus we say 'Return us, our Father, to Your Torah'.

In the same sense [R. Moses] Alshikh understood the verse in Psalm 51: 1: 'A song by David. When Nathan the prophet came to him, after he came to Batsheva.' Then, at last, David understood his sin and could begin to repent. For until then he had believed his actions were permitted since she was legally divorced, as the Rabbis taught [BT *Shab.* 56a]. Indeed, so it is when one sees the face of the *tsadik* and becomes bound up together with him. The encounter with the *tsadik* repairs one's soul and leads to complete and true repentance. *The famous story of R. Hayka Amdura attests to all of this.* And so, too, in the case of Joseph's brothers. They had sold him into slavery, but it didn't occur to them that they had treated him unjustly. And for that reason they were utterly unable to repent. So it was until they came to Joseph himself and beheld his countenance—for Joseph was the *tsadik* of the generation, the 'pillar of the world'.[62] Seeing his face awoke them; it made their wrongs known to them. All at once they set to wondering how they ever could have committed such terrible deeds—as they confessed: 'But, truly, we are guilty' [Gen. 42: 21]. . . . Then, at last, they were able to take upon themselves the yoke of heaven and begin to repair. All that is hinted in what they said: Had we not delayed in beholding his radiant countenance, we could long ago have begun our return.[63]

A reading focused on elucidating hasidic ideology would point out that this *derashah* uses the idealized figure of the '*tsadik* of the generation' as a template for reading the biblical narrative. The typology of the righteous Joseph, or Joseph the *tsadik*, named already in kabbalistic teaching as 'pillar of the world', does invite such a direct translation of terms. And, indeed, in the case of R. Solomon of Radomsk, a hasidic leader in Poland in the first decades of the nineteenth century who ardently believed in the power of the hasidic *tsadikim*, such a reading virtually imposes itself.

But I think this *derashah* does more than personify an ideological doctrine or esoteric concept in the figure of Joseph. What R. Solomon portrays is a

---

[61] See Zohar iii. 23*b*; a similar formulation appears in *Shenei luḥot haberit*, iii. 192.

[62] The phrase 'Joseph, the pillar of the world' is drawn from the Zohar. See e.g. Zohar i. 45*a*.

[63] *Tiferet shelomoh*, 'Mikets', i. 115; emphasis mine. Note that this passage begins and ends with the same verse—R. Solomon opens by citing its plain meaning; in his conclusion he rereads the verse figuratively, in light of the connotations of return as repentance and amending that he developed in the *derashah*.

human drama fraught with emotion. That drama reaches its climax and final resolution in the biblical narrative with the encounter between Joseph and his brothers. In terms of social realism, Joseph clearly models the new mode of connection between *rebbe* and follower that hasidism developed. On a wider horizon, however, R. Solomon's commentary suggests that the dynamic of that connection, played out here between Joseph and his brothers, really comprehends all questions of understanding—of life and of sacred texts. This idea underlies the *derashah* as a whole. A closer look at its component parts will help clarify how R. Solomon communicates his message.

Not only the story of Joseph and his brothers, but all the scenarios that this *derashah* recalls are inlaid with trauma and healing. Each of them speaks, in one way or another, of how we live our lives trying to make sense of events and of our private suffering. R. Solomon sets out those scenes to explain the inner workings of repentance and its ethical and spiritual bearing. The process he describes begins with a feeling of alienation—from God, from the Torah, or from one's whole self and true being. This nameless sense of having somehow 'missed the mark' drives one to search for its root cause. Most crucially, R. Solomon suggests that in order to understand it the mediation of an 'other' is needed. The other breaks in on the closed world of consciousness to challenge one's defences and resistance and misconceptions. That encounter can then open out towards the discovery of new meanings of one's experience —and maybe even further, to repair and 'return'.[64]

R. Solomon presents four instances in which such an encounter takes place. The first is with the Torah itself, in the personified sense that the Zohar portrays. 'Whoever rises at midnight to learn Torah, reflects bitterly on his deeds, and regrets all those empty, wasted days—the Torah itself will make that person's wrongs known to him.'[65] In the second, strikingly related instance, it is Nathan the prophet who makes King David's wrongs known to

---

[64] In these terms Thomas Ogden comments on psychoanalyst D. W. Winnicott's unfinished last paper, "'the fear of breakdown is a fear of a breakdown that has *already happened*, but has *not yet been experienced.*" In other words, we have ways of experiencing or not experiencing the events of our lives' ('Fear of Breakdown and the Unlived Life', 210–11). See also E. Frankel, *Sacred Therapy*, 129; Caruth, *Unclaimed Experience*.

[65] This passage in the Zohar ostensibly interprets the unclear formulation in the verse, 'If the sin that he committed becomes known to him' (Lev. 4: 23, 28). Rashi (on Lev. 4: 23) resolves its meaning thus: "'becomes known to him"—when he sinned he thought his act was permitted; later he found out that it was forbidden'. On the more radical reading in the Zohar, it is the Torah itself, when studied authentically, that brings one to realize the import of one's actions. The intimate moment of disclosure that the Zohar describes is won through intense and engaged learning, in which the reader searches for a message with personal relevance.

him. The harsh moment of recognition—'You are the man!' (2 Sam. 12: 7)—marks the dramatic turning point of that biblical narrative, and sets off the arduous course of repentance that will take up the rest of King David's life. The third scenario is R. Hayim Haykl's story: 'still his soul was plagued with a feeling of incompleteness, until he came to the sainted Rebbe, our master Dov Baer of Mezhirech. Then he attained his *tikun* [soul repair] and finally became whole.' The fourth instance concerns Joseph and his brothers: 'Seeing his face awoke them; it made their wrongs known to them.' From that point the brothers begin to amend and return—not, in the plain sense of the verse, to Canaan and their father's home, but towards a spiritual rebuilding and the healing of wounds.

The overarching theme of this *derashah*, then, is how, from a place of not knowing, one can come to know. Understanding emerges through encounter and relationship and community. Each of these scenarios describes the ways in which such a meeting can engender a crucial shift in consciousness, one that enables a new self-understanding. Its effect on the course of a life is potentially transformative. The hasidic *tsadik* is a master of traumatic experience and of interpretation (of self and world and texts).[66] He has the power to awaken the soul to the world, to reveal what had been concealed and help people understand things otherwise. The new kind of relationship that developed between the *tsadik* and his hasidim surely enhanced that effect. But R. Solomon's *derashah* makes it clear that the relation between the *rebbe* and his followers takes place not only within that social contact. In a more primary sense, the hasidic masters discovered the healing power of a mutual bond mediated by Torah and lived out in the interrelation of learner and teacher. Hasidic commentary on the Torah hermeneutically performs this bond as well. The reconciliation and amending, the *tikun* that it teaches, are initiated by human agency. They are offered to anyone who yearns for inner change, who reads and listens for guidance on the way, illuminated by the master's 'radiant countenance'.

Finding the Words: R. Ze'ev Wolf of Zhitomir, *Or hame'ir* on R. Dov Baer, the Magid of Mezhirech

'For the meaning that the *tsadik* gives to one's labour—that is essential like nothing else.' The last two passages we have considered referred obliquely but

---

[66] On traumatic experience and 'the complex relation between knowing and not knowing' implicit in it, see e.g. Caruth, *Unclaimed Experience*, 3–5, 117 ff.

specifically to R. Dov Baer, the Magid of Mezhirech (1704–72). The following *derashah* puts him at centre stage. One of the most creative thinkers in the early generations of hasidism, the Magid deeply influenced the learning dynamic taking shape between *rebbe* and disciple. An erudite Talmud scholar and contemplative, traditional pietist steeped in esoteric lore, he is also re-membered as a charismatic religious figure and spiritual mentor. The Magid's teachings abound with parables about children and parents, teachers and learners, and have much to say about how knowledge can be communicated. Hasidic stories recount his own first, transformative encounter with his pre-eminent teacher, the Ba'al Shem Tov. Other tales describe the Magid's extraordinary personal presence, his astonishing exegetical skills, and his penetrating, paranormal insight into the human soul. Reliable historical in-formation about his life is much more sketchy.[67] We know that he served as official preacher or *magid* in Mezhirech and the nearby community of Korets, but his fame was not won in that public role. The Magid's home was his *beit midrash*, or house of study, and it was in that ambience that his teachings took shape, in dialogue with students, contemporaries, and variegated visitors who found themselves in Mezhirech. Over the years an elite circle of disciples was drawn to him. Their age, life stage, social status, and personal talents varied widely. Some spent months or years in the Magid's proximity; others, only a day or two. Regardless of their ideological differences and the geographical distance that separated them, R. Dov Baer's impact on his followers was immense. The writings of his closest disciples integrate valuable accounts of the Magid 'speaking Torah'. While many issues remain in dispute, historians recognize that the Magid of Mezhirech and his followers played a central role in developing hasidic theology and models of spiritual leadership during a formative, transitional stage as hasidism evolved into a powerful social and religious movement.[68]

R. Ze'ev Wolf of Zhitomir was a prominent member of the Magid's circle.[69] The following passage from his commentary *Or hame'ir* is part of

[67] Two recent and major studies with critical reviews of scholarship on the Magid are Mayse, *Beyond the Letters*, and Lederberg, *The Gateway to Infinity* (Heb.).

[68] Polonsky (*The Jews in Poland and Russia*, ii. 281) writes: 'A key role in this process [the spread of hasidism] was played by Dov Baer, who sent his followers over the whole area of the former Polish-Lithuanian Commonwealth, Menahem Mendel to Vitebsk, Shneur Zalman to Lyady, Levi Isaac to Berdichev, Elimelekh to Lizhensk.'

[69] He was a preacher and founder of a dynasty (d.1797), and had close personal ties with other central figures of his time—among them R. Jacob Joseph of Polonnoye, R. Nahum of Chernobyl, and R. Levi Isaac of Berdichev. See Piekarz, *The Hasidic Leadership* (Heb.), 94–102.

a long *derashah* on the opening verse of Deuteronomy: 'These are the words that Moses spoke to all Israel' (Deut. 1: 1). Identifying deeply with his protagonist, R. Ze'ev Wolf begins his sermon with some thoughts on what Moses must have experienced just then in his role as paradigmatic teacher. He describes the tiresome struggle that every public speaker knows all too well. Before him sits a heterogeneous and critical audience. Their individual needs are at radical cross-purposes. And so he spends his strength in an endlessly frustrating, fruitless attempt to satisfy the demands or expectations of even one of them. That is the context in which R. Ze'ev Wolf places the following account, featuring his own *rebbe* and mentor, R. Dov Baer of Mezhirech.

Once we were in the Magid's home. People of all kinds, old and young, had come to join us at his table. After a while he began to speak: There is a story [BT *BK* 60*b*] about a man who had two wives, a young one and an old one. The old wife would pluck the dark hairs from his head; the young wife, the white hairs—until he was bald all over. So it is with words of Torah. As the Rabbis said, the Torah was given as black fire on white fire [JT *Sot.* 8: 3]. Black fire—this refers to what strikes awe and fear in young hearts, words of reproof meant for those who aren't yet confidants in God's secret counsel. For youth need to be threatened with the sting of the strap.[70] White fire—that's everything that has to do with love, all the Torah's hidden signs and hints that are meant only for the enlightened few, to grant them wisdom and draw them closer in knowing the Creator. Now, when people of all kinds come to consult with the *rebbe*, some of them need to understand about awe and 'black fire'; others, about love—until he's bald all over, at a total loss for words. But if he is truly a wise man, expansive of spirit and deeply intuitive—such a *rebbe* can find the right words for each person. And each of them will find solace for his soul by discerning what the *rebbe* means to tell him about his own life's work.

Read as a biographical source, the Magid's *derashah* is clearly self-referential, even self-revelatory. It speaks directly about the challenges he faces in his role as religious leader, and lends itself to speculations about his ambivalence towards the demands that role imposed on him.[71] Read as a historical document, this internal hasidic source offers important information about the demography of the Magid's *beit midrash*. It documents R. Dov Baer's intent to give his audience spiritual and religious instruction, and testifies to his ability

---

[70] Cf. *Tikunei zohar* 12a.

[71] Haviva Pedaya discusses the biographical and autobiographical aspects of the Magid's activity: 'The Baal Shem Tov, R. Jacob Joseph of Polonnoye, and the Maggid of Mezhirech' (Heb.), 25–73; 'Two Types of Ecstatic Experience in Hasidism' (Heb.) 73–108. On these aspects of this *derashah* in particular, see also Green et al., *Speaking Torah*, 48–9; Mayse, 'Beyond the Letters', 474–6.

to formulate a polysemous message open to individual interpretation. As historians have indeed shown, all this is corroborated by the unique first-hand testimony of an outsider to the hasidic world, Solomon Maimon, who had visited the Magid's court as a young man.[72]

These are important perspectives to keep in mind. Yet I think there is more going on in this *derashah*. It illuminates something fundamental about hasidic teaching, and about the *eros* that might truly make the encounter between teacher and learner a 'world-shaking' event.[73] Before taking a closer look at the passage, I need to point out that the Magid's teaching here is embedded in another text—R. Ze'ev Wolf's own commentary on the Torah. And so my reading will relate to the Magid as a literary figure portrayed by his disciple, and will then consider the scene above as R. Ze'ev Wolf frames it in a broader exegetical context of his own making.

Most evidently, the Magid's teaching depicts a meeting between teacher and students. It addresses the well-known dualisms built into that meeting—between self and other, subject and object, speaker and audience—and recognizes the tensions implicit in those dualisms. The scenario of the harried husband at the mercy of his jealous wives sets all that out humorously, from the teacher's vantage point, to startle his students into self-awareness. Not coincidentally, in its original talmudic context the scene serves the same rhetorical purpose:

Rabbi Ami and Rabbi Asi were sitting before Rabbi Isaac the smith. One of them said, 'Will the master please tell us some legal points?' The other one said, 'Will the master please give us some homiletical instruction?' When he started to say something homiletical, one of them cut him off. When he began a legal discourse, the other

[72] In his autobiography (*Lebensgeschichte*), Maimon wrote about that visit: 'Every one of the newcomers believed that he discovered, in that part of the sermon which was founded on his verse, something that had special reference to the facts of his own spiritual life. At this we were of course greatly astonished' (*Solomon Maimon: An Autobiography*, 169).

[73] Richard Palmer notes that a central element in the meaning of hermeneutics is that it is a mediation between worlds. 'And in the strongest instances, Hermes' message is "world-shaking": it brings, as Heidegger says, "a transformation of thinking"' ('The Liminality of Hermes', citing Heidegger's *On the Way to Language*, trans. Peter D. Hertz (New York, 1971), 42). Educational theorist Joseph J. Schwab, in his classic essay of 1954, introduced the concept of *eros* to speak of the desire, yearning, and love for knowledge that a true teacher seeks to foster in students: '*Eros*, the energy of wanting, is as much the energy source in the pursuit of truth as it is in the motion toward pleasure, friendship, fame, or power.' Schwab's vision of educational reform calls for a shift in emphasis from the acquisition of (passive) knowledge to engendering an active, dynamic interrelationship between teacher and student, in which emotion and experience play a real part. See 'Eros and Education', 109.

one kept him from continuing. Finally he said, 'I have a parable for you. There was a man who had two wives, a young one and an old one . . .'

In a basic sense, R. Isaac's parable gives voice to the difficulty of asserting a sense of control and personal agency; it even acknowledges the teacher's secret anxiety about being depleted by students' pressing needs and demands. But the Magid's *derashah* does more than portray a speaker's rhetorical situation and an audience's reception of his message. On a deeper level it also enacts a way of teaching.

To the image of the man bereft of black and white hair, the Magid attaches a second, remarkably incongruous allusion: 'So it is with words of Torah. As the Rabbis said, the Torah was given as black fire on white fire.' What inner logic could be linking together the images of hair and fire? The proof-text that reveals their continuity of meaning seems to be this one. On the verse 'His curly locks were black as a raven' (S. of S. 5: 11), Rashi comments: '"Black as a raven", for the Torah was first given as black fire on white fire. Another interpretation: "His locks were black"—when God revealed Himself at the parting of the sea, He appeared to them as a young warrior. At Sinai He appeared to them as a white-bearded ancient filled with mercy.'[74] Here indeed, the Magid's two images are superimposed upon one another. Black-white hair and black-white fire speak, equally, of the infinite, ungraspable essence of the Divine and the Torah. Both images affirm that human beings are unable to apprehend such fullness of being. Any single moment of revelation, then, can be no more than partial, subjective, situational—some sort of monochromatic message that fits the receiver's capacity to contain it.

All this is reflected in the position of the *tsadik*. He knows all too well that his own fullness of being and the sources of his wisdom cannot be transmitted as he knows them. But faced with an audience with such diverse and conflicting needs, after some moments of silence the *rebbe* catches sight of a solution. His teaching must embody the essential nature of the Torah itself. It too needs to be a dynamic revealing and concealing, ablaze with black and white, love and awe, plain and esoteric meanings. This, then, is the *rebbe*'s own 'Torah'. More than concepts or doctrines or esoteric wisdom, it is an experience that he wants to communicate to his listeners. Like fire, the inner vitality of that message, its passion and transforming, purifying force cannot be given over to the intellect in abstract discourse. The encounter itself is the main thing: the immediacy of a human relationship between teacher and learner,

---

[74] Following the midrash *Mekhilta*, 'Shirah', 4.

between *rebbe* and hasid. By the parable he retells, the Magid highlights the reciprocity at the heart of any genuine learning experience.

Here the listeners themselves are embedded in a potentially powerful rhetorical situation. Some kind of need has brought these people to him, and the hope that his words will speak to them in some way. What the Magid tells them is that true learning of anything (including Torah) begins there: with questions, lack, and searching. The desire to know is what enables each of them to discern, in the shifting flames of the Torah's infinite possibilities, what's meant for them, every one separately, in any given here and now. Thus understanding, when it is achieved, is always personal in that it responds to what the learner seeks. All this makes the *rebbe*'s teaching unlike 'any other wisdom'—both in content and in the mode of engaged learning that it mandates.

The larger meaning of this scene emerges when we take account of the 'frame story' in which it appears. Notably, the last lines of the Magid's *derashah* subtly blur the boundary between inner and framing texts: 'But if he is truly a wise man, expansive of spirit and deeply intuitive—such a *rebbe* can find the right words for each person'. Is this the Magid still speaking (of himself), or are these reflections R. Ze'ev Wolf's? Reading on, we see that the boundary between textual elements dissolves. The dynamic that inhabits the Magid's *derashah* is manifest in the biblical narrative as well, in the figure of Moses. As I noted at the outset, R. Ze'ev Wolf's commentary opens with a portrait of Moses rendered mute by his audience. How, then, did he finally summon words—words that would become immortal and forever relevant, the words of the Torah? R. Ze'ev Wolf concludes his commentary by resolving this tension. He links the figure of Moses with that of the hasidic *tsadik*, embodied, in this *derashah*, in his own master, the great Magid. The activities of those figures are bound together in a shared mission:

And so, to return to our verse: 'These are the words that Moses spoke' . . . 'These words'—from the time he spoke them, their power endures. Now, every person who recognizes the Creator is called 'Moses'.[75] What proves that this is so? Words that come from the heart enter the hearts of all Israel—the great according to their greatness, and the small by their smallness. Each of them finds solace for the soul in his words, guidance and instruction to serve their Master. Then may peace be upon His

[75] An allusion to *Tikunei zohar* 69, 104*a*: the phrase in question is *itpashtuta demosheh bekhol dor vador* (the spreading forth of the aspect of 'Moses' in each and every generation). More on this below. The same formulation appears in the passage we read from *Teshuot ḥen*, 'Tetsaveh' in chapter 1. There, the phrase from *Tikunei zohar* is cited explicitly.

people and upon those who love Him. All of them are equal in goodness; they turn [to the *tsadik*] for advice and follow his instruction; his words are surely true and worthy, may he be blessed.[76]

As he merges the Magid's *derashah* with his own, R. Ze'ev Wolf performs a second merging as well. Moses' task as educator is to be taken up and carried out by the righteous in times to come, in the Torah that they teach. Every *tsadik* serves as Moses for his generation. Here, then, the images of Moses and the Magid converge. But R. Ze'ev Wolf's main purpose is not to sing his own master's praises. Rather, his experience as a hasid and as a *rebbe*, as both a student and a teacher, enables him to enact a living pedagogical situation through his *derashah*. Not only orally but in written form too, it revisits the vital moment of saying 'These are the words'. Such an event is bound to no one place now lost in time—be it the plains of Moab or the *beit midrash* in Mezhirech. Against the misdoubt that in hasidic Torah commentary the face of the listener is lost,[77] R. Ze'ev Wolf writes that 'words that come from the heart enter the hearts of all Israel'—if only they want enough to hear them again.

Hasidism put the bond between the *tsadik* and his followers at the heart of religious life. The passages we have been looking at attest to the power of that bond. When they are read with a historian's orientation, these 'relics of the past' do involuntarily disclose something useful about their own contemporary social reality, and about the doctrines and concepts that underlay that reality.[78] In studying them here, I have attempted to understand these commentaries using another approach and different tools. Beyond their compelling real-life dimension, they also help us to discern the ways in which the hermeneutic of the *derashah* itself enacts that fundamental bond. The encounter between *rebbe* and hasid—and, more generally, between teacher and student, text and reader—is potentially a founding event. It may bring about profound understanding or spiritual 'awakening', emotional healing and repair, a paradigm change, perhaps even self-transformation. In what sense, though, is all this redemptive? To address that final question, we need to revisit our terms at their origins.

---

[76] *Or hame'ir*, 'Devarim', 227a–228a.   [77] See Introduction, p. 19.

[78] In light of Gadamer's critique of historical method: 'Thus for the historian it is a basic principle that tradition is to be interpreted in a sense different than the texts, of themselves, call for. He will always go back behind them and the meaning they express to inquire into the reality they express involuntarily. Texts must be treated in the same way as other available historical material—i.e., as the so-called relics of the past.' See *Truth and Method*, 330–2.

The Secret of Exile: R. Jacob Joseph of Polonnoye, *Toledot ya'akov yosef*

This was the reason for the exile in Egypt. They did not know what they lacked—in exile, knowing [*da'at*] was no more. We learn this from the writings of the holy Ari [R. Isaac Luria].[79] And so Pharaoh could imprison them—for **Pharaoh** signifies *ohreph* [the back of the neck], the place of forgetting. As Pharaoh retorted, 'Who is God? . . . I do not know him' [Exod. 5: 2]. . . . Thus Egypt confined them in a state of spiritual exile—they forgot what they once knew; they sank into blind unawareness. And then their spiritual exile dragged them into physical exile as well. . . . Until Moses appeared, who represents the aspect of knowing.[80] . . . Then at last they could begin to repent, to amend their deficiencies. And then the course of redemption began. . . . So I heard [from the Ba'al Shem Tov] on the verse 'Draw near to my soul, redeem it' [Ps. 69: 19]—once that has happened, national redemption will also come.[81]

The idea that R. Jacob Joseph of Polonnoye sets out in this *derashah* is one of hasidism's most central innovations: the concept of personal exile and redemption and its interrelation with other exiles and redemptions that take place on more distant ontological planes.[82] In terms of method, the description of exile as an existential and cognitive state makes this *derashah* an excellent example of the way that hasidism transmuted kabbalistic theosophy to

[79] See R. Hayim Vital, *Sha'ar hapesukim*, 'Shemot' on the words *ki sar lirot*. And compare Zohar ii. 161*a* on knowing, unawareness, and the nature of exile. R. Jacob Joseph cites that passage from the Zohar in his commentary: *Toledot ya'akov yosef*, 'Kedoshim', 8.

[80] See Zohar ii. 221*a*; on the association between Pharaoh and *ohreph* see *Ets ḥayim*, 26: 3; *Sha'ar hapesukim*, 'Vayeshev'.

[81] *Toledot ya'akov yosef*, 'Pekudei', 75*a*. Compare a similar formulation of the Ba'al Shem Tov's teaching by R. Nahum of Chernobyl: 'The secret of exile, the meaning of Egypt, is that knowing [*hada'at*] was in exile. For one must know that there is a Creator. But they knew nothing of Him.' *Me'or eynaim*, 'Shemot' (*vayakom melekh*).

[82] Moshe Idel analyses this basic 'threefold categorization', which appears already in medieval philosophical and kabbalistic texts: 'the material exile and redemption, the spiritual exile and redemption, and the exile and redemption of the Shekhinah'. He notes that 'what distinguishes the kabbalistic triad from the Hasidic one is not so much the nature of the three exiles/redemptions as the specific concatenations between and among them. . . . Hasidic "spiritual redemption" is essential preparation for the "general" one . . . Thus the spiritual accent on individual redemption in Hasidism is not divorced from a national one but is in fact conceived of as indispensable as it is preparing the latter' ('Multiple Forms of Redemption in Kabbalah and Hasidism', 65). Morris Faierstein discusses ideological trends in later hasidic schools of thought, with changing views on 'personal redemption' and the agency of the *tsadik* in attaining it. See Faierstein, 'Personal Redemption in Hasidism'. See also Jacobs, 'Pesach and the Exodus in the Thought of Two Hasidic Masters'.

psychological terms.[83] Beyond discursive statements such as these, however, the larger meaning of the passage comes to the fore when we take its historical context into account. It appears in the first published volume of hasidic commentary on the Torah, a work that was the cornerstone of R. Jacob Joseph's entire exegetical project. Ideas and insights that he had learned from his master, the Ba'al Shem Tov, figure prominently in the hundreds of pages of homilies that he wrote. R. Jacob Joseph's central interpretative and theological concern, which he often reiterated, was to bring home the relevance of Scripture 'to every reader at every time in history'. That project, and the exegetical techniques that he developed to carry it out, Shaul Magid proposes, distinguish R. Jacob Joseph as 'a major architect of early Hasidism'.[84]

Once the notions of exile and redemption have been reconceived as metaphors, the first chapters of Exodus recount a charged meta-historical process that speaks to countless facets of human experience. Most relevantly at the moment, this *derashah* also revisits many of the topics explored in this chapter. On R. Jacob Joseph's reading, the biblical verses map an epic journey. The Israelite nation's exile starts from a place of not knowing, estranged from the past, from a sense of self, and from what had been a transcendent source of meaning. That state of disconnection and paralysing unawareness will later be mitigated (this particular passage only gestures towards that future event) by the appearance of Moses. He is the intermediary who will restore 'knowing', reconnect all that has fallen asunder, and gather together the Jewish people in the next stages leading to the final redemption.

The 'secret of exile' disclosed in this *derashah* in the name of the Ba'al Shem Tov was a foundational insight in hasidic thought. R. Jacob Joseph presents it exegetically here with uncommon directness. Other hasidic masters developed its thematic and emotional valences further in their own commentaries. The following *derashah* focuses on the point of resolution—the second half of the dialectic just out of sight.

The Secret of Redemption: R. Shneur Zalman of Lyady, *Torah or*

'Therefore say to the Children of Israel: I am the Lord. And I shall take you out from your enslavement in Egypt' (Exod. 6: 6). The dramatic event of the

---

[83] See Scholem, *Major Trends in Jewish Mysticism*, 340–4; Idel, *Hasidism: Between Ecstacy and Magic*, 227–38.

[84] Magid, 'Hasidism: Mystical and Nonmystical Approaches to Interpreting Scripture', 146.

Exodus is rooted deep in Jewish self-consciousness. But what makes that miracle primary above all others—so much so that 'for all generations, every individual must realize anew, morning and evening, that the time of "going out from Egypt" is here, right now?' R. Shneur Zalman of Lyady (1745–1812), founder of the Habad Lubavitch hasidic dynasty, opens his sermon with this acute question.[85] On his reading, three parallel narratives are encoded in the biblical verses. The straightforward, literal one recounts how the event of the Exodus was played out in historical time. In a more esoteric sense, the 'going out' will ultimately take place in the cosmic realm. Finally, an exodus might take place 'here below, in the human soul, in religious life', day by day. To elicit the meanings involved in the 'here below', R. Shneur Zalman intimates certain everyday experiences of emergence—the first dawning of emotion; a ray of insight on the dark horizon of consciousness; intuitions that begin to stir long before they are fully 'revealed in the heart'. Crucially, however, he notes that what precedes all of these moments of emergent reality is an antithetical period: a time of 'oblivion and hiddenness . . . in gestation, still unborn'. He continues:

For all manner of exile, estrangement, and suffering are called 'pregnancy' [*ibur*] . . . and redemption is 'birth'—the infant emerges, revealed into the world. And the pangs of the messiah's coming, they are the pangs of bearing. As it is written, 'Like an expectant woman in the throes of birth, so are we before You' [Isa. 26: 18]. And so the time of pregnancy and exile will lead, finally, to the revelation of divine light. But for that to come, first there have to be birth pangs. Deep, bitter pain must be felt from all that obstructs that light—all of life's petty needs . . . all its pleasures and its trickery that capture us and prevent Godliness from emerging, revealed into the world. And when the time of birth comes at last, and with it the fullness of revelation, then 'Israel will rejoice in its Makers' [Ps. 149: 2]. Then all the barriers and impediments will be as naught before that utter happiness with God.[86]

---

[85] *Torah or*, 'Va'era', 113. He refers to Mishnah *Pes.* 10: 5 and to the familiar phrase in the Passover Haggadah, where the Rabbis prescribe remembering the Exodus as a personal religious obligation. The third section of the Shema prayer (Num. 15: 37–41), recited morning and evening, was added to that end; see BT *Ber.* 12*b*; Maimonides, *Mishneh torah*, 'Hilkhot keriyat shema', 1: 3. In his *Tanya*, ch. 47, R. Shneur Zalman develops many of the elements found in this *derashah*. See Naftali Loewenthal's insightful discussion of that chapter and its importance for understanding the Habad school: 'Finding the Radiance in the Text'.

[86] *Torah or*, 'Va'era', 114. His interpolation of this particular verse from Psalms seems to follow the exegesis in Zohar iii. 219*b*. Medieval commentators explain the plural form 'Makers' to refer to God. Yet the author of the Zohar infers a real plurality involved in the 'making' or engenderment of the Jewish nation, drawing on kabbalistic notions of 'father' and 'mother';

Here, most of all, is a 'metaphor we live by'. The raw, primary experience called birth evokes facets of human creativity that all of us know. Our hopes, books, babies, a nation are conceived and gestate over time; we labour, often painfully, to bring them to life, out into the world. Formally defined, what R. Shneur Zalman is talking about are the concepts of exile and redemption. The metaphor of birth links together those two distant points of primordial beginning and end-time. Additionally, 'birth' as a metaphor clears a channel between the everyday moments of our lives and larger spheres of national, historical, and cosmic significance. R. Shneur Zalman does not elaborate here on possible causal connections between these spheres of meaning. Rather, he highlights the correspondences they share by transferring meaning from one to the other.

R. Shneur Zalman's conception and method in this *derashah* are evidently informed by earlier hasidic teachings on personal exile and redemption, while the more esoteric elements that he integrates show the influence of even earlier kabbalistic traditions. And yet a diachronic textual analysis of this passage against its sources would leave something important unsaid. The literary resonances and rhetorical potential of these images—remoteness, pregnancy, the throes of childbirth, opening, emergence—cannot be contained in theoretical constructs.

On closer examination, this *derashah* actually focuses less on the ultimate end point called redemption (whether individual or general) than on the way it unfolds as a process in time. And so the far more urgent problem being addressed is the arduous intermediary stage before 'birth' finally comes: everything that has to be passed through to reach the fortuitous outcome. How can that pain be understood in a way that might unleash its redemptive power? 'Therefore say to the Children of Israel: I am the Lord. And I shall take you out.' What is R. Shneur Zalman telling his readers, through the biblical verses and his commentary on them, about their own enslavement in 'Egypt' and about becoming free?

Habad historiography contains a wealth of material that sheds light on its founding figure, the author of this *derashah*. A brief look at some details of his life might give us insight into the issues that concern us now. The onset of R. Shneur Zalman's leadership, and the point at which Habad was established as a school of hasidic thought and practice, are dated to 1783 or 1786.

these notions fit in with the motif of birth in this *derashah*. My reading here is very partial. It leaves many sections of this complex text undiscussed and does not touch on the esoteric elements or terms that inform R. Shneur Zalman's commentary.

In the early years of his career R. Shneur Zalman expressly had not seen himself as an autonomous leader or *tsadik* responsible for a defined hasidic community, but rather as a mentor who offered personal guidance to individuals. Yet from that time onwards, both his teachings and his leadership reflect a new stage of self-definition, combining theosophical mysticism, uncommon psychological acumen, and practical religious instruction.[87] R. Shneur Zalman's biographers, academic as well as hasidic, distinguish a clear pedagogical agenda in his activity. Its overarching goal was to construct a programme of spiritual growth that would be inviting and accessible to Jews of all kinds. As R. Joseph Isaac Shneerson, the sixth *rebbe* of Habad Lubavitch, famously put it, 'The Ba'al Shem Tov taught how one *should* serve God, and our master, our great Rebbe [R. Shneur Zalman], taught how it is *possible* to serve God.'[88]

R. Shneur Zalman's role as educator comes to the fore in the *derashah* we have been reading. Most evidently, he explains how the rabbinic imperative to 'remember the Exodus' can meaningfully be fulfilled. Normative, mindful action—the Shema prayer recited morning and evening, with its explicit mention of the Exodus—offers an immediate opportunity to revisit, in some sense, that founding historical event. On a more contemplative level, he illuminates an inner dimension of that precept to guide his listeners on the path of hasidism. Here, the mandate to 'remember the Exodus' is a call to conscience. It summons one to see that one's soul is imprisoned in exile, and to recognize that material existence (physicality, the evil inclination, 'all of life's petty needs and pleasures') is what constricts and oppresses the soul and blocks its path to true freedom. Pursuing the metaphor one step further, the pangs of birthing are the counterforce that breaks through all barriers. Clearly here both the labouring body and the unborn infant, passing through narrow straits in the struggle to be born, must endure them.[89] But when that traumatic process has been reimagined, all of life's suffering—'the pangs of the messiah's coming'—will then open towards redemption.

Reread in this way, the moment of exodus takes place in a far more

[87] On the techniques that R. Shneur Zalman developed to convey his teachings and create a hasidic community, see Loewenthal, *Communicating the Infinite*, 39–63.

[88] The statement appears in a letter to his son-in-law, R. Menachem Mendel Schneerson (1932). This letter was later published in *Hatamim*, 2 (1935), 150–9. Loewenthal writes: 'Rabbi Shneur Zalman made communication of spirituality his central endeavour, and created a form of Midrash that presents esoteric, cosmic perceptions in the apparently exoteric, accessible medium of the Habad Hasidic discourse' ('Midrash in Habad Hasidism', 438).

[89] Some pages earlier, in his first *derashah* on 'Va'era', R. Shneur Zalman describes the unborn infant's perspective in great detail. *Torah or*, 109.

encompassing context of meaning. The biblical narrative now recounts the immemorial past and gestures towards the illimitable future. But more than marking either of those extreme points, 'remembering the Exodus' is meant to arouse the sense of living an emergent reality—one in which something vital is just now coming to be. 'For all generations, every individual must realize, morning and evening, that the time of "going out from Egypt" is here.' R. Shneur Zalman shows a way that passage to ultimate freedom can be endured, with all the pain and confusion bound up in it. Seen in broader perspective, leaving one's personal exile, enabling the light of holiness to be revealed in the depths of the human heart is, most essentially, to carry out God's plan for the world.[90] So the Ba'al Shem Tov taught: 'Redemption is always called "birth" . . . for birth is the secret of redemption.'[91]

Summing Up

The hasidic commentaries that we have been considering speak compellingly of alienation and relations, brokenness and mending. Along the way, they suggest something important about how understanding can be won and about its hidden redemptive power. Some of those texts portray the *tsadik* and the *rebbe* as a living presence; his face, in others, is absent. Either way, all that we have are his words on the printed page. I have tried to show that these words nonetheless seek to convey a living teaching. It is engendered by listening attentively to sacred texts and detecting their sonorities in the world outside and within. An engaged reader, through the same practices, can revive that teaching. These passages, in addition, tell of teachers and students who, together, breathe life into the texts of Jewish tradition and draw them into the community of memory, obligation, and practice. The poetic of these commentaries creates a bond between teacher and learner, author and reader; that bond, as we have seen, is a powerful conduit for conveying meaning to live by.

The encounter with a *rebbe*, or with the books that preserve his teachings, might help those who wish to cross over a threshold of spiritual life. This is the transformative potential of any learning process. The evocative power of the *derashot* we have read inarguably serves to draw one closer to that threshold. But as the Irish poet John O'Donohue put it so well, threshold is a 'testimony to the fullness and integrity of an experience or a stage of life that it

---

[90] *Torah or*, 'Va'era', 110.

[91] Cited by R. Gedaliah of Linits in *Teshuot ḥen*, 'Vayeḥi', 57; see ibid., n. 474 in reference to the writings of the Maharal of Prague.

intensifies toward the end into a real frontier that cannot be crossed without the heart being passionately engaged and woken up'. That event, the heart's awakening, is conceived in the hasidic world of thought as a moment of 'personal redemption'. To experience it one must be ready to have one's beliefs provoked and challenged, to put one's preconceptions at risk. The encounter with the sacred texts of Jewish tradition can offer such provocation. Understanding, however, begins only when something addresses me, when I believe a text is telling me something.[92] To find such inner attunement is no simple matter, at least not for most of us. As Michael Fishbane writes of his own project of hermeneutical theology: 'we are beset by other enclosures of thought . . . And thus another breakthrough is needed. I would call it the consciousness of natality, the spring of beginnings that comes with a reborn mindfulness. . . . Natality is the route to transcendence.'[93]

[92] This is Gadamer's contention, *Truth and Method*, 269, 299, 388. On the transformative potential of Jewish text study, in dialogue with philosophical hermeneutics, see Holzer, 'Ethical Dispositions in Text Study'.   [93] *Sacred Attunement*, pp. ix–x.

THREE

Responses to a Shifting Landscape

THE YEARS 1815–81 marked a period of growth and dramatic expansion, both demographically and geographically. Hasidism gained financial patronage and drew followers from across the Jewish social spectrum, from worldly urban businessmen to impoverished *shtetl* dwellers. The courts of the *tsadikim* branched into dynasties and grew institutionalized. It was in this period that hasidism became a movement with hundreds of thousands of adherents. By the mid-nineteenth century, as Moshe Rosman puts it, hasidism had 'the power and the sophistication of a confident and influential movement that actively engaged the other elements in modern society and exploited modern expedients in its drive to achieve its earthly program of dominating the Jewish community, and its heavenly program of thereby bringing near the Redemption'.[1]

During the same period, political and economic developments made their mark on the intellectual and religious domains of Jewish life. Enlightenment-inspired reform penetrated to eastern Europe, pressing for acculturation; the influence of the Haskalah spread in ever-widening circles. Voices advocating emancipation, social integration, and political rights for Jewish residents became increasingly strident within the Jewish world. Cracks widened; traditional society was slowly disintegrating. By the late 1880s hasidism was beleaguered from without and within. On the regnant, outspoken view in eastern Europe, contemporary hasidic culture was 'an atavistic survival' entrenched in stubborn battle against the inevitable modernization of Jewish society.[2]

Early scholars of hasidism, influenced in various ways by their own conflicts with Jewish tradition and their political convictions, gave voice to that animosity. A case in point is the path-breaking history of hasidism presented by Simon Dubnow (1860–1941). It celebrates an early period of dynamic,

---

[1] Rosman, 'Hasidism as a Modern Phenomenon', 215.

[2] See Deutsch, *The Jewish Dark Continent*, 40.

innovative renewal of traditional Judaism in the first and second 'genera-tions'—the Ba'al Shem Tov and his circle of disciples—a period ending in 1772 with the death of the Magid of Mezhirech. But as hasidism grew into a mass movement, Dubnow contended, deterioration set in. The 'period of the predominance of tsadikim and the struggle against the Haskalah movement' began, during which 'the cult of tsadikism obscure[d] the light of Jewish rationalism and arous[ed] fanatical hatred of freedom of thought'. By his own time, hasidism had entered its terminal phase of degeneracy, and was now a fossilized spirituality, uninspired and obscurantist.[3] Jacob S. Minkin, author of the first history of hasidism in English (1935), was no kinder in his own description of this late phase, his own day: 'The movement . . . has become weak and impotent. . . . External circumstances linked to internal corruption hastened the destruction of the movement. . . . [I]t is an empty shell the contents of which had been blown away by the wind, never to be revived again.'[4]

Dubnow and other pioneering critical scholars of Jewish culture and his-tory utilized contemporaneous historical documents for the authentic, first-hand testimony about the hasidic world that they provided. Their primary resources included the libellous documents circulated by *mitnagedim*; Yid-dish and Hebrew secular journalism; belles-lettres, lampoons, and satires by *maskilim*. Modern and postmodern academic attitudes have been far more self-consciously critical towards their source materials. Yet the same historical evidence, written by Jews estranged from the religious world being studied, remains central to their work. Thus, as one historian puts it, despite his 'ellip-tic and ungenerous reading' of hasidism, Solomon Maimon is 'one of our great informants about early modern East European Jewish life'. Maimon's memoirs, published serially in 1792 and 1793, provided German salon circles 'both slapstick amusement and credible confirmation for their prejudices against those who came to be known as *Ostjuden*'.[5] Other voices—of rebels

---

[3] Dubnow, *The History of Hasidism* (Heb.), 37, cited in Polonsky, *The Jews in Poland and Russia*, ii. 281. Ironically, Allan Nadler notes: 'But while the rabbinic war on Hasidism was, in the course of the nineteenth century, rapidly eclipsed by this unified religious resistance to the haskolle [Haskalah], a major confrontation about Hasidism emerged within enlightened Jew-ish circles almost a full century later. Rather than a war between the parties themselves, this was a struggle among the liberal Jewish historians, essayists and intellectuals of late imperial Russia over the true meaning and legacy of Hasidism' ('Rationalism, Romanticism, Rabbis and Rebbes', 5).

[4] 'Hasidism', *Universal Jewish Encyclopedia*, cited by Nehemia Polen in his introduction to *The Rebbe's Daughter*, p. xxvii.

[5] Levine, '"Should Napoleon Be Victorious . . .": Politics and Spirituality in Early Modern

and seekers who had liberated themselves more or less from the 'beloved-despised' tradition—have also provided valuable resources for incisive new studies of nineteenth- and twentieth-century hasidic life. Inarguably, they speak volumes in exposing the 'untold tales' hidden in the darker corners of the hasidic world.

The following pages will not retell those testimonies nor review the recriminations and defences from any side. Rather, I would like to reach what could be called a more gracious understanding. Arthur Green, in his own re-examination of hasidism in this historical period, makes an important move of reframing that deserves our attention:

When Eastern Europeans are considered at all in discussion of Jewish intellectual modernity, it is generally secular national alternatives to religion that they are thought to offer. Pinsker, Ahad Ha-'Am, Borochov and others are treated in this way. But the religious thought of Polish and Russian Jewry in the later nineteenth and twentieth centuries has seldom been considered or thought to have broader significance. . . . The early period of Hasidism of course has been very widely treated by scholars. After that time, Hasidism was supposedly so wholly engaged in its life-and-death struggle against haskalah and every incursion of modernity that its energies were dissipated and its creative powers diminished. If it innovated, it did so in a retrogressive way, re-reading its own earlier tradition to eliminate or lessen the religious radicalism of the BeSHT and the early Hasidic masters so that Hasidism would be a fitting weapon with which to fight off all modern, non-Jewish, and 'external' influences. But the picture in fact is much more complicated than that.[6]

This chapter seeks to address these broader cultural dimensions of Jewish intellectual modernity. Its starting point is the conviction that for an authentic understanding of hasidism in its 'late' phase as well, we need to pay serious attention to homiletical works. They offer a crucial voice from the inside that is largely absent from historical accounts. Reading hasidic *derashot* from this period, however, what interests me is not programmatic statements in relation to contemporary socio-political events or typologies of leadership, nor explicit directives for pragmatic action. Traditional Jewry needed to discover novel forms of religiosity and spiritual meaning in a world that was being trans-

Jewish Messianism', 3. See also Ross, *A Beloved-Despised Tradition* (Heb.); Assaf, *Untold Tales of the Hasidim.*

[6] Green, 'Three Warsaw Mystics', 1. Rosman suggests a new periodization: 'As a successful framework that helped many Jews to negotiate their way in the modern world, Hasidism deserves to be classed with other "modern" phenomena of Jewish history and studied, not as a block to modernization, but as a version of it' ('Hasidism as a Modern Phenomenon', 224).

formed. Some hasidic masters rose to the occasion. They sought—through ritual, community, and engagement with the Torah—to create a space in which they and their followers could maintain traditional religious practice and faith while renewing them from within. In times of crisis and suffering, their sermons were meant to be a source of empowerment for listeners and readers—at times, audibly, for the author himself as well. Innovative hasidic commentary on the Torah, read in that light, has much to teach about this project.

In the first part of this chapter I will focus on certain foundational elements in the developing hasidic ethos. These elements endured and also evolved through the nineteenth and twentieth centuries as hasidic masters responded to challenges posed by modernity, including secularization and assimilation, violent political upheaval, rupture, and catastrophe. My discussion is arranged in more or less historical order. Having said that I stress that it is not meant to be a comprehensive survey of hasidic homiletical activity during that complex and traumatic period. My focus is on leading figures who entered into some kind of dialogue with their times, who tried to respond to their community's needs, and who discovered new interpretative attitudes to do so effectively. Their Torah commentaries contain, I believe, moments of greatness and rare vision.

The Space in the Middle: R. Israel ben Shabetai Hapstein, the Magid of Kozienice, *Avodat yisra'el*

We'll begin with a *derashah* by R. Israel ben Shabetai Hapstein, known as the Magid of Kozienice (1733–1814). During his lifetime hasidism came to play an important role in the religious life of Galicia and the Kingdom of Poland. Two major dynasties became established in Galicia in the first decades of the nineteenth century: the first centred on the court of R. Elimelekh of Lizhensk. Two of his disciples, R. Jacob Isaac Horowitz (the Seer of Lublin) and R. Israel, the Magid of Kozienice, brought hasidism to the Kingdom of Poland.[7] A high-profile hasidic leader in those years, R. Israel was also a renowned talmudic scholar and kabbalist. He embodied book culture: a prolific author, he also spearheaded the printing of rare books and manuscripts and, to encourage literary activity among his contemporaries, he issued more than thirty approbations for both hasidic and non-hasidic books.[8]

---

[7] Polonsky, *The Jews in Poland and Russia*, ii. 292.

[8] A number exceeded only by his contemporary, R. Levi Isaac of Berdichev, who wrote

Hagiographical accounts, some of them grounded in historical reality, have much to say about his instrumental role, together with other religious leaders, in influencing the government's Jewish politics and policies.[9] Alongside his public activism and scholarly pursuits, R. Israel won fame and affection in the wider community among simple people, Jews and non-Jews alike, as a healer and holy man.

For thirty years R. Israel served as preacher, or *magid*, in Kozienice and nearby towns. His most well-known homiletical work, *Avodat yisra'el*, is a traditionally structured commentary that follows the weekly Torah portions. There are signs that some of these *derashot* had originated as sermons that R. Israel delivered orally. Yet the published volume is a composition with inlaid textual layers; clearly, it reached that final form only in writing. The passage I have selected for a close reading showcases its author's inventive and insightful thought; moreover, it seems to be addressing one of traditional Jewish society's most central contemporary concerns. My aim in the following pages, however, is not to decode veiled references to specific events or personalities, but rather to consider how R. Israel presents the hasidic ethos by means of exegesis.

seventy-one approbations over his lifetime. R. Israel's oeuvre includes commentary on the Talmud, responsa, and kabbalistic and hasidic writings. He initiated the republication of major works, some with his own glosses and approbations, among them the early kabbalistic treatise *Raziel hamalakh* and *Likutim* by R. Hai Gaon. He effectively reintroduced the thought of the Maharal of Prague to the Jewish learning community, in the role of both interpreter and critic; see Hershkowitz, 'Geulat Yisrael by the Koznitzer Maggid' (Heb.), 15–31. On his commentary on *Pirkei avot* see Gries, 'R. Israel ben Shabbetai of Kozienice' (Heb.). The most comprehensive discussion of the Magid of Kozienice, his life and works, is Rabinowicz, *Between Przysucha and Lublin* (Heb.), 159–253. A brilliant scholar, he studied in yeshivas of the foremost Torah figures of Poland. A formative influence on him as a young adult was R. Abraham of Przysucha (d.1806), a learned scholar, kabbalist, and community preacher. It was Samuel Shmelke Horowitz (later of Nikolsburg) and his brother R. Pinhas Halevi (later of Frankfurt am Main) who first travelled with him to the Magid of Mezhirech. There, he met other disciples of the Magid: R. Elimelekh of Lizhensk, R. Shneur Zalman of Lyady, and R. Levi Isaac of Berdichev, with whom he had a lasting friendship. After the Magid's death he became a disciple of R. Elimelekh. At his court in Lizhensk, he met the Seer of Lublin.

   [9] Social historians have examined the phenomenon of nineteenth-century Jewish activism as hasidic leaders developed new tactics of intercession, or *shtadlanut*, in their dealings with Polish and Russian authorities to resolve anti-hasidic government measures favourably; Wodziński, *Hasidism and Politics*, 165–217. Additionally, historians have stressed the role played by Jewish mercantile elites in these activities. Wealthy Jewish patrons sympathetic to hasidism subsidized and promoted hasidic interests in conflicts with *mitnagedim* and in their struggles against religious and social reform. See Dynner, *Men of Silk*, 89–116; id., 'Merchant Princes and Tsadikim'.

The context of this *derashah* is the biblical scene in which Moses receives the second Tablets of the Law. After forty days and sleepless nights, God tells him: 'Write these words for yourself, for according to all these words have I sealed a covenant with you and with Israel' (Exod. 34: 28). With the new stone Tablets in hand, Moses descends a second time from Mount Sinai. R. Israel's *derashah* begins at this juncture.

'Moses did not know that his face was radiant' [Exod. 34: 29]. In the midrash: 'Where did the rays of majesty come from? The Sages said the radiance was from the cave. [Another opinion:] Rabbi Berakhyah Hakohen said in the name of Rabbi Samuel, 'The Tablets were six handbreadths long and six handbreadths wide. Moses grasped two spans of their length and the Shekhinah two more. It was from the two spans left between them that Moses received the rays of majesty.'[10] This is what it all means. The cave—it signifies connection [*ḥibur*]: Moses merited that radiance by his devotion and ceaseless bond with the Creator, blessed be He.[11] . . . Now, as we know, God gave the Torah to Moses in [the four exegetical dimensions know as] PARDES and he was to teach all of them to the Jewish people. But the root source of the Torah— what cannot be revealed—remains with God on high. The latter aspect is thus called 'two spans in the hand of the Holy blessed One', while the former is the 'two spans in Moses' hand'. Now, everything that seasoned scholars and the righteous will ever innovate—the Torah insights they generate continually, drawing them down through the soul of Moses, which shines within each and every *tsadik*—all that is 'the two handbreadths in the middle'. It was from there that Moses received the rays of majesty. And through Moses all manner of effluence and new understanding is revealed to the righteous of each generation.[12]

[10] *Exod. Rab.* 47: 6; a parallel with variations in *Tanḥuma* 37. The motif of six handbreadths divided into three appears in other sources, e.g. JT *Shek.* 6: 1. To avoid a blatant anthropomorphism, the Rabbis replace 'the Holy blessed One' here with the Shekhinah (divine presence) grasping two spans.

[11] R. Israel continues: 'And so the Rabbis spoke of "the cave where Moses and Elijah stood", for the *gematria* of "Elijah" is 52; it signifies the Name YHVH, which means union [*devekut*]. "And Rabbi Berakhyah said, The Tablets were six handbreadths long, etc." As I wrote elsewhere, [in the Kedushah prayer, we say of the heavenly hosts that] "They praise You threefold"—for effluence descends in triad form, as we know; and in triad form it is received from below. Then, when Giver and receiver enjoin, between them they share six. And so "six handbreadths long" alludes to the Giver, and "six handbreadths wide" alludes to the receiver.' Concerning the numerical value of 'Elijah' and the divine Name that corresponds to it, see e.g. *Shenei luḥot haberit* iii. 364 (with cross-references there to additional contexts in the same work). An early instance of the kabbalistic concept of emanation in triad form is *Sefer yetsirah* 3: 7; cf. R. Moses Cordovero's commentary on that section. *Tikunei zohar* 114a, an important source to be discussed below, also conceives of the 'emanation of Moses' in triad form.

[12] R. Israel ben Shabetai Hapstein, *Avodat yisra'el*, 'Ki tisa', 82. A similar reading appears in his work *She'erit yisra'el*, 'Ki tisa' (Lublin, 1895), 68. Elements of this reading recall the thought of

As an opening, R. Israel presents the midrash with two rabbinic opinions, each with an accompanying metaphor. Its apparent purpose is to explain why or how it was that Moses' face radiated (*karan*) light. Transmuting the verb into a noun, the Rabbis create the poetic image of rays of beauty, or glory, or majesty (*karnei hod*) that emanate from Moses' forehead. On the first view, their provenance was 'the cave'. But what cave are the Rabbis referring to?

Most evidently, the midrash draws on the biblical verses that stage this scene: 'God said, There is a place near Me; you may stand on the rock. When My glory passes by, I shall place you in a cleft of the rock; I shall shield you with My hand until I have passed. Then I shall remove My hand and you will see My back, but My face may not be seen' (Exod. 33: 21–3). This cleft in the rock, at first sight, must be the cave in question. But just a bit earlier in the same midrashic collection the Rabbis evoke another cave image, placed in a wholly different setting. Not coincidentally, a page earlier in his own Torah commentary, R. Israel remarks on that other cave as well. This association is important; as we will soon see, the two caves are interrelated. The Rabbis strategically insert that first midrashic cave image into the larger biblical narrative and invest it with a powerful emotional charge. To appreciate their intent in this contextualizing move, we need to recall that the Giving of the Torah (for the second time) took place in the shadow of an abysmal national failing. Following the sin of the Golden Calf, the atmosphere heavy with ambivalent anger, Moses struggles to reanimate and ultimately to restore the connection, the primary and totally unexplainable affection that had once been between God and his chosen people. The Rabbis take note of the unusually dynamic rhythm of the dialogue between God and Moses in the Bible (Exod. 33: 12–20), and offer this remarkable metaphor to touch on its meaning: 'Like a cave at the edge of the sea: the sea's waves rise and fill the cave and recede and rise again' in an unending buoyance of giving and receiving. 'And so', the midrash has Moses aver to God, 'You cannot remove Your love for this nation', just as the waters of the cavern cannot be separated from the waters of the sea.[13]

R. Judah Loew, the Maharal of Prague, in chapter 2 of *Netsaḥ yisra'el* (Benei Brak, 1960), 13. Based on the version of the aggadah in JT *Shekalim*, the Maharal named the 'two spans in the middle' as the locus of communion between God and Moses at the moment of giving and receiving the Torah, and identified the 'two spans' in God's and Moses' hands respectively in much the same way. Yet the thrust of the hasidic reading, with its confluence of motifs, is far more radical than the Maharal's.

[13] *Exod. Rab.* 45: 2–3. R. Israel cites this midrash in another *derashah* in the same work: *Avodat yisra'el* 'Ki tisa', 82. There, the cave metaphor, with its connotations of intimate union,

Back, now, to those altitudes so dazzlingly spare and clean, to that fissure between the mountains.[14] R. Israel, it seems, has merged the two cave images, and borrows the emotional overtones of the first cave to say something essential about this second biblical scene. And so 'the cleft of the rock', like the cave at the edge of the sea, becomes a dark space of intimate encounter. There, inside, an originative connection is finally restored. On R. Israel's reading, this scene is emblematic. Its immediate narrative role is to lay the ground for the next episode in Moses' personal story, to explain how he merited the radiance. Yet in a more profound sense it evokes the original bond between God and the Jewish people that was forged long before their fateful lapse. The Torah, given and received here for a second time, thus embodies the promise of restoral in the end, despite anything that might happen along the way—for 'You cannot remove Your love for this nation'. Afterwards, the trace of that encounter lingers to illuminate Moses' countenance. 'From the cave', the rays of majesty recall the long trajectory from sin to repair and the covenant that has been sealed 'with you and with Israel'.

The second midrashic opinion on how it was that Moses' face was radiant is introduced by a blithely anthropomorphic image: 'The Tablets were six handbreadths long . . . Moses grasped two spans and the Shekhinah two more; from the two spans left between them Moses received the rays of majesty.' An evocative scene, to be sure, but its underlying logic is opaque at best. How are 'the two spans between them' related to the 'rays of majesty'? The midrash elaborates no further. It is this gap, the unspoken connection, it seems, that incites R. Israel's associative leap to another rabbinic notion, which he then reads through the lens of an important kabbalistic trope. This hermeneutical gesture, I will suggest, makes a forceful statement about the nature of the Torah itself and the way it remains a living tradition.

The issue R. Israel confronts here is as acute as it is ancient. He signals the midrashic source that sets it out. On the stone Tablets were 'all the words that God spoke' to Moses on the mountain from the midst of the fire (Deut. 9: 10). 'All the words', the Rabbis taught, signifies 'the Bible and Mishnah, halakhah and aggadah, and everything that seasoned scholars will ever teach—all of that was already spoken to Moses at Sinai.' To back their claim, the Rabbis paraphrase the world-weary Ecclesiastes (1: 10): 'One might say "Look, this is

---

draws on yet another association linked with the Song of Songs: 'the kisses [*neshikot*] of His mouth' (S. of S. 1: 2)—the mingling of waters (*meshikin*).

[14] After Dillard, *Pilgrim at Tinker Creek*, 274.

new!"—but his companion will counter, "No, it already was ages before us.""[15] R. Israel marks this source in the phrases, 'Now as we know, God gave the Torah to Moses in [the four exegetical dimensions known as] PARDES' and 'everything that seasoned scholars and the righteous will ever innovate'. This is a very strong claim of rabbinical authority. It means that from Scripture to the Oral Law, which the Sages themselves were just then in the process of instituting, and onwards throughout history, every legal decision as well as the myriad spiritual intuitions in all generations to come will belong, in some supra-rational way, to the original, received divine Word. While such a claim is inarguably central to the task of constructing a sacred tradition, it does sound faintly reductive, even deterministic. Aren't the Rabbis collapsing the vast panorama of human creativity and closing it up in something finite, totalized, already said? How can 'all the words' ever reopen to offer a real, living encounter with the 'saying' of the infinite?[16]

Let's look again at the beginning of the *derashah*, 'Moses did not know that his face was radiant.' Clearly, now, on his rereading of the midrash concerning that verse, R. Israel has subtly shifted the focus from the fact ('his face was radiant') to the moment of 'not knowing'. He sees the 'rays of majesty' as signifying a dimension of the Torah that remains beyond Moses' own grasp—an aspect that cannot be comprehended, contained, fixed in his consciousness. The rays are thus the trace of presence and of absence, of something that has been entrusted and yet withheld.[17] The luminous space left 'in the middle' then becomes the place where Jews of all times can relive the primary experience of receiving as they find new meanings in the Torah's words.

'And through Moses all manner of effluence and new understanding is

[15] JT *Pe'ah* 2: 6; see also *Lev. Rab.* 22: 1.

[16] Borrowing here from Levinas. In *Otherwise than Being* Levinas explores the fundamental distinction between two realms of language which he names the 'saying' and the 'said'. For Levinas, as Susan Handelman explains, 'saying' is 'the realm of equivocation in language, the relation to the other prior to thematization, representation, comprehension, and narrative (the "said"). "Saying" . . . is that "rhetorical" aspect of language prior to philosophy—a primary appeal to and relation with the other before any discourse can even begin. As such, it also disrupts the drive toward conclusive certainties, identities, and representations of the "said".' *Fragments of Redemption*, 248.

[17] R. Israel gestures here to BT *Shab.* 10*b*: 'One who gives a gift to a friend is not required to notify him, as it is written, "Moses did not know that his face was shining".' The 'trace', in the sense that R. Israel evokes here, foreshadows an important concept in the thought of Levinas and subsequently in two of Derrida's early works from the 1960s, *Writing and Difference* and *Of Grammatology*. See Handelman's discussion of 'the trace, the face, and the word of the other' in *Fragments of Redemption*, 202–25; and see Bernasconi, 'The Trace of Levinas in Derrida'.

revealed to the righteous of each generation.' The kabbalistic trope that informs R. Israel's understanding here is found in *Tikunei zohar*, and draws on the same metaphysical poetics of light. 'Through Moses' means, not only in a figurative sense but literally, that some essential aspect of Moses himself is gradually emerging over the course of time. *Itpashtuta demosheh bekhol dara vedara uvekhol tsadik vetsadik*—'Moses' emanates and expands in each and every generation, in each and every *tsadik*.[18] This *derashah*, we now see, is strikingly performative. R. Israel reads the 'empty space' between God's and Moses' hands; at the same time, he puts himself into that very space. This is no doubt a deliberate move: it is the hasidic master's own taking part in the cumulative revelation of the Torah as it unfolds through history, in the person of each and every righteous individual.

What is R. Israel trying to convey to his audience? This passage touches on the shared conviction that Torah study is the living heart of Jewish existence and comprehends spiritual, religious, intellectual, and devotional facets of being. While underscoring the importance of these fundamental beliefs, he refashions the notions of Torah and engagement with it, representing them as a core element of the hasidic ethos. No mention is made here of contemporary conflicts, but we know well that in the first decade of the nineteenth century, hasidic attitudes towards Torah study were a major point of strife. The Magid of Kozienice himself, as one of the most distinguished hasidic leaders of his time, served as a prime target for mitnagedic arrows.[19] Against this polemical backdrop, and maybe even in conscious non-involvement with the most hotly contended issues, R. Israel is making a powerful claim. He describes the very act of Torah study as a taking part in the primordial, living covenant between God and the Jewish people. That sense of belonging to tradition is what matters most. It subsumes any and every particularistic concern. Each individual, through Torah study, thus contributes something essential in the vital task of preserving and sustaining that covenant.

I think there is a second, related dimension of the hasidic ethos that comes to the fore here. The interaction that this passage portrays suggests a mode of spirituality and religious action. Moses' illuminated countenance, as R. Israel

[18] *Tikunei zohar* 69, 104*a*; 114*a*; the phrase appears frequently in later kabbalistic sources.

[19] As noted above, opponents accused the hasidim of undermining the supremacy of Torah study in the hierarchy of Jewish religious values; of neglecting the central domain of traditional Jewish scholarship, the Talmud and legal codes; of using Torah study as a means to attain mystical experience rather than 'for its own sake'; of popularizing kabbalistic practices and encouraging mystical prayer. On R. Israel's place in the conflict, see Wilensky, *Hasidim and Mitnagedim* (Heb.), ii. 27 and index.

conceives it, is an emblem of gradual revelation. Here, the Torah unfolds from within itself as the multiplicity of its potential meanings gradually comes to light. What his reading suggests, on the most personal level, is that a Jew's encounter with God takes place in the midst of tradition, filtered 'through the soul of Moses' in the act of learning. And so the mode of engagement that R. Israel describes in this *derashah* is profoundly generative. It is an active taking part in the continuous realization of the Torah's infinite meaning. Perforce, it happens 'in the middle'. That's where we find ourselves.

'For the Times They Are a-Changin'': R. Levi Isaac of Berdichev, *Kedushat levi*

In the next *derashah* a scenario of even more radical 'not knowing' unfolds as control over the Torah's meaning is effectively wrested out of Moses' hands entirely. With characteristic irony its author, R. Levi Isaac of Berdichev, revisits a primary hermeneutical issue, one that has occupied Jewish thinkers throughout history.[20] In tone as well as content, his sermon illuminates other notable dimensions of hasidic teaching and practice as they continued to evolve in the early nineteenth century.

Teiku. These letters mean: *tishbi yetarets kushiyot ve'ibayot*—'the Tishbite [Elijah the prophet] will resolve all problems and disputes'.[21] But something here needs explaining: isn't that to happen after the Redeemer comes (may it be speedily, in our own days)? Why, then, should Elijah be the one to resolve our difficulties and conflicts? What about Moses? After all, it was he who gave us the Torah with its commandments; won't he be able to work out all the questions and disagreements that it caused?

Well now, *Seder hadorot* writes this about the dispute between Rashi and Rabbenu Tam concerning the *tefilin*:[22] Rashi represented Moses and his camp, but Rabbenu Tam paid that no mind. He countered 'Moses' that the Torah was given to us already.

[20] On R. Levi Isaac see Ch. 1 and references there. Green (*Speaking Torah*, 48–9) comments briefly on part of this well-known *derashah*.

[21] The talmudic term *teiku* marks the unresolved end of a halakhic disagreement. It is a short form of the Aramaic word *teikum*—'it will stand' (upright, leaning towards neither side). The folk etymology that R. Levi Isaac recalls, linking *teiku* with Elijah, is first found in medieval sources, where it is already cited as a popular tradition.

[22] This dispute, most famously associated with Rashi and his grandson Rabbenu Tam, concerns the order of the four scriptural passages in the head phylactery, which contains four separate compartments. Rashi held that they are to be arranged in the order in which they appear in the Torah; Rabbenu Tam held that the second and fourth passages, which begin with the word *vehayah* (Exod. 13: 16; Deut. 11: 18), should be sandwiched between the first and third ones

It is in our hands now, and so we have the right to rule as we understand the Torah's laws.[23]

To explain this, we'll recall what the Rabbis said about the controversy between the House of Shammai and the House of Hillel: 'These and these are the words of the living God' [*Eruv.* 13*b*]. For when a person studies the Torah and tries to discern its plain meaning, that person's essence is the guiding force. If one is from the world of kindness [Hesed], then everything is pure and permitted and kosher—that's how one's mind comprehends what the holy Torah means. The opposite as well: if one's essence is powerful judgement [Gevurah], everything looks the reverse [impure, forbidden, non-kosher]. And because the House of Hillel embodied kindness their rulings tended towards leniency; the House of Shammai embodied power and so their rulings were stringent. In truth, though, both of them taught 'the words of the living God'.[24]

Our Sages, who lived in a generation after the Houses of Shammai and Hillel, realized that their world needed to be conducted with mercy. And so they prescribed halakhah in concord with the House of Hillel, favouring leniency in nearly every case. But who can discern such a thing? Who is able to sense what the world needs and establish the law accordingly? Only someone among the living, here in this world, can know what the world needs. Those who aren't alive have no awareness of all that. Now, Elijah—he lives and endures. He never tasted death; his presence in our world is everlasting. And so it is he who will straighten out all the problems and disputes, for Elijah knows just how the world needs to be run at any given time. Now we understand what Rabbenu Tam was saying to 'Moses': the Torah has been given to us already. It is in our hands now to teach as we see best.[25]

(Exod. 13: 9; Deut. 6: 18). Both conflicting views date, in fact, from tannaitic times. The midrash *Mekhilta* (end of 'Bo') presents the interpretation held by Rashi, while some early rabbinic authorities note that in the Jerusalem Talmud, *Seder kodashim*, they had seen the approach associated with Rabbenu Tam; that text is no longer extant. On the historical stages of this dispute and their reflections in halakhic practice, see Elyashiv, 'Tefillin Times Two'.

[23] *Seder hadorot* (The Order of the Generations) surveys chronologically the transmission of rabbinic law. Written by the Lithuanian talmudist and kabbalist R. Jehiel Heilprin (*c.*1660–1746), it was first published in 1768. The identification that R. Levi Isaac notes in the next lines between the rabbinic figures and the *sefirot* (Hillel—Hesed; Shammai—Gevurah) is found in that work (ii. 212); Heilprin cites Zohar iii. 245*a* and *Hesed le'avraham*. However, a number of elements in this *derashah* seem to be R. Levi Isaac's own invention; the associations between Hillel and Shammai, the figures of Rashi and Moses, and the dispute with Rabbenu Tam do not appear in *Seder hadorot* nor in the sources cited there.

[24] This contention of subjectivity stemming from kabbalistic 'aspects' of being is found in earlier thinkers. Linguistic similarity and some distinctive parallels suggest that R. Levi Isaac is paraphrasing Cordovero, *Pardes rimonim*, 9: 2 (*Sha'ar hamakhri'in*) (Jerusalem, 2000), 143–4. The passage in *Pardes rimonim* is cited in full by R. Isaiah Horowitz in *Shenei luhot haberit*, which may have been R. Levi Isaac's more direct source.

[25] *Kedushat levi, Likutim*, 316–17. The notion of Elijah's immortality is found in *Targum*

First a word about what R. Levi Isaac is doing here. His erudition is audible; the sermon is filled with references, quotes, paraphrases, and allusions to a wide range of sources—aggadic, halakhic, and kabbalistic. And yet this is not a learned review or analysis of rabbinic and post-rabbinic views on the subject at hand. It sounds rather more like a dialogue involving many texts and voices. R. Levi Isaac asks questions, some of them rhetorical; the historical figures that he summons offer partial answers, and he ponders further. As the *derashah* unfolds we find ourselves listening in on this interchange with Jewish tradition as it is being enacted. I believe that this dynamic rhetorical mode contributes something essential to his message—more on that later.

A cipher, *teiku*, announces his theme. In the Talmud, *teiku* is a technical term that marks the unresolved conclusion of a halakhic dispute between the Rabbis. But because it connotes an impasse or incontrovertible cut-off point, *teiku* also bears a certain emotional weight. R. Levi Isaac proceeds to recall some of the most sensational clashes between rabbinic views in Jewish cultural memory. Among them were confrontations that ended on dissonant, even tragic notes with no resolution in sight—a virtual sense of *teiku* if not termed so explicitly.[26] On retelling those incidents, however, R. Levi Isaac subtly reconceives the notion of controversy itself. He mitigates the tension that fuels most real-life conflicts and entrenches adversaries in stances of right or wrong, guilty or innocent, winner versus loser. That binary model is set aside. In its stead he offers an image of multiplicity inspired by kabbalistic teaching. It embodies a different order, in which every individual's perspective

yonatan, Num. 25: 12; see also Zohar iii. 214*a*; in the midrash it is said that he never tasted death: *Gen. Rab.* 21; *Yalkut shimoni* on Genesis 34. An important subtext is at work in this passage. It is one of the most dramatic in all of rabbinic literature. The traumatic conflict between Rabbi Eliezer and his colleagues at the rabbinic court and academy at Yavneh climaxes with these lines: 'Again [Rabbi Eliezer] said to them, "If the halakhah agrees with me, let it be proved from Heaven!" A heavenly voice then sounded: "Why do you dispute with Rabbi Eliezer? The halakhah agrees with him in every instance." Rabbi Joshua got to his feet and exclaimed: "It is not in heaven!" [Deut. 30: 12]. What did he mean? Rabbi Jeremiah said: "That the Torah was already given at Mount Sinai. And so now we pay no mind to heavenly voices."' Compare R. Levi Isaac's formulation: 'the dispute between Rashi and Rabbenu Tam concerning the *tefilin*. Rashi represented Moses and his camp, but Rabbenu Tam paid that no mind. . . . He countered "Moses" that the Torah was given to us already. It is in our hands now.'

[26] On the phenomenon of halakhic dispute in Jewish cultural history and its messianic overtones in hasidic thought in particular, see Magid's review of major scholarly discussions of rabbinic controversy in 'The Intolerance of Tolerance', 328 and n. 5. In our passage R. Levi Isaac's purpose is not to challenge traditional rabbinic and post-rabbinic ontologies of controversy, although he clearly holds that the root cause of difference is not error or negligence or loss of tradition.

is shaped by some integral, wholly unique essence. That essence, whose source is holy, is what guides a person in understanding anything and everything.[27] The Rabbis had the power and breadth of vision to comprehend multiple, variant senses of the world and to validate each of them. And so, R. Levi Isaac concludes, they could affirm with absolute certainty that 'these and these are the words of the living God'.

This is a valuable insight to be sure. It doesn't, however, obviate the troublesome, painful, often destructive reality of controversy. And while every conflicting opinion may well have some intrinsic truth value, rulings still need to be made and legal decisions then upheld for a community to remain functional, if not unified. How, then, is that to come about? In effect, the emblematic controversies that R. Levi Isaac cites uncover a general rule. They show that new developments and practices legitimately deserve to gain the upper hand. And indeed, he concludes, history itself teaches that each figure of authority, no matter how commanding—Moses himself, the House of Shammai, Rabbi Eliezer the Great, and Rashi too—ultimately yielded to make way for the next era and other powers.

This, I suggest, is the core importance of this *derashah*. It cogently reflects R. Levi Isaac's time-consciousness as well as his self-consciousness as a hasidic master. For the questions with which he contends are at the top of the contemporary Jewish public agenda. 'Who is able to sense what the world needs and establish the law in accordance with it? Only someone among the living, here in this world, can know what the world needs.' This recognition seems to imply that the hasidic masters, as spiritual leaders truly in touch with the times, are those best attuned to the overarching, urgent concerns of their generation. Hasidic teaching would then embody the aspect of Torah that is most fully 'among the living'. Read in that light, the precedents cited here authorize and mandate our author's confidence that, indeed, 'The Torah has been given to us already. It is in our hands now to teach as we see best.'[28]

---

[27] This sense of personal differences, diverse perspectives, and varying senses of the world—which R. Levi Isaac brings to the fore in this *derashah* by means of dramatic dialogue—is central in Mikhail Bakhtin's dialogic conception of truth. He describes it as 'a unified truth that requires a plurality of consciousnesses, one that in principle cannot be fitted within the bounds of a single consciousness.... The monologic way of perceiving cognition and truth is only one of the possible ways' (*Problems of Dostoevsky's Poetics*, 81). On polyphony and the 'dialogic sense of truth' in Bakhtin's thought, see Morson and Emerson, *Mikhail Bakhtin*, 234–7.

[28] Green reads this *derashah* as a 'theology of generational change . . . a theological reflection on the phenomenon, not unique to the modern world, of a new generation rejecting the cultural truths passed down to it or, in the case of a very conservative culture like this one, seeking a way

Some closing comments on the rhetorical aspects of these two *derashot*. Like R. Israel, R. Levi Isaac chooses a path of indirection. There are no cutting accusations or innuendos here, no stabs at unnamed enemies and no apologetics. On the long view he sets out, controversy as a phenomenon is transfigured. His meaning emerges gradually as he interacts with the sources he cites. He questions Jewish tradition through its texts. Between the lines, he tries to intuit something about the life experiences recorded in them, and then draws his insights into the present in a way that might make sense here, too, 'in our world'. The power of this dialogical mode, I think, is in its inherent resistance to finalized or absolute truths. Dialogism makes this teaching become what R. Levi Isaac calls 'living Torah'. And so the *derashah* itself enacts his message: it models a way for each generation to define its identity in relation with the past, even while guarding the illimitable right to innovate new modes of understanding. Is this reading 'messianic'? The rabbinic statement from which it sets out ('the Tishbite will resolve all problems and disputes') does refer to an unknown future resolution. Yet R. Levi Isaac makes a strong claim for Elijah's presence here and now. Elijah embodies a sensitivity to the hour, 'knowing what the world needs' in changing times. This attunement teaches something vital about engagement with the Torah, and about understanding and communicating the truths it reveals in every present moment.

Read in their own historical context, these passages seem to share a larger purpose. Both the Magid of Kozience and R. Levi Isaac of Berdichev were charismatic spiritual leaders and renowned Torah scholars. Their *derashot*, composed in the early years of the nineteenth century as hasidism was gaining a foothold in traditional society, seek to create a sense of community. Both authors place Torah study in the foreground as a primary facet of Jewish and hasidic identity. But while they reinforce that most conservative of religious values, they also reanimate its latent potential. These sermons model a compelling and novel mode of engagement with Torah. At its core is the personal dimension: the unique essence of every individual and of every generation. What they are teaching, in effect, is a gesture of appropriation—another important component of the hasidic ethos. We turn now to sermons by hasidic masters over the course of the nineteenth century, and to the ways these elements evolved further.

to recast the meaning of that legacy so that it may at once see itself as both rebellious and loyal' (*Speaking Torah*, 49).

Reason for Hope: R. Tsadok Hakohen, *Peri tsadik*

'For I know the thoughts that I am thinking for you, said the Lord: thoughts of peace and not of evil, to give you a future and a hope' [Jer. 29: 11]. . . . 'Hope'—for times to come. So I heard from our holy *rebbe*, who said in the name of Rebbe Bunim: Yes, the minds of each generation are weaker than those who came before it. But the spark of vitality in the heart grows ever larger and purer. . . . And that is reason for hope in this exile.[29]

These lines give voice to a deeply ambivalent vision of history: on one side, an ineluctable course of intellectual decline; on the other, an optimistic, open-ended movement towards inner refinement. In some incomprehensible way, these opposing trajectories converge to offer 'reason for hope'. After R. Simhah Bunim's death in 1827, deep schisms would divide his followers and drive their own disciples on widely separate paths. Still, this primary counter-intuitive 'reason for hope' endured as a lodestar for many of them, and for hasidic thinkers of other schools as well. We will return to this complex time-consciousness further on in the chapter.

For now, I'd like to take a closer look at the founding conviction, voiced here with great confidence, that, despite everything, 'the spark of vitality in the heart grows ever larger and purer'. This is a central element in the legacy of Przysucha hasidism. It also corresponds with certain broader movements that emerged in the nineteenth century. Charles Taylor, in his subtle and profound discussion of the sources of modern identity, describes 'the massive subjective turn of modern culture, a new form of inwardness, in which we come to think of ourselves as beings with inner depths'.[30] And so, increasingly, 'we find many moderns turning to a retrieval of experience or interiority'. The guiding force of this 'turn inward', Taylor maintains, is the belief that 'each of us has an original way of being human' and that the differences between people have

[29] R. Tsadok Hakohen of Lublin, *Peri tsadik*, 'Va'ethanan', 21, citing his teacher R. Mordecai Joseph of Izbica in the name of R. Simhah Bunim of Przysucha. R. Tsadok cites the image of 'dwarfs on the shoulders of giants' a number of times throughout his works. After much deliberation I decided not to discuss the ideological underpinnings of this theme in R. Tsadok's thought. An important image since medieval days, 'dwarfs on the shoulders of giants' is relevant not only to the issue of halakhic innovation, but in the wider context of the intellectual and cultural history of the Middle Ages. See Melamed, *On the Shoulders of Giants* (Heb.); Leyman, 'Dwarfs on the Shoulders of Giants'. On the motif in R. Tsadok's thought see Brill, *Thinking God*, 351; Elman, 'The History of Gentile Wisdom'. On the motif in post-medieval and hasidic sources, see Nadler, 'The Gaon of Vilna and the Rabbinic Doctrine of Historical Decline'.

[30] *The Ethics of Authenticity*, 26.

moral significance. 'This idea has entered very deep into modern conscious-ness. It is also new.'[31] The authors of the next *derashot* indeed seem to show a heightened interest in the inner self and a concern with personal experience and identity. I will foreground these elements while using certain other developments contemporary to them to illuminate the novel aspects of these hasidic teachings.

The Inward Turn: R. Isaac Meir Alter of Ger, *Sefer hazekhut*

R. Isaac Meir Rothenberg Alter (1799–1866) became one of R. Simhah Bunim's close disciples as a young man.[32] After the master's death, most of his inner circle of followers recognized R. Menaham Mendel Morgenstern, a senior member of the Przysucha group, as his successor and moved with him to Kotsk. In the stormy period that followed, and throughout the twenty years in which the Kotsker Rebbe sealed himself off from public life, R. Isaac Meir formally maintained the role of disciple while he pragmatically managed R. Menahem Mendel's hasidic court.[33] During the same period (the late 1840s to 1860) he emerged as a major leader of Polish Jewry. It was a decade of far-reaching Jewish reform initiatives. Prominent traditionalist leaders, R. Isaac Meir among them, 'proved able to galvanize mass Jewish discontent and neutralize initiatives they felt threatened the distinctive Jewish way of life, notwithstanding the efforts of maskilim and other Jewish integration-ists'.[34] Glenn Dynner concludes: 'A reconstruction of documentary sources presents Isaac Meir Alter as a scholarly, pious, yet politically sophisticated

---

[31] *Sources of the Self*, 461; *The Ethics of Authenticity*, 28–9. Lionel Trilling (*Sincerity and Authenticity*) is an important predecessor who explored the concept of modern identity in eighteenth- and nineteenth-century thought.

[32] His father had been a disciple of R. Levi Isaac of Berdichev and R. Israel, the Magid of Kozienice; his mother, Hayah Sarah, was orphaned in childhood and was raised in the Magid's home. As a young man, R. Isaac Meir continued to travel to the Magid of Kozienice and, at times, also to the Seer of Lublin. After R. Israel's death, for a time he visited the court of his son, R. Moses Elyakim Beriyah (*c*.1777–1828) but ultimately transferred his allegiance to Przysucha.

[33] For a lively quasi-historical account of this period and its central players, see Menashe Unger, *A Fire Burns in Kotsk*. See also Green, *The Language of Truth*, introduction.

[34] Among those initiatives: 'military conscription (1843), agricultural inducements (1843), educational reform (1844), and a ban on Jewish rural tavern-keeping (1844), in addition to the clothing decrees' (1845) that would ban Jewish garb in the Russian empire. Dynner, 'The Gar-ment of Torah', 96, 102, 123–4. Dynner notes (p. 125): 'Alter's careful, coordinated campaigns marked an important stage in the evolution of Polish Jewish *shtadlanut* (political intercession).'

leader cautiously navigating his community's Diaspora existence within a colonized Polish entity.' On the Kotsker Rebbe's death in 1859, his closest followers (including the future leaders of the Aleksandrow and Warka hasidic dynasties) chose R. Isaac Meir as his successor. In 1860 he moved from Warsaw to the nearby town of Góra Kalwaria. Within a few years, his court became one of the most important centres of Polish hasidism and Jewish learning.[35] An accomplished Talmudist and respected halakhic authority, R. Isaac Meir also played a central role in establishing hasidism in the mainstream.

For a fuller understanding of this key figure, his homiletical writings are a critical yet largely unexplored historical resource. They open a rare window into his inner world and have much to teach about a powerful hasidic group in its formative early stages.[36] In his writings R. Isaac Meir expresses a cogent historical consciousness. He articulates the hermeneutical project that would come to underlie Ger hasidism and sets out its founding ideas. One conviction central to that project is that Torah learning is inextricably linked to contemporary circumstances. Religious leaders, he maintains, must be attuned to the spiritual needs of the hour. 'New meanings of the Torah are revealed in each generation—the meanings that are needed just then to guide them on the path. And so, indeed, our own insights into the Torah may at times be more profound than ever before.' R. Isaac Meir also makes a strong claim for the democratization of study. The Torah, he affirms, opens itself to every Jew and thus mandates a highly personal way of engaging with it. 'Every single generation has its own interpretation of the Exodus. And not only every generation. Within every person is an inmost point of freedom, the secret sense of what "leaving Egypt" really means, and that individual alone can discover it.'[37] These assertions seem to articulate the strikingly modern consciousness that

[35] By the mid-nineteenth century the schism between hasidim and *mitnagedim* about conventional Torah study had greatly narrowed. R. Isaac Meir's novellae on the Talmud and the *Shulḥan arukh*, entitled *Ḥidushei harim* (Warsaw, 1875), were widely studied and are still recognized as classic works.

[36] *Sefer hazekhut* is an intellectual diary of sorts in which R. Isaac Meir recorded insights, thoughts, and teachings, some of them dating from the early 1850s. A second collection of his discourses is *Ḥidushei harim al hatorah*, which includes parts of *Sefer hazekhut* and other records, written and oral, of R. Isaac Meir's teachings.

[37] *Sefer hazekhut*, 5–6; on the notion of democratization, see p. 10. Taylor (*Authenticity*, 47) notes that the ideal of authenticity results from the decline of hierarchical society and entrance to a democratic social order. As the ideal of authenticity 'emerges, for instance with Herder, it calls on me to discover my own original way of being. By definition, this cannot be socially derived but must be inwardly generated.'

Charles Taylor describes—informed by the ideal of authenticity, attentive to the resources of the inner self, striving for an inwardly generated identity. Alongside programmatic statements of this sort R. Isaac Meir integrated his convictions in his homiletical teachings as well.

The following *derashah* voices a number of them. Its textual framework is the *parashah* 'Tazria', and it begins with the opening verse: 'When a woman conceives and gives birth, she shall be impure for seven days' (Lev. 12: 1). In its plain sense, this verse is the first in a long series of halakhic guidelines that the Bible sets out concerning states of ritual impurity and their processes of purification. Yet the Rabbis hear the verse speaking of many other things too. And so, beyond its pragmatic, literal meaning, the phenomenon of child-birth arouses a rich chain of midrashic reflections on what being human is all about. R. Isaac Meir briefly recalls some of those thoughts, adds one more telling insight from the Zohar's commentary, and then proceeds to draw together these far-flung associations to evoke a vulnerable moment of human experience:

'When a woman etc.' In the midrash: 'Before and after have You created me' [Ps. 139: 5] etc. 'I will attain my knowledge from afar' [Job 36: 3] etc. '"From afar"— that is praise for Abraham our forefather: "He saw the place [*hamakom*] from afar" [Gen. 22: 4].'[38] The Zohar says that, on the third day, he saw that God [*hamakom*] was far from him.[39] Indeed, it was a huge trial—here he was on his way to slaughter his only son, at God's command. Had he only sensed that God was near him—but instead, a void of uncertainty [*makom lefakpek*]. And Satan whispers to him: What *I* heard was 'a lamb for the offering'—not Isaac![40] But still he steeled himself to do God's will, even amidst such terrible remoteness. This, then, was the test: God's hid-ing of His light. And its effect is everlasting, for all generations. They might go very, very far away yet God's love for Israel, the innermost essence of that love, will always remain. In the hearts of all Israel too—their love for God endures deep within them, only concealed. That, in fact, was God's promise to Abraham, 'I am your shield' [Gen. 15: 1]; there is a tiny point within every Jewish heart and God Himself shields it, that it

---

[38] *Lev. Rab.* 14: 1–2. The biblical verses integrated in the midrash are heavily allusive and have borne many creative interpretations. R. Isaac Meir just cites those verses cursorily in these opening lines; in keeping with that, my provisory translation of them makes no attempt to reflect their deeper meanings.

[39] Zohar i. 120*a*. R. Isaac Meir seems to be using this reading rather associatively; in the Zohar itself the notion of distance ('from afar') is presented in a temporal sense: Abraham was able to peer into the distant future, but without full clarity—'through a mirror, darkly'. A second reading the Zohar offers is that he glimpsed the resolution that would eventually materialize in some far-off time to come.   [40] See *Midrash agadah*, 'Vayera', 22: 12; BT *San.* 89*b*.

never be lost. For this reason, 'a Jew, though he has sinned, remains a Jew'.[41] And so in our prayers we praise God as 'shield of Abraham'. And Abraham himself—when his trial was finally over, he gave thanks to God for the very remoteness he had endured. Then, at last, he understood everything, why all of it had happened. Thus [the midrash] learns that praise is due to Abraham from the verse 'He saw . . . from afar'.

Now we too, in all our generations, must continue to recognize this. 'I will attain my knowledge from afar'—for knowledge rises and emerges from far away, as it is written, 'His sister waited at a distance, to know' [Exod. 2: 4]. Awe [*yirah*] is remoteness. And inside every Jew there is something called 'far' and 'near'. This verse speaks of it: 'Peace, peace for the far and near' [Isa. 57: 19].

Here, then, is the difficulty that the midrash is trying to resolve: How can it be that the birth of a Jewish child brings on impurity? The answer the midrash offers is that being far away is also part of Creation, and that it really is a great good. And so a true servant of God must never despair, even when the distance seems immense. For this, too, is surely for the best.[42]

Were I compelled to name the ideas this passage discusses, they might well include the theological tension between immanence and transcendence; existential dilemmas of faith and doubt, double-mindedness; the hasidic doctrine of 'divine service through corporeity'; and the central concept known as the 'inner point' (*dos pintele yid*, or *hanekudah hapenimit*).[43] All of them are surely important. But I am quite convinced that R. Isaac Meir's primary aim here was not to elucidate any of those abstract topics. In any case, to read this *derashah* through the narrow lens of ideational content alone would lose sight of its singular hermeneutical force.

We must keep in mind, then, that the passage before us is a commentary on the Torah. Specifically, it relates to the biblical portion of 'Tazria' and sets out from its opening verse, 'When a woman conceives and gives birth'. The midrash on that verse concerns the endless miracle of how humans come into being and the unnoticed hand of Providence behind it all. Here, the motif of

[41] BT *San.* 44a.

[42] *Sefer hazekhut*, 'Tazria–Metsora' (5623 /1863); the passage also appears in *Ḥidushei harim*, 'Tazria' (p. 293).

[43] Valuable studies have been devoted to these important concepts, in conjunction both with the ideology of Ger hasidism and with hasidic teachings on the binding of Isaac. Mendel Piekarz traces the historical roots of the 'inner point' in the thought of R. Judah Halevi and the Maharal of Prague, where it is conceived as the seed from which redemption will sprout. Piekarz notes that the idea of the 'inner point' was used by modern non-hasidic thinkers as well; see '"The Inner Point" of the Admorim of Gur and Alexander' (Heb.); Gershon Greenberg further investigates the motif of the 'inner point' in 'Hasidic Thought and the Holocaust'. See also Gellman, *The Fear, the Trembling, and the Fire*.

'far and near' gives voice to the sense of wonder that is aroused by processes of becoming as they unfold in space and in time. By association Abraham is named, for he 'saw the place from afar'. Notably, the midrash on 'Tazria' is concerned only with the themes of engenderment and birth. It totally disregards the second half of the verse: 'she shall be impure for seven days'. Yet when the whole verse is reconsidered through the prism of hasidic sensibility, it raises a deeply troubling human issue. R. Isaac Meir presents that difficulty in the name of the midrash but the question is really his: 'How can it be that the birth of a Jewish child brings on impurity?' It is a striking statement, in that 'impurity' here does not refer to the evident halakhic category but to unseen realms of being. To such a disquieting question, it would seem, no theoretical response could mean enough. Lived experience alone can illuminate the role of 'impurity' in the 'true servant of God'. For this reason R. Isaac Meir turns to Abraham's spiritual journey.

Juxtaposed with the themes of 'Tazria', Abraham's trial on the way to Mount Moriah comes to show how the experience called impurity plays out in the human soul. On R. Isaac Meir's retelling of that trial, the notions of 'far' and 'near' grow denser. The midrash on 'Tazria' that we saw above focused on the primary senses of those terms—distance and proximity, beforehand and afterwards. Now 'far' and 'near' take on more and heavier meanings: hiddenness and clarity, estrangement and intimacy, disloyalty and faithfulness, incomprehension and knowing at the end.[44] All of these connotations touch on the ways in which impurity might be experienced as an inward state— a sense of alienation or loneliness, tinged perhaps with the spectre of sin, riddled with uncertainty. What finally gets Abraham to the other side of that vast distance is a presence concealed from conscious knowing—ironically, from Abraham's most of all. R. Isaac Meir names that presence as 'a tiny point within every Jewish heart, shielded by God Himself, that it never be lost'. We will return to the larger meaning of this seminal idea later on. For the moment, we need to consider more closely the meaning that he draws from Abraham's trial as lived experience.

Here, I think, the most innovative and distinctly modern aspect of R. Isaac Meir's reading comes to the fore. His recounting of Abraham's pri-

---

[44] Needless to say, he draws on midrashic tradition and medieval biblical commentary, but goes beyond them. R. Isaac Meir does not spell it out, but the biblical account of the binding of Isaac clearly seems to be the subtext here. In rabbinical literature the associations between far and near, impure and pure, sin and repentance are explicit; see Mishnah *Edu.* 8: 7; BT *San.* 99*a* and parallels.

vate spiritual journey suddenly opens out onto a wider existential vista with a remarkable transition: 'And inside every Jew there is something called "far" and "near".' The radical undertones of such a statement should not be ignored. In medieval and mystical sources the trope 'far and near' is used to speak, decidedly not of 'every Jew' or the inner realms of human sensibility, but of the Creator, who is 'infinitely distant, infinitely close'.[45] R. Isaac Meir underscores the reordering that he's proposing with the proof-text, 'Peace, peace for far and near [said the Lord, and I shall heal him].' Read in a straightforward manner, the verse is naming disparate groups—penitents and the righteous, the impure and the pure—each defined by their relationship to God. But here, all that becomes a metaphor to evoke the psychological dynamic that takes place endlessly within a single self. This is a deeply intuitive poetic of perspective. It is, moreover, fundamentally generative. Now, looking back on the stages of the *derashah* as it has unfolded, we see that R. Isaac Meir's object is to show how difficult, painful, and troubling life situations—here called 'impurity'—might be integrated into some kind of larger, encompassing whole. Reconsidered in this larger context, Abraham's trial becomes an essential moment of self-affirmation—of knowing, having lived through the experience personally, that 'being far away is also part of Creation, and that it really is a great good'.[46]

In sum, this *derashah* models a novel mode of commentary on the Torah that is informed by a strikingly modern consciousness. R. Isaac Meir's interest in the inner life leads him to read both the story of Abraham's trial and the laws of impurity in a new light. His object in this *derashah* is not abstruse complexities of elite wisdom known only to Torah scholars or mystics. Rather, what he is communicating is the most central and elementary of values: regard for every Jew's mundane, unexceptional effort to live in loyalty to God and the

[45] Cf. Ibn Pakuda, *Ḥovot halevavot*, 'Sha'ar hayiḥud', 10; Alshikh on Ps. 91: 'The Creator has two aspects, as it were: far and near [*raḥok vekarov*]'.

[46] 'For Romantic and post-Romantic culture generally, such self-affirmation is the essence of psychic health' (Holbrook, *Shakespeare's Individualism*, 106). Charles Taylor (*Sources of the Self*, 447–55) discusses self-affirmation, or 'the capacity to affirm goodness', as a response to the 'crisis of affirmation' at issue in the thought of Kierkegaard, Dostoyevsky, and Nietzsche. Self-affirmation meets that crisis through 'a transfiguration of our own vision, rather than simply through a recognition of some objective order of goodness. The recovery may have to take the form of a transformation of our stance towards the world and self, rather than simply the registering of external reality. Put in yet other terms, the world's being good may now be seen as not entirely independent of our seeing it and showing it as good, at least as far as the world of humans is concerned. The key to a recovery from the crisis may thus consist in our being able to "see that it is good"' (ibid. 448).

Torah; recognition of the bond of love between God and the nation of Israel, along with the obligations that covenant imposes. All this should be seen as part of a larger project of awakening and empowerment, a pragmatic vision of a way to help his contemporaries attain self-understanding and spiritual awareness, to appropriate the Torah 'as a living truth of existence'.[47]

R. Isaac Meir served as a hasidic leader in Poland until his death in 1866. His outstanding talmudic erudition helped him establish contacts with prominent rabbinic figures and halakhic authorities throughout eastern Europe. Through his efforts, hasidism attained respectability and asserted its place as a leading force within the mainstream Jewish community as 'the former lines between Hasidism and their onetime opponents virtually disappeared'.[48] R. Isaac Meir's sole surviving descendant was his grandson, R. Judah Leib Alter (1847–1905), then 19 years old. For four years, the court of Ger was led by R. Hanokh of Aleksandrow, a senior member of the Przysucha circle. Upon his passing in 1871, R. Judah Leib, now 21 years old, took over leadership of the dynasty. Over the following three decades, his social acumen and political skill built Ger hasidism into a decisive and influential presence in Orthodox Polish Jewry.

Modernity and Its Discontents

The closing decades of the nineteenth century saw European Jewry faced with formidable and unprecedented challenges. Major studies of hasidism have focused on the dramatic socio-economic developments, new political ideologies, and accelerating trends of secularization and acculturation that were rapidly fragmenting traditional society in that period. The common judgement has been that 'the Orthodox struggle against these new currents only heightened their inclination to close ranks in defense, painting their leaders with a conservative, even fanatical color. Hasidism gradually lost its attractiveness.'[49] Considered within a wider context, however, we see that the advance of modernity was exerting a massive cultural force in all areas of European intellectual creativity. Emergent trends in philosophy, psychology,

[47] As Fishbane puts it ('A Jewish Hermeneutical Theology', in *Jewish Hermeneutical Theology*, 159): 'It is only when the textual content is humanly appropriated as a living truth of existence that our own life fills out its exegetical spaces, and its linguistic features infuse our consciousness with challenge and possibility. Then the scriptural text offers models of theological living, of life lived in the context of God.'

[48] Green, *The Language of Truth*, pp. xxv–xxvi; see also Polonsky, *The Jews in Poland and Russia*, ii. 312.　　　　　　　　　　　　　　　　[49] Assaf, 'Hasidism'.

literature, and the arts vividly reflected the conflicts, anxieties, and spiritual dilemmas of the modern condition. Perspectives from these fields are equally necessary for an appreciation of that complex and highly ambivalent era.

A founding theorist of modernity, Max Weber (1864–1921), came of age in those critical decades. He bore witness first-hand to the widespread sense of the fragmentary and problematic character of modern life. He sensed, as well, an undercurrent of longing to recover some form of spiritual wholeness. Weber's 'exemplary model of the world as a place that had lost its magic, from which the super-natural had disappeared, and in which nature had been replaced by man-made, artificial, cultural production, was thus a very contemporary conception of the state of the world and an expression of modern self-doubt and cultural critique already in the 19th century'.[50] Modernity is a slippery term, and it has been given many conflicting definitions. My purpose here is only to suggest some directions of thought, a broader horizon of experience that I will try to keep in sight as I consider some contemporary trends in hasidic teaching. Reading the following *derashot* in light of the cultural discourse of their times means, in a sense, to look at them anew from other, perhaps less common vantage points. One gain might be a more circumspect, and perhaps more sympathetic, understanding of hasidism—which, after all, is more than a social ideology or a form of political activism.

'God is in the Detail': R. Judah Leib Alter of Ger, *Sefat emet*

Throughout nearly thirty-five years of his leadership, on sabbaths and festivals R. Judah Leib Alter of Ger addressed large audiences. He delivered his

---

[50] Hagen Schulz-Forberg, *London–Berlin*, 11–12. As eloquent testimony to those cultural trends, Schulz-Forberg cites a travel diary written around 1855: 'Throughout her account, Niendorf continuously mentioned her fatigue, her confused senses and her incapability of gaining an overall picture of London. Furthermore, despite the speed and the sentiment of temporal acceleration, she already complained about her time's repetitiveness, blaming her age for being void of original ideas, for simply producing copies, and for a far too rigid discourse of perception. . . . The most disturbing experience of the metropolis, however, was the constant growth of restlessness, the feeling of uncertainty and contradiction, the notion that one was somehow always slightly, or even grossly, out-of-place. . . . [Niendorf] would want to escape from the tumult of the big hub of confusing sights that the London of her present represented, searching for sensual and sensitive refuge at places endowed with a different temporal quality that provided her with stable narratives.' On Weber and the cultural milieu of the late nineteenth–early twentieth centuries see Hughes, *Consciousness and Society*.

talks in Yiddish and recorded them later, in his own hand, in Hebrew.[51] After his death, the *derashot* were arranged according to Torah portions and the yearly cycle of Jewish festivals, and published in the volumes entitled *Sefat emet*. His writing style is laconic, at times nearly cryptic. Frequently, these passages read more like personal notes than a proper communicative discourse. Rendering them in English was unexpectedly difficult. But the attempt to put together a good enough translation has given me insight into the associative nature of his thinking and its lithe resistance to being parsed. It also led me to wonder if these qualities might be part of his message. I'll return to that idea presently.

R. Judah Leib read and interpreted the Torah within the fertile matrix of his religious sensibility. One effect of that is the associative, frequently digressive character of his homilies, which complicates any linear narration of their themes and contents. Another distinctive feature of his *derashot* is the presence of trenchant poetic images, iconic figures of a sort, which took shape over his career—among them: the gate, the journey, the word, the face, the book, the desert. He revisited each of these figures over and over again, impressionistically, always partially, in many shifting contexts. I'd like to focus now on one such poetic image as it appears in some of his homilies. The following three passages, selected not too deliberately from among dozens throughout his commentary, in diverse exegetical settings, invite us to reflect on the language of inwardness that pervades these teachings, a language as evocative as it is elusory. The import of all this in light of R. Judah Leib's objectives as a hasidic leader contending with the spiritual challenges of his times will become clearer as we go along.

The following verses are the textual base for the first two passages: 'All the wells that [Isaac's] father's servants had dug in the days of Abraham his father, the Philistines stopped up and filled them with earth. . . . And Isaac dug anew the wells of water that they had dug in the days of Abraham his father . . . and he called them by the same names that his father had called them' (Gen. 26: 15–18).

My grandfather of blessed memory, about the wells. To dig and find the light that has been hidden away, the radiance that is obscured in materiality and appearances. [One of the wells] was called 'wide open spaces' [*reḥovot*]—this is the holy sabbath. For on the sabbath the innermost point emanates to illuminate the outside as well. Thus the

---

[51] On his oral discourses, their various methods of transcription, and questions of translation see Reiser and Mayse, '*Sefer Sefat Emet*'. Green addresses some of these questions in 'On Translating Hasidic Homilies'.

verse says, 'Now God has widened our spaces' [Gen. 26: 22], because the point of light concealed in every thing grows larger on the sabbath, and that point is the source of life itself. Now, the other wells are called 'quarrel' [*eshek*] and 'enmity' [*sitnah*]—these are the profane days of the week. On those days the light is hidden. But even so, if heart and soul strive hard enough, and if one utterly opposes the evil inclination —with all those efforts, even in the everyday we can find the hidden light.[52]

The wells that our forebears dug. My grandfather of blessed memory said: it means that the debris of outer appearances needs to be moved away to discover the hidden light. For everything contains an innermost point. . . . Indeed, wells are being dug each day—when one silences selfish desires and the heart's clamouring and surrenders everything to God. Then, afterwards, on the sabbath there is an ascent. Then the wellspring means discovering new understanding and holiness. For 'the Philistines had covered it over with dust' and so those living waters need to be uncovered all over again, every time anew. That's how it is when a Jew resolves to start serving God. At first there's a surge of love and desire to cleave to the Holy One—like 'Abraham my beloved servant' [Isa. 41: 8]. But then other, earthly loves come crowding in and the wellspring gets stopped up. The remedy is through 'Isaac'—that is, fear of heaven.[53]

'He looked, and behold—a well in the field. And three flocks of sheep were resting nearby, for from the well the flocks were watered. But the stone was large on the mouth of the well. When all the flocks had gathered there, they would roll the stone off the mouth of the well' [Gen. 29: 2–3].
  'A well in the field'. The well: it signifies the Oral Torah that is planted inside us. Something of it lies deep within every Jew. All that is needed is to find the strength to speak. And so we plead, 'Lord, open my lips' [Ps. 51: 17]. This comes about when the stone is moved from the mouth of the well. Thus there are three times for prayer each day, 'three flocks of sheep'. And when all the prayers of the Jewish people are gathered together, then the fountainhead above can open at last—as it is written, 'all the flocks gathered'. And so the verse says, 'O heeder of prayer—unto You all flesh comes' [Ps. 65: 3]. For only when one joins oneself together with all of Israel—only then can one hope for opening.[54]

These, to be sure, are allegorical readings of the biblical narratives. To say it differently, they fit into the parabolic method of exegesis known in Jewish tradition as *remez*. There is nothing too original in this approach itself, of course; the same verses inspired a wealth of allegorical readings in midrashic and

---

[52] *Sefat emet*, 'Toledot' 5632/1871. Compare *Kol simhah*, 'Toledot', 7; *Sefer hazekhut*, 'Hayei sarah', 7. Piekarz traces the connection here between the 'inner point' and the sabbath to kabbalistic sources such as the Zohar and *Reshit hokhmah*; *Ideological Trends of Hasidism in Poland* (Heb.), 136.

[53] *Sefat emet*, 'Toledot' 5633/ 1872.   [54] *Sefat emet*, 'Vayetse' 5643 / 1882. Cf. *Exod. Rab.* 21: 4.

medieval commentaries.[55] What is remarkable, however, is the way that R. Judah Leib engages with the biblical text. And so first of all I'd like to look a bit more closely at the poetic aspects of these passages. This will help us evaluate the significance of his hermeneutical project in a larger cultural and historical sense.

A subtle language, sensual and associative, invests these *derashot* with a fullness and intensity of life. The surface of Scripture, its prosaic words and mundane plot, seem to hint at something deeper. Landscape here, as in modernist works, is a projection of interiority. Recesses below, the dust, the heavy stone, waters outflowing—these images, with their metaphorical and symbolic valences, allude to unapprehended realms of being. The analogies that R. Judah Leib evokes, we should note, differ greatly from the abstract concepts and ideas named in traditional allegorical readings. What interests him most are the intimate spaces of a personal cosmos. To gain entrance to such spaces, other, non-discursive modes of expression are required. And so the fragmentary sentences that make up these passages, the biblical verses loosely linked together by a word or phrase or undefined kinship, the reflexive 'we' and 'our'—all these elements combine to suggest an impression, never fully said, of the secret connections between things. This textual dynamic creates what Paul Ricoeur calls a *poesis* of revelation.[56] It means: try to read beyond the verse, beneath the debris of an unexamined life—and suddenly there might be a flash of seeing what was there all along. The key is to be mindful of the details, to take notice of unassuming traces, to decipher the signs scattered about in the text as they are in the world. Such an effort may grant a glimpse into hidden dimensions of reality, into spaces charged with holiness. These *derashot* enact just that sort of deeply engaged mode of reading. But what larger historical significance could all of this have?

To address this question, I'd like to consider a fascinating instance of intellectual creativity that, at first sight, is very far removed from fin-de-siècle Góra Kalwaria. Italian historian Carlo Ginzburg explores a novel model of learning and experience, a 'presumptive paradigm' based on semiotics that began to emerge in the humanities towards the end of the nineteenth century.

---

[55] Albeit with different referents to those of the hasidic homilies. Cf. *Gen. Rab.* 70; Nahmanides on Gen. 29: 2; Zohar iii. 62*a*. In those contexts, the analogues are set out in straightforward, discursive statements. The wells refer to the First, Second, and Third (future) Temples; to the historical exiles of the Jewish people, to the *sefirot*, etc.

[56] Ricoeur, *Essays on Biblical Interpretation*, 20, 34; *The Rule of Metaphor* (n. 64). And see Fishbane's insightful discussion of the four dimensions of exegesis, especially the mode of *remez*, in *A Jewish Hermeneutical Theology*, 193–5.

Its founding notion: what seem to be minor or negligible details, if only they are recognized as signs and correctly deciphered, can reveal 'profound phenomena of great importance', details that provide 'the key for approaching higher aspects of the human spirit'. Ginzburg traces some of the earliest manifestations of this distinctly 'modern attitude' in three evolving disciplines of the human sciences—psychoanalysis, literary fiction, and art history—and notes a primary conviction that they share. 'In each case, infinitesimal traces permit the comprehension of a deeper, otherwise unattainable reality: traces—more precisely, symptoms (in the case of Freud), clues (in the case of Sherlock Holmes), pictorial marks (in the case of [Giovanni] Morelli).' The parallels are more than coincidental. Ginzburg illustrates the real effects of Morelli's iconographical theory on Arthur Conan Doyle, creator of the uncannily insightful detective, Sherlock Holmes, and he demonstrates the intellectual influence that both of them exerted on Freud at the earliest, formative stages of his psychoanalytic method. This new (or newly rediscovered) model for attaining knowledge, which Ginzburg called 'the evidential paradigm', thus marks the historical emergence of a vitally new line of thinking. Close observation of unremarkable clues, followed by conjecture, uncertainty, and speculation—in a word, 'aphoristic reasoning'—might grant one access to mysteries that will forever elude the grasp of systematic thought.[57]

Ginzburg prefaced his incisive essay with the aphorism 'God is in the detail'. Translated more literally, what its author Aby Warburg wrote is 'Dear God is hiding in the detail'.[58] Undeniably, a vast distance separates Warburg, the German Jewish cultural theorist and art historian (1866–1929), from his older contemporary, R. Judah Leib Alter, the Gerer Rebbe. And yet the same intuition seems to have drawn both of them to search for the symbolic powers, perhaps even the traces of divinity, hiding in the detail most of all: in the images and metaphors that inform sacred texts, works of art, and cultural history. The 'evidential paradigm' truly appears to have come to dwell in many and varied areas of modern thought—and R. Judah Leib's commentary, the *Sefat emet*, a prime instance of hasidic creativity, clearly numbers among them.

This brings us back to a larger question. R. Judah Leib was a prominent

---

[57] Ginzburg, 'Clues: Roots of an Evidential Paradigm', 101, 104, 124–5. Fishbane briefly notes Ginzburg's 'evidential paradigm' in *A Jewish Hermeneutical Theology*, 195. That, for me, was an eye-opening reference for which I am very grateful; see below.

[58] 'Der liebe Gott steckt im Detail'; see Wuttke, 'Nachwort des Herausgebers', 619. Christopher Johnson (*Memory, Metaphor, and Aby Warburg's Atlas of Images*, 45) translates: 'God hides in the details' and suggests that Warburg's intent was indeed to the presence of 'divinity'—this in spite of the clearly areligious nature of Warburg's project.

spiritual leader of a large religious community in an age when the project of modernity was making deep inroads into Polish Jewry. What overarching purpose might he have envisioned for these *derashot*—and how was their uncommon manner of poetic expression meant to further it? My limited study here focuses on three short sermons, but a closer look at this sample alone suggests that he was well aware of actual realities.

Some of the concerns that can be detected between the lines of these passages are the unsettling influences of modern urban life and the growing pull of materialism, with its valuation of external effects and attraction to baser aspects of social life. And so R. Judah Leib speaks of what is 'obscured in materiality and appearances', 'the debris of outer appearances', 'the evil inclination', 'selfish desires and the heart's clamouring', the 'earthly loves that come crowding in'. Other concerns include the secularizing effects of modernity.[59] He acknowledges the difficulty of maintaining an authentic and vibrant religious life: 'on some days the light is hidden'; 'the stone is large on the mouth of the well', 'and so those living waters need to be uncovered all over again, every time anew'. When all this is reframed as a known and shared experience, a clear mode of spirituality and action emerges. The realms of profane and sacred, secular and holy, the 'days of the week' and the sabbath, emerge as purposeful facets of religious being.

The meaning that R. Judah Leib conveys in these sermons, then, is addressed to every Jew. Without dogmatism, and eliding the obscurities of theological or mystical discourse, he communicates it by reading otherwise. Finding traces of holiness in the Torah's simplest words—here, the image of the wellspring and its attendant details—he evokes a privileged kind of experience. He touches on it repeatedly, calling it an 'opening', 'discovery', 'illumination', 'ascent'. With awareness of the richer field of meaning that these words contain, the notion so central to Ger hasidic teaching—that 'everything contains an innermost point, the source of life itself' and that 'it

[59] The notion of the modern and its secularizing effects is linked to many factors: ideas of evolution and progress; a critical attitude towards traditional practices; the fading of religious experience; estrangement from the sacred texts of tradition, and a sense of alienation from religious community structures. Breaking with the past, in all the forms it took in Jewish ideologies of the twentieth century—liberalism, socialism, Zionism, etc.—depends on progressivism of one kind or another. See de Vries, *Religion: Beyond a Concept*, 1–98. Concerning the hasidic milieu, Green maintains: 'In the later years of R. Yehudah Leib's reign, both Zionism and socialism became major factors in the lives of a great many Warsaw Jews. While statistics are hard to come by, it is fair to say that between 1871 and 1904 an increasingly significant percentage of Warsaw Jewry was less and less faithful to the norms of Jewish practice and the old way of life that Hasidism had come to represent' (*The Language of Truth*, xxxi).

lies deep within every Jew'—suggests something more.[60] At issue is not an abstract concept to be contemplated, but a real and pressing directive. Well-springs await their opening; the 'inner spark of vitality' must be rediscovered endlessly, day by day, as a real presence. To take on such a challenge means to find oneself on an enduring path towards God-mindedness.

On a longer view, this new attentiveness to the 'heart's understanding' reflects an aim shared by many of R. Judah Leib's contemporaries—figures as diverse as Marcel Proust, James Joyce, Virginia Woolf, and Franz Kafka—to reconfigure 'the sacred', to uncover religious meanings in the everyday, secular world. A *derashah* from the last years of the *rebbe*'s life revisits the familiar image. Perhaps it was meant to give courage to his listeners on journeys yet to come:

All the places where there was no water to be found—those are places where holiness is not easily revealed. For God took the generation of the wilderness through desolate vistas, the lairs of serpents and evil powers. Yet even in the wasteland, the wells of Torah can open. . . . So it is written: 'Those who pass through the valley of tears—they make it a place of flowing springs.'[61]

Prophets of the Past, Prophets of the Future: R. Joshua Heschel Rabinowitz of Monastyrishche, *Divrei yehoshua*

Our locus moves now from the Kingdom of Poland to late imperial Russia. 'The year 1881–2, as a major watershed in modern Jewish history, looms large over what came after. In that year the problem of Russian Jewry was first revealed in something of its true magnitude and menace; the vision of the exodus caught the popular imagination and at the same time became an issue of wide-ranging political debate; and Jewish nationalism became a significant political force.'[62] Of the forces driving the young Jewish revolutionaries of eastern Europe, David Biale writes: 'They wanted to escape from what they considered the oppression of an obscurantist, medieval religion and to create a new Jew and a new society. . . . Their ideologies ranged from Communist to Zionist, from Yiddishism to assimilation. But one thing characterized all of

---

[60] Piekarz surveys the ideational meanings of this core concept: it denotes the indelible mark of Jewish identity; the unity of the Jewish people despite all differences; the chosenness, eternity and indestructability of Israel. Green defines Piekarz's thesis on the role of the 'inner point' in twentieth-century hasidic thought: 'it served as a strategy to continue to claim the loyalty of Jews who in their outward lives were no longer loyal to tradition' (*The Language of Truth*, xxxii–xlviii; see also id., 'Three Warsaw Mystics', n. 33).

[61] *Sefat emet*, 'Ḥukat' 5663 (1903), citing Ps. 84:7.   [62] J. Frankel, *Prophecy and Politics*, 5.

them: a generational revolt against a world in which the Jewish religion, economic plight, political impotence, and cultural backwardness seemed wrapped up together in one unsavory package.' That revolt, however, did not mean a total rupture with, or negation of, tradition. A far more complex dynamic was at work: a pattern of rebellion, loss, and retrieval that David Roskies has called 'creative betrayal' in the effort to redefine Jewishness and forge a new identity out of the shards of the past.[63] The following *derashot* foreground this dialectic between the secular and the religious, sacred and profane, tradition and modernity.

R. Joshua Heschel Rabinowitz of Monastyrishche (1860–1938), scion of a distinguished hasidic family, took on the role of *rebbe* after his father's death in 1885.[64] For the next three decades of his life, he served as religious figurehead for many *shtetls* scattered throughout Ukraine. One of the rare *tsadikim* in Russia in those years who put pen to paper, R. Joshua Heschel was keenly aware of the many crises confronting Russian Jewry. Incidents of antisemitic violence shadow his letters and memoirs; these and other works, including his sermons, also reflect the urgent issues on the public agenda. Among them were nationalism and the Jewish struggle for equal rights; Zionism and the renaissance of the Hebrew language; Jewish secularization and other powerful currents of modernity that had violently uprooted the younger generation.[65] His works—all of them written in strikingly modern Hebrew—offer uncommon insight into the life of a hasidic thinker and preacher deeply engaged in the historical experience of the era. We will look at three passages from his works, composed at two very different points in time. The first *derashah* was written in the 1890s, in the early years of his leadership. I will try to read it with an eye to some of the larger contemporary concerns hinted at between the lines.

The setting is the founding biblical narrative, 'Moses was shepherding the sheep of Jethro, his father-in-law . . . He guided the sheep far into the wilder-

---

[63] Biale, *Not in the Heavens*, 14; Roskies, *A Bridge of Longing*, 4.

[64] His father was the great-grandson of R. Gedaliah Rabinowitz of Linits (a disciple of the Ba'al Shem Tov and R. Aryeh Leib of Polonnoye, introduced in Ch. 1) and of R. Pinhas of Korets; his mother's ancestry stemmed from R. Meshulam Zusha of Zinkov, grandson of R. Abraham Joshua Heschel of Apt.

[65] His published works include homiletics, rabbinic essays, an autobiography, and poetry. Some of the passages I cite here are from a substantial collection of unpublished personal letters. My gratitude to R. Gedaliah Rabinowitz for enabling me to study them. For more on this important hasidic figure see my discussion in 'Rebbe Yehoshua Heschel Rabinowitz of Monastyrishche' (Heb.).

ness . . . until he arrived at the mountain of God, towards Horev' (Exod. 3: 1). Following the well-known midrash on those verses R. Joshua Heschel notes, with some irony, that it's no easy matter to understand people and how they work. We judge only by what meets the eye, while every human heart forever remains a mystery to every other.

But as for God, He has thought everything out so that no Jewish soul, come what may, will ever be totally lost.[66] And so it sometimes happens that even the lowest of the low, someone who seems devoid of all spirituality, as tasteless and scentless as a willow frond—even such a person might suddenly burst aflame with the desire to do God's will with all his heart, just like the most perfect servant of the Lord. As the Rabbis said, 'even a [Jewish] thief, as he is breaking in, calls to the Merciful One.'[67] . . . 'He arrived at the mountain of God, to a place that was parched and barren [*ḥorevah*]'—where hardly a trace of holiness remained. And yet 'an angel of God appeared to him in the blaze of fire from amid the bush'—thorny, utterly fruitless, but still it might burn for a moment with a sacred fire, all alight with longing to do something good. And he marvelled: 'This bush is on fire yet it is not consumed'—the emptiness inside it remains: the excitement fades, the flames abate, and nothing has really changed! That is what astonished Moses. He went closer to look: 'Why is it that the bush doesn't keep on burning'—continually, without cease?[68]. . . And God answered, 'Do not come closer'—for you cannot understand this hidden mystery. . . . 'The place upon which you stand'—the idea that you are contemplating—'it is holy ground', one of 'God's profound, concealed mysteries'.[69] Then, in an influx of prophetic vision, God showed Moses the reason that a Jew might suddenly awaken, alive with spiritual fire: 'I am the God of your father'—it is their inheritance from their forebears, a vital spark of holiness, God's own essence planted deep within every Jewish soul. And so, in truth, 'the bush *will* burn'—somehow, always.[70]

The central motif of this *derashah* is the biblical image of the burning bush. In Jewish exegetical tradition it figures as a metonymy for the nation of Israel, oppressed yet surviving. The 'bush that burns but is not diminished' also

---

[66] Cf. 2 Sam. 14: 14.   [67] BT *Ber.* 63a.

[68] As R. Joshua Heschel notes, his reading draws on the medieval biblical commentary *Akedat yitsḥak*, *sha'ar* 31. There, R. Isaac Arama detects a contradiction between two verses (Exod. 3: 2 and 3: 3) and proposes an original rereading to resolve it. Moses marvels not because 'the bush is on fire yet it is not consumed' but because 'the bush does not keep burning'. R. Joshua Heschel adds psychological and existential dimensions to that reading to further his larger message.

[69] The Talmudic phrase *kivshei deraḥmana* refers to incomprehensible aspects of human life and to the suffering they incur. See BT *Ber.* 10a.

[70] *Divrei yehoshua*, 'Shemot', 131. The *derashah* follows the order of the verses in Exod. 3: 1–6. He draws on the midrashic reading in *Lev. Rab.* 11.

symbolizes the Covenant—divine, eternal, unalterable. R. Joshua Heschel's allegorical reading, informed by his own hasidic sensibilities, highlights an additional meaning. Alongside the collective experience of the Jewish people, these verses also speak of a private, individual facet of religious life. Interpreting the verses in that way, he relates to the inner turmoil of young Jews caught up in the maelstrom of modernity. To appreciate this *derashah* more fully, I'd like to consider the same idea from the 'other side', through the writings of one of R. Joshua Heschel's young contemporaries, who was standing just then at the crossroads between (west) European modernism and east European Jewish culture.

Son of a poor Jewish family from Noviye Mlini, northern Ukraine, the pioneering Hebrew author Joseph Hayim Brenner (1881–1923) was a figure whose life story mirrors the drama of twentieth-century Jewish life. His was 'the generation that made "the great leap" from Imperial Russia's Pale of Settlement to the metropolitan centers of modernity, and from traditional Jewish beliefs and way of life to secularism and existentialism'.[71] Surely there was no one who 'recorded with such intensity, with such obsessive concentration, the search of the *polu-intelligentsiia* (the half-intelligentsia)—that section of the radicalized youth who had some formal Jewish education, but otherwise were autodidacts, denied access to the *gimnaziia* and the university, uprooted and penurious—for some meaning to life in general and to Jewish life in particular'.[72] And yet, even as Brenner struggled to break with tradition, to engender a radical new and secular Hebraic identity, his very being remained infused with the images, idioms, and religious universe of Jewish sources. His early writings in particular reflect both the urgency and the tense ambivalence of that project, torn between old and new worlds.

Brenner's first novel, *Baḥoref* (In Winter; 1901), written at the age of 19, centres on its author's tortured inner world. And so his protagonist Feierman is drawn at times to a Tolstoyan spirit of 'universalism', at others to the ideals of revolutionary Marxism. But then he falls back, yet again, into dark musings on 'the Jewish world that is mine alone',

my thoughts about 'the sons who have been banished from their father's table'; about the great and strange historical tragedy of an ancient people that has been dying for two thousand years, that burns but is not consumed . . . about its fine young men rotting away in cellars or deserting it for other worlds and forgetting its very existence; about the contempt and the poverty that the entire world heaps onto this bent over

[71] Shapira, *Yosef Haim Brenner*, 1–2.   [72] J. Frankel, 'Yosef Haim Brenner', 148.

but proud people; about its awakening to life and chance for salvation, for redemption; about its literature and its thinking which are so explosive and yet so utterly ethereal.[73]

The dichotomy is harsh, nearly absolute. Tradition looms large here in grim motifs of decay and death, impotence, despair, irreparable loss, and estrangement. On the distant horizon, a promise of arousal and return, transformed, to life. Notably, though, the same 'great and strange' biblical image haunts Feierman's (Brenner's) lugubrious thoughts as well. The Jews are 'an ancient people ... that burns but is not consumed'. Indeed, it is that very paradox, the 'profound, concealed mystery' symbolized in the burning bush, that ensures both the nation's continued, frail existence and its final, longed-for 'awakening to life'.

Three years later Brenner, now in London, wrote of his plan to publish a literary journal. The first issue of *Hame'orer* appeared in January 1906. In his 'To the reader' manifesto (written under a pseudonym), Brenner declared: 'We write in Hebrew because we cannot do otherwise, because the divine spark within us only emerges on its own in this flame, because this spark does not ignite, is not completely fulfilled, except in this language.' On these lines, Anita Shapira comments: 'This was a translation of the poetic pathos of Abramson's reasoning in [Brenner's novel] *Around the Point*, who hears a "divine voice from Mount Horeb" only in Hebrew. There was something mystical and inexplicable in his devotion to Hebrew, but it is a fact; he could not do otherwise.'[74] Other fragmentary images here—the 'divine spark within us', the flame that bursts alive in the holy tongue alone—draw on kabbalistic and hasidic sources.[75] In *Hame'orer*'s second year (1907) an epigraph was added

[73] Jonathan Frankel cites this passage in 'Yosef Haim Brenner', 153–4; see also his *Crisis, Revolution, and Russian Jews*, 109–10. I have altered the first lines of Frankel's translation so that they more accurately represent the talmudic source as Brenner cites it: 'Woe to the sons who have been exiled from their father's table' (BT *Ber.* 3a). The original manuscript of *In Winter* was lost in a fire; Brenner rewrote it and it was published in *Hashilo'ah*, 12 (1903). See Brenner, *Ketavim*, i. 176.   [74] Shapira, *Yosef Haim Brenner*, 76–7; 83–5.

[75] Brenner's friendship with Hillel Zeitlin (1871–1942), whom he met in Homel in those formative years and saw as his mentor and guide into European literature as well as Jewish religious traditions, may underlie his engagement here with these motifs. Shahar Pinsker argues convincingly for Brenner's strong sense of religiosity, on which Zeitlin was a major influence; *Literary Passports*, 328–36. Pinsker also foregrounds one of Brenner's most extensive but little-known works in Jewish mysticism and hasidism: an essay he wrote in Yiddish around 1906, entitled *Di beditung fun hasidism in yudentum un zayn obklung in der moderner hebreisher literature* (The Meaning of Hasidism and Its Echoes in Modern Hebrew Literature). In that essay 'Brenner finds an affinity between modernist concerns and hasidic mysticism and its ability to

that explained the journal's name: 'For it is to awaken you, my brother, that I come. To awaken you, saying: Ask, O man, of the ways of the world. Ask: Where,   O where is the road?'[76]

Brenner's voice in these passages is animated with a prophetic spirit. He speaks with visionary certainty and an overpowering sense of mission. As one literary historian puts it, he sought to 'give voice to the pressing issues of concern to his generation . . . a guide to the perplexed' on the existential search they shared.[77] The invocation in Brenner's commanding epigram, 'For it is to awaken you that I come', is in fact borrowed apiece from the language of prophetic revelation that informs kabbalistic works: 'I, it is I who am speaking with you—your own soul . . . for it is to guide you that I come, to guide you on the road that you shall walk.' Or: 'Here, I must awaken you with this, that you may know'.[78] Even more cogently, the core motif in his adjuration, intoned with the heavy urgency of a preacher at the gate, reiterates nearly literally the words of the prophet Jeremiah: 'Thus says the Lord: Stand on the roads; see, ask of the ways of the world. Ask: which is the good road? Walk on that road and find solace for your soul' (Jer. 6: 16). But while in the biblical prophet's lost world of clarity 'the good road' was singular and self-evident, Brenner's summons emerges from a jagged 'tear in the heart'.[79] 'Where is the road, O

penetrate the "mysteries of life." . . . [He] maintains that the *Besht* (and others like him) sensed the impenetrable mystery of existence and that is what made him close to modern man and modern thought. . . . [He] writes that he feels very close to "those shattered, complex, tragic souls that penetrate into the secret, that rise into the mist, the mystery"' (Pinsker, 332, quoting Brenner, *Ketavim*, iii. 179). The purpose of the essay and its unwritten sequel, as Brenner put it, was to explain 'the meaning of Hasidism for Jewry as a whole . . . for us, the children of the present and of the *future*' ('The Meaning of Hasidism', in Pinsker, 404).

[76] *Hame'orer* means 'The Awakener'. I've translated these lines somewhat differently to the English version of Shapira's biography. On the epigraph Shapira notes: 'Brenner placed this in quotation marks, as if he had taken it from the words of one of the ancient Jewish sages. But in fact he was quoting himself, from an article he had published twice, in *Hayehudi* (1905) and in *Hame'orer* (June 1906). The article, *Al haderekh* (On the road), which was published immediately after the October 1905 pogroms, is an extraordinarily Brenneresque mélange containing a call for territory, "acquisition for a place for our wanderings," and a demand for loyalty to the Hebrew language' (*Yosef Haim Brenner*, 100).

[77] Brinker, *Narrative Art and Social Thought in Y. H. Brenner's Work* (Heb.), 20.

[78] Karo, *Magid meisharim*, 148; *Ets ḥayim*, i: 8. A close reading of Brenner's essay 'Al haderekh' shows that he is consciously 'translating' the scenario in ch. 6 of the book of Jeremiah, with overtones of 1 Kings 18 (the story of Elijah on Mount Carmel). Indeed, as Brenner confessed, 'If someone would say about me that I am a "mystic" . . . I would not think of this as an offense' (letter to Shimon Bichovsky, 11 Apr. 1907, cited by Pinsker in *Literary Passports*, 305).

[79] Citing Berdichevsky, Brenner's teacher and mentor; see Pinsker, *Literary Passports*, 282.

where?' Which of the countless paths—ideological, political, literary, artistic
—open before him and his generation in a new world of freedom will lead to
the highest ideals that they wished so desperately to realize: national renewal
and personal redemption, 'the liberation of humanity'—ultimately, to 'find
the face of true being'?[80]

To return to R. Joshua Heschel's sermon: as he points out in its opening
lines, the biblical narrative is framed in a larger context. Moses emerges as
spiritual leader and is charged with the heavy burden of understanding and
guiding each individual in the community. 'And an angel of God appeared to
him in the blaze of fire from amid the bush.' Like Brenner (and Feierman, his
alter ego), the bush burns in a passionate search for truth, only to fall back
again into consuming despair and 'boundless pessimism'. Yet it will awaken to
life again 'because of the divine spark within us'—with the 'latent optimism of
a man who irrationally claims that "despite everything," the Jews' will to live
will prevail'.[81] The understanding that R. Joshua Heschel draws from the
biblical narrative, specifically from the moment of revelation given to Moses
at Mount Horev, is that 'you cannot understand that hidden mystery'—that
is, the secret yearning of a human heart. All that can be done—rather, what
must be done—is to acknowledge the anguished, endless quest driving on the
children who have deserted 'their father's table', and to keep sight of the 'vital
spark of holiness, God's own essence planted deep within every Jewish soul'.
Who knows how or when it might come back to life? Finally, R. Joshua
Heschel reminds his reader of an even greater truth, one that will forever
remain wholly beyond reason: 'As for God, He has thought everything out so
that no Jewish soul, come what may, will ever be totally lost.'

The atrocities of the twentieth century began, for Russian Jewry, with the
1903 Kishinev pogrom. Two years later came the revolution of 1905, bringing
far more widespread and violent pogroms. Then the Beilis blood libel (1913);
mass recruitment of Jewish forces for the Great War; the dislocation and traumatic expulsion of entire communities from the western part of the empire,
the dramatic collapse of the monarchy in the February Revolution of 1917, and
the subsequent fleeting months of democracy. The following two passages
were written that euphoric spring. Both are extracts from unpublished letters
that R. Joshua Heschel wrote from his home in Uman, southern Ukraine, and

[80] Brenner, 'Al haderekh', *Ketavim*, iii. 95–6.
[81] Shapira, citing Brenner, in *Yosef Haim Brenner*, 2. Note that 'Brenner' in Yiddish actually
means 'burner'; his autobiographical character and namesake 'Feierman' is analogously a 'man of
fire'.

copied out for safekeeping. The familiar, traditional genre of Torah commentary combines in these excerpts with a second dimension. Live testimony and reflections on events as they unfold charge these texts with an urgent sense of bearing witness to history in the making. This new emotional register, untempered by the bitter retrospective wisdom that was soon to come, alerts us to another important role of homiletics. More on that below. The first letter was written on 12 March 1917.[82]

Now we have seen God's mighty hand raised against our enemies and oppressors—they who have persecuted us more cruelly than the Egyptian enslavers. My amazement, all my feelings are too intense to express in words. As if 'every fibre of my being says, Who is likened unto you, O God?'[83] But we cannot yet rest content; my heart will still not rejoice. For many, many of our brothers remain in mortal danger on the battlefields. Our choicest forces crouch in pits and trenches, the sword of Damocles hanging over their heads.[84] Whatever will become of them? The situation grieves me deeply. And now this most recent turn of events—it recalls what happened to Israel at the parting of the sea. They, too, saw the mighty hand of God and they were moved to sing. But the great prophet [Moses], in his song, said: 'You will deliver them', 'and replant them on the mount of Your heritage'.[85] At the sight of Pharaoh being overthrown and the Egyptians perishing the people broke into song. Yet at the same time their eyes were set on what was still to come—something even more momentous, the future they had awaited all the years of their enslavement: to return to the land of their forebears, to inherit and possess the Land that God had promised them. Now I'll tell you what I said at the third meal this past sabbath.

On the midrash in *Vayikra rabah* 2: 4, 'Speak to the Children of Israel' . . . What distinguishes those two moments—the parting of the sea and revelation at Sinai—is this. At the sea, Israel witnessed the utter destruction of their arch-enemies, the Egyptians. But their anxiety did not disappear; they still feared that 'Just as we have reached the other side, they, too, are about to emerge out of the sea', as it says in the midrash. So it was until the revelation at Sinai—then God named them as His holy nation. Then, at last, they won total liberty and absolute freedom. As the Rabbis taught: 'Inscribed [*ḥarut*] on the Tablets—freedom [*ḥerut*] from the yoke of the nations'.[86] I write this very briefly so that you might understand my views on our

---

[82] The February Revolution (24–28 February in the Julian calendar then in use) took place on 8–12 March 1917. In the Hebrew calendar it coincided with the festival of Purim (14 Adar fell on 8 March). In this letter Purim themes—abrupt reversals of destiny, with the miraculous defeat of malicious oppressors—figure prominently.   [83] Ps. 35: 10.

[84] The phrase 'sword of Damocles' was often used in contemporary Russian and Polish Jewish journalism. See for instance *Novyi Voskhod*, 37, pp. 16–18; *Hatsefirah*, 17 Sept. 1912 (published in Poland). On the historical reality of this period see Natan Meir, '"The Sword Hanging Over Their Heads": The Significance of Pogrom for Russian Jewish Everyday Life and Self-Understanding (The Case of Kiev)'.   [85] Exod. 15: 17.   [86] *Lev. Rab.* 18: 3.

current situation. For I am not yet content. My eyes pine and yearn for even greater salvation, for us, from God—salvation in a positive and not only negative sense.[87]

Before I finished writing this letter, I was summoned to the Hebrew Bank in town, to lead the Jewish delegation celebrating this Liberation Day. Only so as to uphold the precept 'Keep not aloof from the community' [*Avot* 2: 4], I went along. My friend, what words can describe it? That huge crowd, their exultation, and, even more, the happiness of Israel. Mighty gusts of freedom are shaking the very foundations ... And I—I uttered praise and thanks to the Almighty for having preserved us in life unto this day....

The sight of all that jubilation. The flags, so many different flags, each group with its own. And all of them shouting Peace, Brotherhood, Equality, Liberty, Freedom. The joy of the Russian army and, more, of the Russian folk, moved me profoundly. For their joy and their wonder are the most powerful testimony that God's own hand has accomplished this. His spirit has turned their hearts around and caused them to hate those they once loved—even, now, to glory in their downfall. That is the clearest sign for me that Israel's redemption is very near.[88]

In the days that followed R. Joshua Heschel continued to watch and wait. Another letter, written some weeks later, speaks in a similar mixture of disbelief and uncertainty, clouded by a vague sense of foreboding. The uncanny concurrence of this period with Passover, the Jewish 'festival of freedom', added shadows of hesitation and worry. The following letter is dated 25 Nisan 5577 (5 April 1917).[89]

Truly there is no Rock [*tsur*] like our Lord; there is no artist [*tsayar*] like Him. He creates one form within another—the strange, surreal visions of this illusory world of ours. The proud are demeaned, the humble elevated. One regime passes away and a new one arises; it shines on those who dwell in darkness; prisoners are suddenly freed

---

[87] *Yeshuah beḥiyuv velo bishelilah.* R. Joshua Heschel's contention here calls to mind terms that were made famous many decades later by Isaiah Berlin: 'negative freedom' is the mere absence of something (obstacles, barriers, constraints, interference), while 'positive freedom' means the presence of something (of control, self-mastery, self-determination, self-realization). See Berlin, 'Two Concepts of Liberty', 7–19.

[88] The February Revolution roused other prominent hasidic leaders to similar expressions of outspoken optimism, even to messianic hopes in the immanent future. Compare the real-time public statement issued by R. Shalom Dov Ber Shneersohn of Lubavitch, *Igerot kodesh ... admor moharshav* (New York, 1986), ii. 830–1.

[89] The following passage is densely inlaid with citations and literary allusions. These are the major ones: 'there is no Rock', after BT *Meg.* 14*a*; 'the proud are demeaned', from the morning prayers; 'prisoners are freed', Ps. 68: 7; 'the wolf will graze', after Isa. 11: 7; 'Israel, who strayed', after Hos. 4: 16; 'the lambs, bound together', from a *piyut* by Hakalir recited in Ashkenazi communities on the sabbath of Shekalim; 'while their young', Isa. 11: 7; 'never to be seen again', Exod. 14: 13.

from their chains. . . . Look, God has let us see it: the wolf will live with the lamb—Israel, who strayed like a wayward cow, now grazes with the savage wolf who used to hunt her mercilessly. And the lambs, bound together, walk arm in arm with panthers while their young mingle in harmony. And I gaze with wonder at the sight of our Jewish nation. They have been transformed overnight—slaves have become freemen. And so in amazement I proclaim: 'Truly there is no artist like our God!' . . .

Here is an insight I had—from my sermon this past Festival of Freedom. . . . It seems to me that the miracle of the parting of the sea—its whole purpose was to separate Israel from the Egyptians, irreversibly. For the flood of love that the Egyptians suddenly unleashed on Israel—the brotherhood and the equal rights that they impetuously offered—it was all meant to lure them into staying in Egypt and forgetting about the Land they had been promised. They would choose to assimilate amidst the Egyptians, to dwell in unity with them on the common foundations of democracy. And so God compelled them to pursue Israel into the sea, and then He made them drown in its waters, never to be seen again. Only thus could that democratic bond, that unnatural liaison between Egypt and Israel, be severed forever.

I beg you, my friend, understand what I am saying. Then you will realize why I am so deeply concerned about what's happening in this world of ours. Why, in these days of happiness and rejoicing, I continue to say, 'Please, God, save now!'

These passages seem to me exceptional in several ways. One, of course, is their animated personal voice—the uncommon voice of an early twentieth-century hasidic *rebbe* who was intellectually engaged with current events, and who cared about the lives of ordinary Jews. Another is the dynamic interplay of many genres: social and psychological observations, self-reflection, direct address, homiletics, and historical analysis, all of them woven together with subtly ironic intertextuality. This rich allusiveness, I suspect, is more than a literary flourish. R. Joshua Heschel's experience of reality is clearly mediated through the sacred texts of Jewish tradition. I'll return to that important aspect a bit later. For now, a third element needs to be noted: the dialogue that we overhear in these letters. R. Joshua Heschel is sharing his thoughts and impressions with an unnamed 'friend, an enlightened, astute, and distinguished writer from Kiev', who (as we can gather from other parts of his letter) ardently believed that the revolution heralded 'a future filled with light and hope'.[90] The dissonance between their readings of the map was apparently what incited R. Joshua Heschel to formulate his message. In other words, there is a covert dialectic at work in these passages. To appreciate the

[90] In his memoirs, R. Joshua Heschel cites part of this letter, and notes similar details; *Ḥayei yehoshua, 68*. It's unclear whether both letters were addressed to the same individual, as no name appears on the copies that R. Joshua Heschel made for his records.

undeclared challenge and the counter-view that he is presenting, we need to take a step back for a broader perspective.

The February Revolution brought three centuries of tsarist oppression to a dramatic and sudden end. It was celebrated nearly unanimously by all sectors of Russian society. For most of Russian Jewry, politically, socially, and religiously fractured though it was, 'the solution to the "Jewish question" appeared to be entwined with the success of the Russian revolution'.[91] R. Joshua Heschel's correspondent was in good company. Simon Dubnow, the preeminent Jewish historian of his generation, witnessed the revolution from his home in St Petersburg. His diary entry of 22 March 1917 reads: 'A remarkable day. Today the Provisional Government published its decision to remove all restrictions on nationalities and religion. In other words, it published its decision to *emancipate the Jews of Russia*. After forty years of fighting and suffering, my life's dream has come true. I still cannot actually comprehend the greatness of the moment.'[92] In a similar spirit, another memoirist recalled: 'In 1917, after the February Revolution, a ray of light of freedom penetrated our dark Jewish life. We believed that a new epoch of freedom for all people including Jews was coming.'[93] The popular sentiments of the times also resounded from a Yiddish Bund poster: 'There, where we live, there is our country! A democratic republic! Full political and national rights for Jews.'[94] In the spring of 1917 it seemed as if everything was possible.

R. Joshua Heschel echoes these bounding hopes for the future. Yet they are counterbalanced by a longer historical memory. To understand the larger message contained in these letters more fully, I'd like to note some critical insights by Yosef Hayim Yerushalmi on the relation between history and hope in Jewish consciousness—that is, 'the impact of ongoing historical events, and the ability to endure and overcome them, to see beyond them'.

Biblical religion endowed the Jews with a view of history that is hard to define. . . .

[91] Budnitskii, *Russian Jews*, 42.

[92] Ibid. 49. On Dubnow's changing stance Jonathan Frankel writes: 'He again remained unwaveringly loyal to the basic articles of his faith, to the liberal creed, to his humanist form of Jewish nationalism, to his belief in the ultimate salvation of mankind.' But Frankel notes: 'With the establishment of the Bolshevik dictatorship in October, and during the next four years, his diary entries expressed profound bitterness at the overthrow of the short experiment in liberty' ('S. M. Dubnov: Historian and Ideologist', 22–3).

[93] Cited by Veidlinger, *Jewish Public Culture in the Late Russian Empire*, 288.

[94] Yiddish poster, Kiev, *c.*1918 (YIVO Archives). It urges Jews to vote for the social democratic programme of the Bund in an election following the revolution. At that time, non-Bolshevik parties were still tolerated by the regime.

I cannot find an adequate term for it, and so, *faute de mieux*, I shall call it a midrash of history. It is as though history became a text, capable of interpretation through a hermeneutic that flowed naturally and unselfconsciously out of the fundamental premises of Israelite faith. History was imbued with supreme meaning, but that meaning was most often to be sought beneath its manifest surfaces.[95]

The passages we have been reading seem to offer just the sort of 'midrash' that Yerushalmi describes, set here in the historical context of the Russian revolution. Formative moments from the Jewish past—the Egyptian servitude and exodus, the parting of the sea, the covenant at Sinai, Haman and Esther—are evident paradigms for interpreting the near-miraculous events of the present. They also foreshadow what the future might bring. The intertextual fabric of these letters—densely woven with biblical verses, phrases from the daily prayers, the festival liturgy, the Passover Haggadah—written spontaneously in real time, testify to the central role of Jewish historical consciousness in understanding contemporary reality.

Against that backdrop, the dialectic at work here comes into sharper focus. For so many of R. Joshua Heschel's generation, the entry into modernity seemed to demand a break with the isolated world of uniquely Jewish identity, and a distancing from the heaviness of historical Jewish memories. Yet, as we noted earlier, recent scholarship has shown that these 'movements of departure' were informed by the spiritual and ethical ideals, religious language, and concepts of traditional Judaism, metamorphosed into secular form.[96] R. Joshua Heschel seems to have been keenly aware of this dynamic. When he portrays current events, the cultural bywords of the era with their secularized meanings—brotherhood, equal rights, freedom, democracy, peace, liberty—are a natural part of his rhetoric. But when he replants them, with deliberate anachronism, in the context of his *derashot*, the original, sacred dimensions of those bywords re-emerge. 'At Sinai God finally named them His holy nation. Then, at last, they won total liberty and absolute freedom. As the Rabbis taught: "Inscribed [*harut*] on the Tablets—freedom [*herut*] from the yoke of the nations".' That is a paradoxical and 'difficult freedom', to be

---

[95] Yerushalmi, 'Toward a History of Jewish Hope', 313.

[96] 'Movements of departure' is Pierre Birnbaum's phrase; *Geography of Hope*, 23. Cf. Yerushalmi: 'We will never appreciate the particular passion of the beginnings of modern Jewish assimilation and the struggle for emancipation without examining them as further metamorphoses of Jewish hope . . . Diametric opposites on so many levels, both nineteenth-century assimilation and Zionism intensely craved an end to Jewish exile, the latter by an actual return to Zion, the former by transforming the lands of exile into Zion.' 'Toward a History of Jewish Hope', 314.

sure.[97] Yet the Covenant—'freedom on the Tablets of stone'—is, in R. Joshua Heschel's eyes, the only hope for true, ultimate salvation 'in the positive sense'. Against it, the struggle to be free of the yoke of historical memory along with the 'yoke of the nations' carries a grave danger: the loss of a distinct Jewish identity and with it the very right to national existence.

The Bolshevik revolution that autumn, followed by massive waves of pogroms, bloody civil war, and chaos (1919–21), devastated Jewish life in the southern provinces of Russia.[98] Typhus, starvation, and renewed persecutions in the early post-revolutionary years of Soviet rule decimated the shattered Jewish communities that remained. In late summer 1923, beset with tragic personal losses, R. Joshua Heschel, his wife, their three surviving children, and four grandchildren left 'the valley of slaughter'.[99] They reached the shores of New York early in 1924, as the gates of immigration were closing. One of the first hasidic *rebbe*s of eastern Europe to resettle in the United States, he devoted his remaining years to American Jewry.

Deep Blue Sky and Yellow Stars: R. Moses Kahlenberg, *Yedei mosheh*

So long as the visible text of history was in conflict with its invisible subtext (and, except for a few intervals of ancient glory, this was always the case), Judaism regarded the latter as decisive. From such a perspective the triumphs of empires could be viewed as transient episodes, mundane victories a sign of error rather than truth, the degradation of Jewry a badge of honor, its suffering a mark of its chosenness. Only at one juncture is visible history decisive—the coming of the messiah and the manifest redemption of Israel and the world, for then the gap between visible and invisible will exist no more. . . . This midrash of history was always potentially available as a bulwark against the terror of history.[100]

Yosef Hayim Yerushalmi concludes his lecture with an admitted sense of malaise: 'But even if I have understood it correctly, it remains a generalization that cannot satisfy the historian within us. The task remains to see how this midrash functioned in specific historical contexts.' The following *derashah* was delivered in one of the twentieth century's darkest moments. It invites us

---

[97] Levinas, *Difficult Freedom*, 284.

[98] In Ukraine between 60,000 and 250,000 Jews were murdered and countless communities ravaged. See P. Kenez, 'Pogroms and White Ideology in the Russian Civil War', 293–313.

[99] Citing his poem 'The Day I Left Uman' (15 Elul 5683/1923), in *Erekh avot*, 36.

[100] Yerushalmi, 'Toward a History of Jewish Hope', 314.

to engage, partially at least, with the neglected history of Jewish hope that Yerushalmi envisioned.

R. Moses Kahlenberg (1882–1942) was born in the town of Skalat, eastern Galicia. His family was associated with the hasidic courts of Kopyczynce and Ruzhin. As a young man he served as community rabbi. When the First World War began and Russian forces advanced deep into Austrian Galicia and Bukovina (1914–15), masses of Jews were expelled or fled westwards. R. Moses, his wife Hayah Gittel, and their two young sons were among them. They found refuge in Budapest; five years later, forced to flee again, they resettled in Vienna. It was there that he became a follower of R. Israel of Husiatyn, the *admor* of Ruzhin. In 1928 R. Moses was invited to become a religious leader for the large émigré community that had gathered in Metz, northern France. It was composed of refugees from Russia, western Galicia, Poland, and Germany. In the course of the 1930s R. Moses gained acceptance in Metz, serving as both rabbi and *rebbe*. He and his family became naturalized French citizens.[101]

In mid-1940 there were some 330,000 Jews in France. Less than half of them were native French. The majority were foreigners: some had fled Nazi persecution during the 1930s; others were more recent arrivals, Jews seeking asylum from German-occupied Belgium, Luxembourg, and the Netherlands. With the German invasion of northern France in June 1940, many of these refugees, along with the resident Jews of Alsace-Lorraine, joined the mass exodus as some four million French citizens fled to south-western France. R. Moses, his wife, and his elderly father, R. Abraham Judah Leibush, found refuge for a short time in Bordeaux. Near the end of 1940 they were interned in the La Lande camp, which had been set up near Monts in the Indre-et-Loire district, north-central France. By October 1941 it had officially become a prison camp for Jewish 'aliens' and 'undesirables'—men, women, and many children. The largest number were from Poland; others were from Austria, France, Germany, Romania, Belgium, and Holland.[102]

---

[101] Sermons he delivered in those years were published in the volume *Darash mosheh* (Biłgoraj, 1935).

[102] In early 1941 La Lande functioned as a 'refugee camp' with a variety of internees, Jews and non-Jews. In late 1941 the camp was enclosed with barbed wire and the inmates became prisoners; most of the non-Jews were moved from the camp at that time. La Lande had been built to house 300 inhabitants; from 1940 to 1942 more than 500 Jews were interned there. For a detailed account of the camp based on archival sources, see Paisot-Beal, 'Le Camp de La Lande'. As foreign nationals, R. Moses and his wife may have been able to escape internment; their two sons survived the war in France's Free Zone. Contact between them was cut off at the end of 1941; when the parents were finally located in late summer 1942 it was too late to save

R. Moses spent twenty-one months in La Lande. During that time he gave public sermons. The original manuscript of nine of them—delivered in Yiddish, written out in Hebrew, and bound with a thread to other writings of his—was discovered in 2005 in the YIVO archives and published in Jerusalem.[103] The passage we will read is part of his last recorded *derashah*, given on 13 June 1942. Earlier that week the decree had been issued compelling Jews in France's occupied zone to wear the yellow star.[104] What followed were the blackest weeks in the history of modern France. Mass arrests of Jews of both foreign and French origin were carried out under Nazi order by French police forces, in collaboration with the Vichy Government. By the end of September, nearly 38,000 Jews had been deported from France to Auschwitz. Transports from La Lande to death camps in the east began on 19 July 1942. R. Moses, his wife, and his father were murdered at Auschwitz in September 1942.

The *derashah* bears the title, with its pointed double meaning, "'Israel, a Marked People—Israel, the Eminent Nation" [*yisra'el metsuyanim*]: A sermon for the *parashah* "Shelaḥ", the sabbath sanctifying the month of Tamuz 5702, in the prison La Lande. On the order to wear the green badge and the closure of the school'.[105]

them. See Schwarzfuchs, 'The Long Road from Metz to Auschwitz' (Heb.), 16; H. M. Kahlenberg, 'Divrei ḥayim', 39–40.

[103]   Esther Farbstein discovered the manuscript and published it in a two-part critical edition, which she entitled *Yedei mosheh*. The author himself had chosen this title for his collected manuscripts, as he attests in the summer of 1942: 'I name this scroll *Yedei mosheh* after my own name, after the verse "Moses' hands grew heavy and so they took a stone and put it under him" [Exod. 17: 12]—now, in the hour of Israel's distress, embattled with Amalek, for "God will be at war with Amalek for all generations" [Exod. 17: 16]. And I, too, am in deep distress, along with the entire Jewish people; my hands are heavy with suffering, my body broken with troubles [after BT *Ket.* 62a], but "seven eyes turn toward the stone" of Israel [after Zech. 3: 9]. So "Moses writes in tears" [after BT *BB* 15a], "for a remembrance in this book", yet "Moses' hands remained steady until sunset" [Exod. 17: 14].' See *Yedei mosheh*, 278–9. In addition to his *derashot*, Farbstein's volume contains R. Moses' introduction to the book of Lamentations, part of his supercommentary on Ibn Ezra's commentary on the book of Lamentations; an eyewitness account of the transport of Jews from La Lande to Drancy in July 1942, and some of his father's Torah novellae. The first section of the volume provides historical and biographical information and a substantial essay by Farbstein summarizing R. Moses Kahlenberg's activity and thought. An English version of that essay appears in 'Sermons Speak History'. To the best of my knowledge, those resources are the only scholarly treatment to date of R. Kahlenberg's oeuvre.

[104]   The order to wear a distinguishing mark was imposed on Jews in the occupied territories of Poland in November 1939. On 1 September 1941 the order was extended to all Jews in the German Reich (in the form of the yellow star), and on 7 June 1942 to the Jews of France.

[105]   *Yedei mosheh*, 209–28. R. Moses consistently refers to the yellow star as 'the green badge' (*ḥatelai hayarok*) or 'the green stain' (*haketem hayarok*). On the significance of this deliberate

They persecute us ceaselessly. Our letters are opened; 'outside, the sword bereaves' and more captives arrive here; 'within, there is dread' [Deut. 32: 25]—others are taken away and sent to even worse places. We know not what today will bring, and so 'each morning we say, if only it were night'—the night already past, for each day is worse than the ones before, without respite.[106]

Now, this week, another contemptible decree: Every Jew 5 years and older in occupied France must securely sew onto the outer garment, on the upper part against the heart, on the left side, a green badge in the shape of a Star of David, and on it the word *Juif* (which means Jew) is written. And this disgrace as well—we will bow our heads and accept the stain with love, as a mark of honour. Of course, we are told that there are good and intelligent people among the French who remain sympathetic to those bearing the green stain, who continue to speak words of kindness and encouragement.

But all that, he continues, is meagre comfort.[107] In the next part of his sermon, he searches for a deeper understanding of his generation's experience and its place in the larger course of Jewish history. Looking back at the past ten years of mounting Nazi persecution, flooding Europe with blood and suffering, he asks the timeless, anguished question: Why has this befallen us?[108] After some lines of moral stocktaking, he focuses on two developments in contemporary Jewish society. First: decades of assimilation, bringing many Jews to abandon the Torah and cast off all visible signs of Jewish identity. Their efforts proved to be futile. Animosity towards Jews has only intensified; modern virulent antisemitism makes it clear that no one can escape their Jewishness. The second movement is secular Zionism. R. Moses concentrates here on the political use of the 'Jewish star'. In centuries past, he contends, the six-pointed star meant something holy: it embodied the concept of absolute divine sovereignty over the world in all dimensions, spatial as well as metaphysical.[109] But now it has been profaned. Jewish nationalists use the Star of David to symbolize a programme in which God and religious tradition play no part. R. Moses'

misnomer, see below. The title of the *derashah* alludes to the Pesach Haggadah; he returns to this motif at the end of his sermon. R. Moses established the *talmud torah* (school) in La Lande himself; the thirty-some children who learned there were his pride and joy. Disputes among the school's (Jewish) authorities had led to its closure earlier that week, and this pained him greatly.

[106] An allusion to Deut. 28: 67; see also BT *Sot*. 49*a*.

[107] *Yedei mosheh*, 209–10. Here and in other *derashot* R. Moses comments with overt respect and censured irony on relations between the French and the Jews interned in La Lande. On the complexity and diversity of reactions to Jewish persecution in French society in those years, see Zuccotti, *The Holocaust, the French, and the Jews*.   [108] After Esther 4: 5.

[109] His contention is based on kabbalistic symbolism related to the number six; cf. Halevi, *Kuzari* 4: 25, in reference to *Sefer yetsirah*.

voice in this section is that of a traditional preacher. Social commentary alter-
nates with an urgent call to conscience and acceptance of collective responsibility. But instead of unity and mutual support, petty disputes are fracturing
the La Lande community.[110] A shift in register, and R. Moses segues to the
final part of the *derashah*:

This brings us back to the Torah reading of this week, to the section concerning the
tsitsit. It is written: ['They shall make for themselves fringes on the corners of their
garments, throughout their generations, and they shall affix a thread of *tekhelet* (blue)
on the fringe of each corner. This shall be *tsitsit* (fringes) for you], and you will see
it and you will remember all of God's commandments and perform them' [Num.
15: 38–9]. The Rabbis commented: 'For *tekhelet* resembles the sea and the sea resembles the sky, and the heavens resemble the throne of divine glory' [BT *Sot.* 17a].
But really, what is the need for all those comparisons? Why not simply say 'Raise your
eyes on high [and see who created these things]' [Isa. 40: 26]—isn't that enough to
bring any thinking person to remember the throne of glory? But just as the heavens
are God's handiwork, so God desires the work of our hands: the deeds that we perform to serve Him. And so the commandment is to make the *tsitsit* with a thread of
tekhelet like the heavens, that it should arouse us to action. This is His holy will. Thus
Scripture emphasizes, 'and you will see it'—the sky-coloured thread—'and you will
remember all of God's commandments and perform them', in the most literal sense.
The verse continues [Num. 15: 40]: 'You shall not wander after your hearts'—off into
emptiness, like those who say: We are Jews at heart and that's enough; 'and after your
eyes that would lead you astray'—yet they declare: What we see is all there is. But in
truth, 'their eyes have been plastered over' [Isa. 44: 18] and they have wandered very,
very far away. Indeed, to our sorrow, many of our fellow Jews have abandoned the precept of *tsitsit*, along with all the other commandments. For some, it is out of shame.
To wear the fringes would humiliate them, for then they would be recognized as Jews.
And so, measure for measure, the green badge has been imposed on us all. It is to be
affixed to our outer garment: 'to learn, to teach, and to comprehend'[111] that, indeed,
Jews we are. We stood, all of us, at Sinai, and there we received the Torah, to guard it
and to uphold it. . . .

Now we are about to bless the fourth month [Tamuz]. Zechariah the prophet
heaped words of consolation upon Israel, assuring them that in time to come, all their
days of mourning and fasting would become festivals of joy and gladness.[112] . . . And
so we read in the Torah portion that, after so much chastisement and suffering, the
Holy blessed One promised that they would enter the Land. The book *Benei yisaskhar*
offers proof that all this is so. The divine Name in the permutation that corresponds
with the month of Tamuz is found in the final letters of the verse 'All this is worth

---

110   *Yedei mosheh*, 210–23.   111   Reference to Mishnah *Avot* 4: 22.
112   See Zech. 8: 18–23.

nothing to me' [Esther 5: 13].[113] These words were uttered by the evil Haman in an hour of terrible darkness; the Face was utterly hidden. But the book of Esther was divinely inspired, and it was written down after God had reversed everything for the good. 'Then the Jews had light and gladness, joy and honour'—and so it will be for all time. 'Those days of Purim can never be taken from the Jews, and their seed will remember them always.'[114] So we hope, as in the days of our exodus from Egypt, that God will show us miracles. And just as, in the days of our freedom, we sit with our children and recount through the night how we were redeemed, the story 'begins with disgrace but ends with glory'. '"There they became a nation"—it teaches that in Egypt, Israel was distinguished.'[115] Indeed, so are we today: set apart, marked—we, the eminent Jewish people. But so, too, may we celebrate our ultimate liberation, soon and with great joy. In gladness and song we will tell of the days of our exile and oppression, of the green badge that distinguished us. We will raise a banner towards Zion, singing a new song. May it come speedily and in our days.[116]

What is R. Moses saying in this *derashah* and what is he doing in a hermeneutical sense? His overt message seems clear enough; it is set out directly in the middle part of his sermon, in the section I have paraphrased above. 'Measure for measure' causality links the misjudgements of Jewish assimilationists and secular Zionists to the Nazi order, just now issued, compelling the Jews of France to wear the yellow star. In R. Moses' religious world-view the true purpose of the decree is to rouse Jews to self-awareness and to take up their Jewishness with dignity. That message, Esther Farbstein notes, resembles one that was voiced by Robert Weltsch nearly a decade earlier. First of all we need to consider Weltsch's famous polemic more closely. This will help us catch sight of other facets of meaning that R. Moses has planted between the lines of his *derashah*.

Boycott Day, 1 April 1933, marked the official beginning of the Nazi party's nationwide campaign of aggression against German Jews. Weltsch, then editor-in-chief of *Jüdische Rundschau*, one of the most widely read inter-war publications in the Jewish world, reacted in a highly influential article entitled 'Tragt ihn mit Stolz, den gelben Fleck!' (translated literally: 'Bear it with pride, the yellow stain!'):

1 April 1933 can become a day of Jewish awakening and Jewish rebirth. *If the Jews wish it.* If the Jews are ready and have greatness in them. If the Jews are *not* as their opponents portray them to be. Jewry, under attack, must come to acknowledge itself. . . .

---

[113] *Benei yisaskhar* was composed by R. Tsevi Elimelekh Shapira of Dinov. On his meaning here, see below.

[114] Esther 8: 16; 9: 28.   [115] Citing the Pesach Haggadah.   [116] *Yedei mosheh*, 223–7.

Today they accuse us of having betrayed the German people; the National Socialist press calls us the 'enemy of the nation' and we can do nothing about it. It is not true that the Jews have betrayed Germany. If they have betrayed anyone it is themselves, the Jews. Because the Jew did not show his Judaism with pride, because he tried to avoid the Jewish question, he must share the blame for the degradation of the Jews. . . . The boycott leadership gave orders that placards 'with a yellow stain on a black background' were to be pasted on the boycotted shops—this is a powerful symbol. The order is meant to be a branding, a sign of contempt. We will take it up and make of it a mark of honour. . . . We remember all those who for five thousand years have been called Jews, who were stigmatized as Jews. Now we have been reminded that we, too, are Jews. 'Yes,' we say. We shall bear it with pride.[117]

By the time Hitler rose to power, Weltsch had become 'one of the most important and articulate interpreters of the situation of German Jewry'. In the early years of the Nazi regime, the *Jüdische Rundschau* under his leadership aimed to encourage Jews facing exclusion and terror. Yet his criticism was harsh towards those who continued to deny the existence of a 'Jewish question' and clung to their hope for integration into German society, unrecognized as Jews.[118] In this article Weltsch summons his readers to wake up to a harsh new and inescapable reality.

The central image in his message is the ambivalent symbol of the 'Jewish star'. Emblazoned (according to popular tradition) on the Shield of David, the star embodies dignity, might, justice, sovereignty. But throughout the lachrymose history of Jewish suffering, the star and other symbols were inflicted as a mark of shame, a humiliating brand. Significantly, Weltsch refers to the star as the yellow stain or patch (*Fleck*). A weighty cultural emblem, it bears a visceral meaning of which his modern European reading audience may have been only subconsciously aware. Historians have shown that the badge, in the shape of a yellow star, soon to become crucial to the 'visual politics of genocide', was a well-researched Nazi invention. It combined two potent elements. Yellow, the stigmatic colour of antisemitism since the Christian Middle Ages,

---

[117] *Jüdische Rundschau*, 27 (4 Apr. 1933). Later published in Weltsch, *An der Wende des modernen Judentums*, 21–5. Weltsch (1891–1984) was born in Prague. Shortly after the First World War, Zionist leaders in Germany invited him to Berlin to serve as editor-in-chief of *Jüdische Rundschau*, the official journal of the Zionist Federation of Germany. The title (usually translated as 'Wear it with pride, the yellow star'), as Hannah Arendt notes, became 'the most popular slogan of those years' and keenly 'expressed the general emotional atmosphere' of the times; *Eichmann in Jerusalem*, 53–4. The Nazis actually forced Jews to wear a yellow badge only six years later. As for the standard translation of the title, note that the word Weltsch uses is not 'star' (*Stern*) but *Fleck*—a stain, splotch, blob, blotch, blemish. On this, see below.

[118] See Wiese, 'No "Love of the Jewish People"?'

was joined with the Star of David. First proposed in 1897 as the emblem of the worldwide Zionist community, by the 1930s the six-pointed star had become the primary symbol of the Jewish nation.[119] The Nazis sought to pervert that chosen, positive emblem. It was to be a 'badge of infamy' (*Shandesfleck*) of 'Jew-yellow colour' (*von judengelber Farbe*).[120]

The stunning rediscovery of the medieval yellow brand of shame in enlightened Europe, more than a full century after Jewish political emancipation, was a rude awakening. Weltsch read it as a timely call to conscience. German Jewry was being summoned to undertake a radical inversion of values —from universalism to particularism—and a concurrent emotional turnaround, transforming a new sense of shame to pride. To bear the 'stigma' of Jewishness with dignity meant that Jews had willingly to recognize and reaffirm their own national and cultural Jewish identity.

In 1933 that was a courageous gesture of empowerment. Nine long years later, however, all who wore the yellow star were literally marked for death. Weltsch, for his part, had 'very soon realized that the German Jews were faced with a merciless enemy, and the chasm between the liberal cultural nationalism of the Zionists and the criminal Nazi regime could not be bridged'. In 1943, now in Palestine, he wrote a letter to the Hebrew newspaper *Ha'arets* saying that 'he would no longer call upon Jews to wear the yellow badge with pride—it had become a stigma that "reveals its wearer as prey for unbounded martyrdom"'.[121] But if so, we are confronted with a troubling question: What is R. Moses Kahlenberg saying to his own listeners? How are these fugitives from the German Reich, imprisoned now in Nazi-occupied France with no way out, meant to 'wear it with pride'? Moreover, if indeed this is his whole message, it comes across cogently enough in the middle part of his sermon. What need is there for the long, final section of the *derashah* with its dense intertextuality and exegetical moves? All this compels us to think more deeply about what R. Moses is doing in this sermon beyond or behind what he is explicitly saying.

[119] See Kisch, 'The Yellow Badge in History'. Sabine Doran, in a comprehensive and insightful study, traces the long history of yellow stigmatization and explores the multiple roles played by that colour in late nineteenth- and twentieth-century American and European culture. She devotes an important chapter to 'Yellow Stars and the Visual Politics of Genocide'. On the Nazi use of the Star of David, Doran notes that the Nazis showed 'a heightened interest in the symbolism of the star and its black magic, which since medieval times was associated with Jews'. *The Culture of Yellow*, 160.

[120] Phrases used by Nazi speakers and documents; see Friedman, 'The Jewish Badge and the Yellow Star in the Nazi Era', 12, 24–6.   [121] Wiese, 'No "Love of the Jewish People"?', 400–1.

His opening lines offer the first hint that there is an unspoken subtext at work here: 'Now, this week, another contemptible decree: Every Jew 5 years and older in occupied France must securely sew onto the outer garment, on the upper part against the heart, on the left side, a green badge in the shape of a Star of David, and on it the word *Juif* (which means Jew) is written.' R. Moses' listeners may not have been fluent in French. But they surely knew all too well about the star, its yellowness, and Nazi regulations concerning it. This opening, then, must be seen as a calculated rhetorical move. It recalls another sardonic first encounter with the Jewish badge, staged in Jiří Weil's novel *Life with a Star*, set in Nazi-occupied Prague:

They gave me a star. It's not at all nice and there's something special about it. It doesn't shine at night, only in the daytime. . . . And it must be worn precisely over the heart. . . . I went home and stitched down the tips of the star with a needle and thread. There were six tips and a word on the star, all contorted and twisted, in a foreign language that seemed to make a face at me.[122]

Like Weil, R. Moses refers to the badge in ironic echo of the Nazi regulations. This is a covert gesture of defiance: the victim wilfully recasts himself as detached observer, empowered now to examine things from the outside. More fundamentally, these words signal the overall project of revision that his *derashah* proposes. In the opening lines, he appears to be citing the infamous Order no. 8, issued by the SS on 7 June 1942 and plastered on the walls of La Lande and the rest of occupied France.[123] Looking more closely, however, we realize that he subverts its language and imagery. And so, instead of the phrase in the Nazi decree specifying 'Jews from the age of 6', he uses the biblical phrase that defines human valuations, 'every Jew 5 years and older' (Lev. 27: 5). The sign of Jewishness, on his retelling, is to be 'placed on the upper part against the heart, on the left side'—citing the words used by Maimonides to denote the place where the arm phylactery is to be bound.[124] But most incongruous, of course, is his insistence, from these first lines and to the end of the *derashah*, that the yellow star is green. It is this manifest counter-image—'the green patch' (*hatelai hayarok*) or 'the green stain' (*haketem hayarok*) as he names it—that will concern us now. To understand it more fully we need to listen

---

[122] *Life with a Star*, 64–8.

[123] Order 8, section 1 read: 'Il est interdit aux Juifs dès de l'âge de six ans révolus, de paraître en public sans porter l'étoile juive. L'étoile juive est une étoile a six pointes . . . Elle est en tissu jaune et porte, en caractères noirs, l'inscription "Juif". Elle devra être portée bien visiblement sur le côté gauche de la poitrine, solidement cousue sur le vêtement.' Cited in Poliakov, *L'Étoile jaune*, 40–1.   [124] *Mishneh torah*, 'Hilkhot tefilin', 4: 2.

closely to R. Moses' dialogue with many centuries of Jewish exegetical tradition—a dialogue that took place through memory alone, as he had no holy books with him in La Lande. It is these voices from the past that enable him to respond to the wholly unforeseen exigencies of the present.

The immediate present is 13 June 1942. On the Hebrew calendar it is the sabbath preceding the biblical 'fourth month' of Tamuz. In Jewish historical consciousness the year's darkest period of mourning begins in Tamuz. It is a stretch of time haunted by failings and national tragedy.[125] R. Moses' comment in the last section of the *derashah*, 'Now we are about to bless the fourth month', surely touches that nerve. It is a painful reminder to his audience of their own grim reality—inflicted now with the yellow stigma, weighted with the spectre of sins ancient and modern. But beneath the all too 'visible text of history', he quickly reminds his listeners, there is an 'invisible subtext'. Another, brighter vision is also associated with the fourth month: 'Zechariah the prophet heaped words of consolation upon Israel, assuring them that in time to come, all their days of mourning and fasting would become festivals of joy and gladness.' To bring his point home, R. Moses gestures towards a source that, against all logic, contains the tension between these two poles. It is a passage written by R. Tsevi Elimelekh Shapira of Dinov, a prominent leader of Galician and Hungarian hasidism (1785–1841). His classic work *Benei yisaskhar* is structured on a constellation of Lurianic teachings concerning the unique qualities of each Hebrew month. R. Moses uses an insight from *Benei yisaskhar* regarding the connection between Tamuz and Purim to discern a deeper stratum of meaning concealed in his own contemporary reality.[126] Here, indeed, is an innovative 'midrash of history' that demands a closer reading. Let us look again at his words:

The divine Name in the permutation that corresponds with the month of Tamuz is found in the final letters of the verse 'All this is worth nothing to me' [Esther 5: 13]. Those words were uttered by the evil Haman in an hour of terrible darkness; the Face was utterly hidden. But the book of Esther was divinely inspired and it was written

---

[125] Many catastrophes are associated with the month of Tamuz, among them the sin of the Golden Calf; in its aftermath, the breaking of the Tablets of the Law; the sieges on Jerusalem that ultimately lead to the destruction of the Temple, and the exile of the Jewish people to Babylonia.

[126] The passage to which he alludes appears in *Benei yisaskhar*, i. 150. The work is unusual both in its structure and in the resources on which it draws. Its organizing principle is the Jewish calendar, with each Hebrew month treated in turn. The author integrates a wide range of midrashic and kabbalistic lore, including the permutation of the divine Name that is linked, in Lurianic teaching, to each month.

down after God had reversed everything for the good. 'Then the Jews had light and gladness, joy and honour'—and so it will be for all time.

The association between the month of Tamuz and Purim is not chronological (the events of Purim did not occur then) but metaphysical. Both are times of harsh judgement (*din*), R. Tsevi Elimelekh notes, when God's compassionate involvement in the world ('the Face') seems to have faded into oblivion. In the Purim story Haman rises to greatness; the entire land trembles before him. Yet insatiable hatred drives him to plot the total extermination of the Jewish people: 'All this means nothing to me so long as I see Mordecai the Jew sitting at the king's gate' (Esther 5: 13). That phrase marks a nadir of hiddenness and absence. But the same biblical verse, R. Isaac Luria taught, contains a chilling paradox. Encrypted in the words mouthed by the embodiment of evil is God's holy name, written 'absolutely backwards'.[127]

For Jewish refugees in occupied France, June 1942 was that hour of terrible darkness and divine concealment. To face it, R. Moses proposes a wilful act of reinterpretation. It is an attempt, inspired by the kabbalistic and hasidic sources he cites, to read, see, and understand otherwise. Doing so might somehow enable him and his listeners to contain the terrible contradiction between the visible (the ruthless persecution of the Jewish people) and the invisible (the divine covenant, the truth of chosenness, the eternal promise of redemption). The yellow star—that is, the 'green patch' or 'green stain'—is the locus of that vital shift in perception and sensibility.

Two thematic elements, both of them rooted in Jewish exegetical tradition, underlie the radical counter-narrative that R. Moses proposes. First, as noted above, in German (as in Yiddish) the Jewish badge was called *Fleck*; in Hebrew, the word for stain or spot is *ketem*. R. Moses uses that word many times to refer to the star. In the consciousness of a learned Jew—which he and at least some of his listeners surely were—stains and spots (*ketamim*) belong to a clearly defined domain: the laws of ritual purity related to menstruation and childbirth. This halakhic subtext is a powerful silent presence in the *derashah* and offers a crucial key to unlocking its meaning. I will try to explain. In the Mishnah, the rabbis distinguish between pure and impure bodily discharges and name five basic colours to classify them. But colours, as we know, are socially defined; their meanings and connotations shift over time. And so later Torah scholars debated the precise meaning of the colours discussed in the

---

[127] 'All this is worth nothing to me'—לי שווה איננו זה וכל. Read in reverse order (from the last word of the phrase to the first) the final letters form the Tetragrammaton in its primary permutation—YHVH.

Mishnah. In the Talmud and among the *rishonim* (early medieval authorities) a more detailed taxonomy developed as the chromatic sphere concerning discharges was filled with hues and nuances. What is relevant for our purposes are three shades called 'green' that the rabbis distinguished in reference to spots and stains: yellowish-golden green, leek green, and azure-blue green. They determined that stains of a yellow-gold shade are tinged with red blood and are thus ritually impure. But if the spot is green like a plant (*yarok kekarti*) or a bluish-green (*yarok ketekhelet*), the rabbis deem it pure.[128]

Refracted back on the subject at hand, what I'm getting at is this. In the Nazis' war against the Jews the yellow star was inflicted to demean its wearers and mark them for violence. By transplanting the badge into the sacred context of Jewish ritual law, R. Moses effectively transforms it. Reading with that wholly other cultural lexicon, a very different self-image can emerge. Once the yellow star has been reconceived as 'the green stain', its degrading symbolism is inverted. Look at it again. It is not a 'yellow stain'; the badge is green. The 'spot' is pure and so are those who bear it. Pure, without shame, worthy of being redeemed.

The second element that re-envisions the star is planted in the weekly Torah reading, *parashat* 'Shelaḥ'. Throughout his *derashah* R. Moses returns, from a variety of directions, to one of its central topics, the *tsitsit*. This is the relevant biblical section:

> They shall make for themselves fringes on the corners of their garments throughout their generations, and they shall affix a thread of *tekhelet* on the fringe of each corner. This shall be *tsitsit* [fringes] for you, and you will see it and you will remember all of God's commandments and perform them, and not wander after you heart and after your eyes, after which you stray. So that you may remember and perform all My commandments and be holy to your God. I am the Lord, your God, who has taken you out of the land of Egypt to be a God unto you; I am the Lord, your God. (Num. 15: 38–41)

This passage was made part of the liturgy—the final section of the Shema prayer recited every day, morning and evening. It sets out a compound and vital religious obligation: to remember (the Exodus, Sinai, the Torah), to recognize the eternal, supernal truth that those elements represent, to remain loyal to them always, and to do so actively. But because humans find it impossible to imagine the Absolute, these verses specify the concrete object that offers an alternative mode of access to infinity. 'They shall make for them-

---

[128] The talmudic discussion stems from the biblical verse Deut. 17: 8. Cf. Mishnah *Nid.* 2: 6; BT *Nid.* 19*a*–*b*; BT *San.* 87*b*; *Shulḥan arukh*, 'Yoreh de'ah', 188: 1.

selves fringes . . . and affix a thread of *tekhelet* . . . and you will see it . . . and remember.' The tangible element in this chain of actions, the 'thread of *tekhelet*', is what enables that metaphorical movement from the visible to the invisible, divine realm.[129] As the Rabbis put it, 'For *tekhelet* resembles the sea and the sea resembles the sky, and the heavens resemble the throne of divine glory.' R. Moses stresses that at issue here is not only an abstract article of faith; these verses prescribe positive action: 'God desires the work of our hands.' The *tsitsit*, with the thread of *tekhelet*, are meant to be a metonymy for all of the commandments; their role is to rouse Jews to action, to live their identity outwardly, with confidence—'This is His holy will.'

Up to now, admittedly, there is nothing very innovative about R. Moses' reading. But the 'thread of *tekhelet*' among the fringes—what colour is it really? Reasonably enough, *tekhelet* is most often associated with colours in the spectral field of blue—more specifically, a dense and deep shade of blue like sapphire, azure, ultramarine, or perhaps indigo.[130] Jewish exegetical tradition comprehends those shades and one more. Rashi, the foremost medieval commentator, on the 'thread of *tekhelet*'—and, in fact, in every relevant instance in biblical and rabbinic sources where the word appears—says that *tekhelet* means 'green'.[131] We won't quibble with Rashi just now about what the sky over eleventh-century Troyes really looked like. What matters is how the notion of *tekhelet* as green plays into R. Moses' hand—how he reads it back into the biblical verses, and then uses them to reconceive the star and everything it represents:

Indeed, to our sorrow, many of our fellow Jews have abandoned the precept of *tsitsit*, along with all the other commandments. For some, it is out of shame. To wear the fringes would humiliate them, for then they would be recognized as Jews. And so, measure for measure, the green badge has been imposed on us all. It is to be affixed to our outer garment: 'to learn, to teach and to comprehend' that, indeed, Jews we are. We stood, all of us, at Sinai, and there we received the Torah, to guard it and to uphold it.

---

[129] B. Dov Hercenberg presents this idea masterfully in his essay 'La Transcendance du regard'.

[130] On changing historical conceptions regarding colours in general and blue in particular, with some insightful paragraphs on *tekhelet*, see Pastoureau, *Blue: The History of a Color*.

[131] See Rashi on Exod. 25: 4; Rashi on BT *Ber.* 9*b*, 57*b*; *Git.* 31*b*; *Sot.* 17*a*; *Ḥul.* 89*a*. A likely basis for his reading is the variant chain of associations in JT *Ber.* 1: 2 and textual parallels: '*Tekhelet* resembles the sea, and the sea resembles vegetation and vegetation resembles the sky'. We saw this association between *tekhelet* and a shade of green above in the context of spots and

In other words, the 'green badge' takes on the role of the *tsitsit*: 'And you will see it and you will remember all of God's commandments and perform them'. Like the thread of *tekhelet*, now the star as well can engender the vital act of seeing and remembering that 'indeed, Jews we are'—bound by the Covenant, connected to God. Here, to be sure, is a bold and radical moment of reappropriation, a positive reclaiming of Jewish identity. Now it will be self-determined rather than inflicted by an inimical Other. The title of the sermon, 'Israel, a Marked People' or 'Israel, the Eminent Nation' (*yisra'el metsuyanim*), reiterated in its last lines, sets this in high relief. How should it be read? Branded, stigmatized, shamed? Or distinguished, chosen, worthy of being redeemed? Pure or impure, green or yellow? In the course of this *derashah* R. Moses shows his listeners a way to transform their own reality—if not outwardly then inwardly, through a far-reaching, symbolic act of reinterpretation.[132] And so the deadly stigma of the yellow star can be subversively transmuted to a sign of resistance and the beginning of hope.

The *derashah* ends with many phrases of comfort. They echo the stock tone of rabbinic sermonizing through the ages: '"There [in Egypt] they became a nation" . . . And so, too, may we celebrate our ultimate liberation, soon and with great joy. In gladness and song, we will tell of the days of our exile and oppression, of the green badge that distinguished us.' Truthfully, though, in the grim circumstances of La Lande in the summer of 1942, what comfort could those unremarkable words of 'hope in the future' possibly bear? It is unlikely that R. Moses was trying to convey any prophetic sense of optimism about an imminent positive outcome for himself and his listeners. Nor does he seem to understand this moment of re-envisioning the yellow badge as something powerful enough to affect historical reality in any objective sense.[133] Most likely, his purpose was more modest and down to earth. As a religious leader and a man deeply in touch with the suffering of the Jewish people, he

---

stains. Later commentators continued to debate the link between *tekhelet* and green in a variety of contexts; see Tosafot, *Suk.* 31*b*; Ritva on BT *Ḥul.* 89*a*.

[132] On the widely documented reaction 'Wear it with pride, the yellow badge', Phillip Friedman, a pioneering American scholar of the Holocaust, remarked: 'Historically, there is nothing surprising in this story. Jewish history knows of many instances where the wisdom of the Jewish people transformed originally vicious devices, intended for social degradation and humiliation (the Jewish hat, the special Jewish garb, and so forth), into sanctified institutions, helping to maintain and protect Jewish identity and Jewish traditions' (*Roads to Destruction*, 24–5).

[133] Compare reactions discussed by Greenberg, 'Hasidic Thought and the Holocaust'. My focus here, in contrast, is on the hermeneutical aspects of this *derashah*; the change that R. Moses envisions is on the cognitive and psychological level.

clearly hoped to rouse his audience to a spiritual accounting, to bring about a return and repair on the most basic level of religious identity. In his redemptive reading, the 'green badge' invites those who hear him to make themselves part of the 'community of fate' as well as of hope, reunited by the invisible subtext of sacred history.

Song of Dust and Ashes: R. Kalonymus Kalman Shapira of Piaseczno, *Esh kodesh*

The last figure in this chapter is R. Kalonymus Kalman Shapira (1888–1943), the Rebbe of Piaseczno. His ancestry stemmed from two hasidic dynasties: on his father's side, from R. Elimelekh of Lizhensk, the Magid of Kozniece, and R. Hayim Meir Yehiel Shapira, 'the Seraph of Mogielnica'; forebears on his mother's side include R. Jacob Isaac, the Seer of Lublin, and R. Kalonymus Kalman Halevi of Kraków, author of *Ma'or vashemesh*, his maternal grandfather, after whom he was named. His father, R. Elimelekh of Grodzisk Mazowiecki, an important hasidic leader in nineteenth-century Poland, died while he was still a child. R. Kalonymus knew him only from his writings, which he cites often and with reverence.[134] He was raised by his mother, Hannah Berakhah, while R. Yerahmiel Moses Hapstein of Kozienice, a cousin who later became his father-in-law, took charge of his education. At the age of 24 he inherited the role of *admor* and then of community rabbi in Piaseczno, a town just south of Warsaw. Some years later he was appointed head of the rabbinical court there. A gifted author, he composed three books of religious guidance, collections of *derashot* which he recorded himself in Hebrew, and a spiritual diary.[135] The uncommon rhetorical force of his writing, along with rare dimensions of self-reflexivity, make the Piaseczner Rebbe's works an extraordinary testimony to hasidic life in Poland, seen from

---

[134] *Divrei elimelekh* (Warsaw, 1890); *Imrei elimelekh* (Warsaw, 1876).

[135] For an extensive biographical sketch see Polen, *The Holy Fire*, 1–6. All of R. Kalonymus' works were written in Hebrew. The only one published in his lifetime was *Hovat hatalmidim* (Warsaw, 1932), directed to hasidic young men; another work, a pamphlet entitled *Benei mahshavah tovah*, was circulated (in only six copies) among an inner circle in the early 1920s. Three other works composed in the 1920s and 1930s remained in manuscript: *Hakhsharat ha'avrekhim*, *Mevo hashe'arim*, and the Rebbe's spiritual diary entitled *Tsav veziruz*. They were discovered in the early 1950s in the ruins of the Warsaw ghetto and published in Israel. The Rebbe's sermons from the 1920s and 1930s were preserved in copies made by a scribe. Those sermons, together with other material related to the Rebbe from disciples who had survived the Holocaust, were published in two volumes: *Derekh hamelekh* (Tel Aviv, 1976); *Derekh hamelekh*, ii (Jerusalem, 1992). On the Rebbe's ghetto sermons, see below.

the inside in an era of profound crisis. We will begin with a look at his inter-war activity and then read one sermon that he composed in the Warsaw ghetto, set in the broader context of his life's work.

The Great War—'the catastrophe that hit Europe between 1914 and 1918, as well as the revolutions, civil wars, and new nationalisms that came in its wake, shattered the world of the nineteenth century and ushered in moment-ous ideological, cultural, and social changes that would shape the interwar period and beyond'.[136] Mass expulsions, flight, and exile led millions of east European Jews to become homeless refugees. The traumas of war casualties, relocation, poverty, and antisemitic violence took their psychic toll. The fol-lowing passage, an entry in R. Kalonymus' diary, reflects his sense of Jewish experience in interwar Poland. It was written in the late 1920s in response to a current wave of suicides in the Jewish community.

Mourn—but not only for those who have done away with their lives. Weep bitterly for the walking dead. . . . They haven't killed themselves, yet they are dead all the same. Life is cheap. To be or not to be, it makes no difference any more. In former times, the evil inclination had to make an effort to bring a person to apostasy, to lose faith in God—it wasn't easy and he didn't always manage. But now, I look around and I see people . . . whose selfhood [*ha'anokhi*] has become worthless to them. Live or die, heaven or hell—for whom? Only for their pitiful selves—what an utterly miserable and meaningless thing to care about. 'So it happened, along the way'—he froze your soul, chilled your whole being.[137]

Cutting psychological observation informs these lines. Later, amidst the growing horror and trauma of life in the Warsaw ghetto, R. Kalonymus would express deep concern for the 'walking dead'—victims of what Polen calls 'psychic disintegration' and Seeman 'depersonalization', taking place by then on a massive scale. Here, he names the agent that sets the process in motion as the 'evil inclination', personified (by allusion) in the figure of Amalek. R. Kalonymus gestures towards the biblical verse that, together with its midrashic gloss, tells the whole story: 'So it happened, along the way, he struck you . . . when you were faint and weary, and did not fear God' (Deut. 25: 18). 'So it happened' (*korkha*), the Rabbis comment, hints at a deeper mean-ing. Read otherwise it says: 'he froze you'. Translated into emotional terms, 'he froze your soul, chilled your whole being' refers to an immobilizing inner

---

[136] Wodziński, 'War and Religion', 283.

[137] *Tsav veziruz*, 16–17, s. 25. A marginal note there links the wave of suicides to an economic crisis in the Jewish community between 1926 and 1928..

coldness, detachment, indifference, loss of feeling.[138] As we will see, 'cold' as a metaphor of spiritual deadness figures prominently in the work of emotion that R. Kalonymus taught.

Equally alarming in his eyes was the rapid corrosion of the old hasidic world of faith. Marcin Wodziński outlines some major historical factors at work, from 1914 and throughout the interwar years: 'The destruction of courts and *shtiblekh* and the deaths of tsaddikim shook the very foundations of Hasidic socio-religious life and dealt an incomparably heavy blow to the functioning of the tightly knit Hasidic communities. With no access to the tsaddik, with no place for prayer and daily gatherings, Hasidism lost much of its essential experience for many.' The dislocation and migration of huge populations, rapid urbanization, poverty, revolution, and intellectual change also made their mark.[139] With vivid literary realism, R. Kalonymus sketches the portrait of a contemporary middle-aged hasid. His children have abandoned him, lured away by secular politics and the uncensored freedom that modernity promised:

The father sees it all. His heart shrivels, his mind is exhausted; all his lofty spirituality deflates, sadness overwhelms him. At first he is furious, then bitter; his life is utterly loathsome. But after a while he gets used to having fallen so low . . . a man with no more aspirations, empty even of longing for something better. Maybe, from the pit of despair, in a fleeting moment he recalls his former self. The thought crosses his mind: I'll travel to my *rebbe*, I'll spend the holy sabbath there with him. More weeks go by; worries and burdens beyond number keep him from it. At last he sets out—but when? Late on Friday, almost nightfall, and then straightaway afterwards he will have to rush off, back to cook some more in the hell of his torments. . . . Now, what is it like for him there, with the *rebbe* during Shabbos? . . . The *rebbe* is 'saying Torah'. Preoccupied, drowsy, he nods off, or maybe not; he just cannot concentrate . . . can't grasp what his *rebbe* is talking about. Broken words clatter about in his head like potsherds—*ḥasidus*, sublime awe, inferior awe, love, purifying and repairing the self, feelings, *sefirot*— and all of it just agitates him even more. Shabbos is going by and he feels so totally distant—what does hasidism and serving God have to do with him? And he wonders how the *rebbe* can still expect so much of us, such piety and devotion. Then Shabbos is over. He races to deliver the *pitka* with his requests to the *rebbe*, to pour out his troubled, shattered soul, bowed to breaking under his load of troubles, and scurries away. Later, on the journey or back at home, darker thoughts confuse him, thoughts

[138] See *Tanḥuma*, 'Ki tetse', 13; Rashi on Deut. 25: 18.

[139] Wodziński, 'War and Religion', 297–311. The Piaseczner Rebbe addressed many of these issues in a public speech delivered before a meeting of Orthodox leaders that took place in Warsaw in the early 1920s. It was published in *Derekh hamelekh*, ii. 418–20.

bordering on heresy. Perhaps they only come from time to time but, to our sorrow, such thoughts do haunt him. Because he has fallen so low and grown so alienated from hasidism, the journey has left him unmoved. And so he broods: What good did the *rebbe* do me at all? . . . Once, the *tsadikim* had the power to elevate the hasid, to inspire him with the spirit of repentance, with hasidism. But now—look, I'm no different than before I went, nothing at all has changed.[140]

To combat the ongoing deterioration of traditional Jewish values and practice, R. Kalonymus took action on a number of fronts. In 1923 he founded the Da'as Mosheh yeshiva in Warsaw, and served as its head until the war broke out. With some 300 students a year, it was one of the largest hasidic yeshivas in interwar Poland.[141] During the 1920s and 1930s he also developed a comprehensive philosophy of education and a programme for religious renewal, which he outlined in three successive works. They are phrased in intimate, personal address, and intended to encourage students and young adult readers to set out on a journey of spiritual and moral growth. More broadly, R. Kalonymus strove to strengthen the religious (and specifically the hasidic) identity of his generation and to reanimate their connection to Jewish tradition and history.

Several excellent studies have analysed major topics in his interwar writings. These include techniques of meditation and guided imagery that he taught to develop mindfulness and emotional self-awareness and, on a higher level, to enhance mystical experience; his conception of prophecy and its redemptive power; the role of his educational project as part of a larger messianic vision; the elite spiritual fraternities that he organized in the hope of revitalizing the hasidic world. Viewed through a wider cultural lens, the Piaseczner Rebbe's oeuvre was clearly part of the dialogue of modernity that took place in those decades. A growing body of scholarship compares and

---

[140] *Mevo hashe'arim*, 40a–42a.

[141] Antony Polonsky points out that during the First World War 'almost all pre-war hasidic yeshivas on the territory of Poland within its 1921 frontiers ceased to operate . . . As a result, such institutions had to be created from scratch after the end of hostilities' (*The Jews in Poland and Russia*, iii. 188). The Piaseczner Rebbe's initiatives were, in fact, part of the shared effort of hasidic leaders in Poland 'to establish educational institutions that would protect their young people from what they regarded as the corrosive impact of the modern world and of secular Jewish ideologies, above all Bundism and Zionism' (ibid. 185). Indeed, Shaul Stampfer notes that 'one of the most striking phenomena of inter-war hasidism in Poland was the dramatic rise in the number of yeshivas, their ubiquity, and their role in the education and socialization of the young males of the hasidic elite' ('Hasidic Yeshivot in Inter-War Poland', 253). On the founding of Da'as Mosheh see Reiser, *Rabbi Kalonymus Kalman Shapira* (Heb.), i. 14.

contrasts his vision of religious renewal with the efforts of his contemporaries —Hillel Zeitlin, Menahem Ekstein, Abraham Joshua Heschel, Martin Buber, and others—to engender a rebirth of Jewish spirituality from within, by means of hasidic ideas and teachings translated to a modern idiom.[142]

These, to be sure, are important and central subjects. Along with them, however, I think there are other dimensions of R. Kalonymus' work that demand more attention. These come to the fore when we consider his writings within the matrix of concerns that have been at the centre of this book. In the following pages I would like to look more closely at the hermeneutical, literary, and rhetorical aspects of his works, and highlight the interplay between those elements and their author's self-understanding as it is revealed-concealed between the lines. Awareness of these dimensions of his interwar writings is essential, I believe, for a circumspect reading of his ghetto sermons in *Esh kodesh* and for a more comprehensive understanding of his life and thought.

Mavo hashe'arim was the last composition that the Piaseczner Rebbe wrote before the Second World War began. Over a number of pages he presents hasidism in a vast intellectual panorama spanning from biblical prophecy to rabbinic teaching, to the Zohar and kabbalistic lore, and leading finally to the following (now familiar) scene:

When the Ba'al Shem Tov of holy blessed memory had a soul ascent in the year 5507 and came to the chamber of the messiah, he asked, 'When is the master coming?' The messiah answered, 'When your wellsprings flow forth'—as we know from the 'Holy Epistle' at the end of the book *Ben porat yosef*. Hasidism is the final stage of revelation before the coming of the Messiah, and it brings the first rays of his luminous holiness. The coming messianic revelation—its essence is foreseen in the verse, 'The world will be filled with knowledge of God as the waters cover the earth' [Isa. 11: 9]. Now, the Ba'al Shem Tov's entire teaching is founded on this verse, on its simple meaning: 'The whole earth is filled with His glory' [Isa. 6: 3]. And there were many—great Torah scholars among them—who persecuted him for that. They accused him of corporealism, of profaning the honour of the Most High.[143] But 'the holy angel who came

---

[142] See Green, 'Three Warsaw Mystics'; Leshem, *Between Messianism and Prophecy*, 197 ff.; and work by Reiser and Mayse. Recent reviews in English of scholarship on the thought and works of the Rebbe of Piaseczno can be found in Seeman, 'Ritual Efficacy, Hasidic Mysticism and "Useless Suffering" in the Warsaw Ghetto', n. 3; Reiser, '*Esh Kodesh*: A New Evaluation', n. 1. For an extensive discussion of primary and secondary source material, see Reiser's introduction, *Rabbi Kalonymus Kalman Shapira* (Heb.), i. 13–80.

[143] The accusation of corporealism (*hagshamah*), voiced by the Vilna Gaon (some thirty years after the Ba'al Shem Tov's death), seems to have been spurred by a certain passage first

down from heaven', our saintly Ba'al Shem Tov, knew that the opposite was true.[144] ... He affirmed not only that divine vitality dwells in every dimension of reality, enveloped and hidden by materiality. Far more: matter and earthliness themselves are but an illusion ... All that is needed are eyes to see and a body striving towards holiness. Then, when you contemplate the world you will see God and God sees you. 'The whole earth is filled with His glory': everything, even earthliness, garments, vessels— all of them are imbued with His sacred radiance. ... The revelation that the Ba'al Shem Tov and his followers brought to the world—it is completely novel. For they drew the supernal light down further than ever before, into the very substance of the vessels, until the vessels themselves are transformed, become luminous. It's not that they transmute and turn into light; rather, now we are able to apprehend that the vessels are actually made of light. ...

In truth, however, already in ancient times our holy Sages disclosed that this would be the form of service leading to the messianic revelation. So it says in *Bereshit rabah* 26: 'In this world, the spirit is instilled in one of the organs'—according to commentators, the midrash refers to the intellect—'but in time to come, it will flash throughout the entire body, as it is written, "I will put My spirit within you" [Ezek. 36: 26].' And so the Ba'al Shem Tov's revelation is the first rays of the Messiah's dawning light. Now, holiness is to be found in every aspect of bodily existence and physicality, not only in the intellect or in mystical intentions.[145]

Put in standard academic categories, this passage presents a number of seminal hasidic concepts, among them worship through corporeality (*avodah begashmiyut*), raising the sparks of holiness, and the dialectic of 'lights and vessels' (*orot vekelim*). It sets out a historiosophical model with 'Hasidism as the culmination of a graded historical process in which biblical prophets, later rabbis and kabbalistic sages each contributed to a unique phase of cosmic *tikun*

---

published in *Tsava'at harivash* (Żółkiew, 1793), s. 194. Cf. Wilensky, *Hasidim and Mitnagedim* (Heb.), i. 188–9. R. Kalonymus' source here is likely to have been R. Shneur Zalman of Lyady's famous defence of hasidic teaching issued soon afterwards in his *Tanya*, ch. 7 (*Sha'ar ha'emunah vehayihud*).

[144] The honorific 'holy angel', after the verse in Dan. 4: 10, was used by R. Hayim Vital in reference to his own master, R. Isaac Luria. See '*Sha'ar hahakdamot*.

[145] *Mevo hashe'arim*, 18a–20b. The Ba'al Shem Tov's teaching cited here appears in *Keter shem tov*, ii. 20a; *Tanya*, 3b; *Likutim yekarim*, 17c. The midrashic source is *Gen. Rab.* 26: 6. R. Kalonymus develops this idea further some pages later, in *Mevo hashe'arim*, ch. 5. Earlier formulations of this contention, also citing the Ba'al Shem Tov's 'Holy Epistle', appear in other of his works, e.g. *Hovat hatalmidim*, 85–6; 109; *Hakhsharat ha'avrekhim*, 56b–57a. *Mevo hashe'arim* was written or completed around 1937. A comparable historiosophical presentation of hasidism was written by R. Gershon Hanokh Leiner of Izbica-Radzyn in the late nineteenth century; see Magid, *Hasidism on the Margin*, 72–108.

or repair'.[146] Having said that, though, the style and tone of these lines make it clear that something far more urgent than theoretical constructs is at stake here. R. Kalonymus not only introduces the fundamentals of hasidic doctrine. He performs them as well, in a brilliant array of rhetorical and hermeneutical moves. Embodied metaphors of revelation and discovery animate this passage; the emotional language of transformation and becoming informs it. Adjuration, phrased in direct address ('when you contemplate the world you will see God and God sees you'), creates the effect that an intimate and essential message is being communicated. The overarching intent of the passage, then, is to arouse the reader, to awaken the desire to attain a radically different mode of consciousness. Beyond any specific intellectual or spiritual content, what hasidism teaches is the work of self-transformation. 'All that is needed is eyes to see and a body striving towards holiness.' This, R. Kalonymus contends, is the spiritual practice or *avodah* that was the Ba'al Shem Tov's founding innovation. It offers an entirely new mode of emotional and experiential knowing that is profoundly empowering.

The evocation of the 'Holy Epistle' nearly two centuries after it was written seems to disclose something at the heart of R. Kalonymus' own project. The world's redemption, so the messiah promised the Ba'al Shem Tov, will come 'when your wellsprings will flow forth'. As we saw in Chapter 1, hasidic masters in the generations after the Ba'al Shem Tov took up the task. Thanks to their efforts, hasidism spread throughout eastern Europe and developed into a religious movement that profoundly affected Jewish society. The mission—spoken or unspoken—of bringing the messianic era closer by the means of hasidism thus became an integral part of the hasidic ethos. The Piaseczner Rebbe, as we know from his writings, was acutely aware of his eminent lineage. Here he voices a sense of his own role, following his forebears, in making the messiah's promise become a reality. Indeed, the sense that he is a spokesman for the entire body of hasidic tradition permeates his interwar writings. But when we juxtapose all this with the historical reality in which he lived, the picture turns immeasurably more complex. I have noted R. Kalonymus' frank recognition of the crisis taking place in the Jewish world, with hasidic faith and society crumbling before his eyes. This passage, then, presents a seemingly irreconcilable dialectic: on the one hand, the vision of an evolutionary historical process moving in rising levels of perfection, a cumulative revelation; against it, ongoing stages of descent and degeneration taking

---

[146] Seeman, 'Ritual Efficacy,' n. 47; Seeman here paraphrases Schweid (*From Ruin to Salvation* (Heb.), 112–14). Compare Leshem, 'Between Messianism and Prophecy' (Heb.), 62–5; 92–

place relentlessly on the ground. R. Kalonymus addresses this paradox in a number of creative and unexpected ways. I'd like to consider some of them first in his interwar writings. This will help us hear their resonances in his later ghetto sermons.

In his attempts during the 1920s and 1930s to reanimate hasidism and restore its power as a living tradition, R. Kalonymus brings to the foreground one of its central innovations: the figure of the *tsadik* and the interconnection with his hasidim. Here he draws heavily on written texts, above all on sermons by his father, grandfather, and earlier ancestors, who numbered among the most famed *tsadikim* in nineteenth-century Poland. Their works—*No'am elimelekh*, *Avodat yisra'el*, *Ma'or vashemesh*, and *Imrei elimelekh*— introduce the classic motifs and imagery related to the *tsadik*. He is the axis uniting heaven and earth, a conduit for divine blessings; he is invested with the power to annul evil decrees and to heal bodies and souls. In *Mavo hashe'arim* especially, R. Kalonymus devotes many pages to descriptions of the *tsadik* amidst his close disciples. For instance,

The Torah that he teaches them contains his essence and theirs as well, for they are a part of him. As it says in holy books, his Torah and his counsel for them are a spark of prophecy—because in prophecy as well, the needs of the people, of the nation, are what shape the prophet's words. So powerful is the bond between them that even when they are not with him, when the *rebbe* sits alone and writes his Torah insights, thoughts of his hasidim, their lives and their trials, enable him to find the words of guidance that each of them needs to hear.[147] ...

And the *rebbe*—to his inner circle, the holy company, he spoke of his own labours, of his spiritual flights and falls, his efforts to ascend again . . . They heard something far greater than the words he said. His soul emerged in speaking with them and they sensed it, until they themselves saw his visions and were enflamed with his fervour. . . . So much radiance concealed in the *rebbe* shone forth; it was revealed both to him and to them. An influx of new light opened before them all; together they were elevated towards holiness.[148]

The idyllic, romantic atmosphere of the works he cites combines here with a personal voice tinged with nostalgia. As a hasid whose own sense of self was

105. James Maisels presents a thorough review of scholarship on these subjects, and of the Piaseczner Rebbe's thought in that context: *The Self and Self-Transformation*, 145 ff.

[147] *Mevo hashe'arim*, 29a–b, citing *Ma'or vashemesh*, 'Tetsaveh', 343 and *Avodat yisra'el* on *Avot* 2: 7.

[148] *Mevo hashe'arim*, 45b, citing *Ma'or vashemesh*, 'Mikets', 157. Allusions here are to kabbalistic motifs such as *or mekif* (encompassing light) and *mayim nukvin* (feminine waters).

deeply influenced by the *tsadikim* he had known, R. Kalonymus is evoking something that he believes is authentic and very precious. In counterpoint, past and present tenses alternate in these lines, giving voice to the author's own sensibilities as community leader and spiritual guide. Yet a significant shift in terms has taken place: the individual of whom he writes is not the *tsadik* but the *rebbe*. This alerts us to the second side of the dialectic. The Piaseczner Rebbe clearly saw it as his mission to teach and preserve the ethos of hasidism against the corrosion of modern times. Implicit in that task, as his sources emphasize, is the imperative to embody the ideal of the *tsadik* in real life. Here, the dissonance between the glowing past and the impoverished present becomes painfully acute. Can anyone still fulfil that noble role in the current sorrowful reality? R. Kalonymus' reflections, written in the mid-1930s, are strikingly candid and revealing. Consider, for example, this portrait—shifting back and forth between narrative and inner voices—of the *rebbe* trying hard to play the part:

Sometimes he wonders about himself: how can it be that the Holy blessed One hears the prayers of a man so unworthy as I, worse than the very worst? . . . Even when God helps the *rebbe*, when his teachings, his prayers, his service, his devotion to God are received with favour and his own soul is filled with light—still he sees himself as the lowliest of creatures. At times he is nearly brought to tears: What a *rebbe*! He is nothing like the *tsadikim* of times past, the Rebbe of Lublin, the Magid of Kozienice. Isn't he lying to himself and to the entire world? . . . Oh, how my life is filled with deception and falsehood![149] . . .

But when his morale falls, that, too, is because he is bound up with his hasidim; their souls are intertwined with his. . . . He strives ceaselessly for their sake, to respond to their every lack, material and spiritual, to pray for them, to illuminate them in the ways of God and to elevate them . . . But not for them alone. He is responsible for the needs of all of Israel; with all his might he must worry for them and sustain them. And now Israel is in grave distress. Terror and darkness engulf them, body and soul. Who will care for them if not those who, after all, are called the leaders of the Jewish people? The saintly Shepherds of Israel from bygone days have been taken away from this world. Into whose hands have God's poor flocks been delivered in these desperate, terrible times? His soul bends under the burden of such worries, until all his efforts seem to him utterly worthless.[150]

[149] These lines are especially telling when read against R. Kalonymus' later writings. Compare *Esh kodesh*, 'Haḥodesh' 5702 (14 March 1942): 'Sometimes the man wonders about himself, have I not broken, am I not almost always in tears . . . with what do I find the strength to develop new interpretations in Torah and hasidism? . . . is my entire life not dismal and dark? This man is confused about himself' (Reiser's translation in '*Esh Kodesh*: A New Evaluation', 69 n. 14). Polen discusses this passage from *Esh kodesh* in *The Holy Fire*, 27–35.   [150] *Mevo hashe'arim*, 30a–31a.

Within its broader narrative context, this excerpt is meant to depict the *rebbe* as an objective category. At the same time, the internal experience being portrayed is quite evidently the author's own. A second passage, the final one that I'd like to consider from the Piaseczner Rebbe's pre-war writings, offers a rare glimpse into his inner world and his self-understanding as spiritual leader and as *darshan*. It is a handwritten note that was found among his papers, dated '*motsei shabbos*, first night of Selihot, 5689' (29 September 1929).

I am so weary of talking to people, of proclaiming in their ears, 'The Lord is God!' I shout, 'Don't you see? He's right there in front of you. In your every deed and thought His holiness is revealed; your world is His—the world of the Holy One, blessed be He.' But they hide their heads along with their whole being, hide inside themselves and do not listen. . . . I roar: 'Hear the word of the Lord, hear what you must do with every movement of your souls and your bodies!' But their eyes are plastered over with emptiness; their hearts are sealed by their own false imaginings. My throat is hoarse, my thoughts falter, my soul's most precious visions are confounded. I am nearly paralysed, about to stumble.

   Shabbos night, coming back from the *tish*.[151] So very weary, no one listens. I open my window and there is the whole world stretched out before me. I shall speak to the world itself. With all my heart I called out to it, 'Hear, O Israel, etc., the Lord is One!' The whole world seemed to shudder. Then, what—'May the earth shine with Your glory!' 'Praised be God, night and day!' 'Master of the universe, whose kingship is everlasting!' . . . The world—it swallowed up each sacred utterance as it emerged from my mouth, welling up from deep within me. All at once my soul was restored. My thoughts and feelings came to life again. From now on, at home and outside, whether anyone listens or not, I shall speak ceaselessly to the world itself, the world of the Holy blessed One. And when the world is made holy, maybe then the Jews in it will become holy as well. 'From the edge of the earth, songs will be heard' [Isa. 24: 16].[152]

The Piaseczner Rebbe's interwar writings contain many reflections on the figure of the *tsadik*. Their value as autobiographical revelations is evident. But in a second and more far-reaching sense, they disclose R. Kalonymus' most

---

[151] Traditional hasidic gathering around the *rebbe*'s sabbath table.

[152] *Tsav veziruz*, 53, s. 48. The Isaiah citation that closes this passage seems to be chillingly self-referential and prophetic. The verses continue: 'From the ends of the earth songs will be heard: "Glory for the *tsadik*!" But I say, "My secret is with me! My secret is with me! Woe is me! The treacherous have dealt with treachery".' My translation of these verses follows Rashi's reading: God has revealed two secrets to the prophet: the secret of Israel's downfall and the secret of their ultimate salvation. 'Woe is me!' for the prophet has been shown the great suffering that will precede the final redemption.

profound beliefs. Hasidism has a crucial historical role, which the messiah himself bestowed upon its founder, the Ba'al Shem Tov. The *tsadikim* of every generation inherit that legacy along with the weighty responsibility to awaken the world with its truth. These convictions, combined with a deeply rooted identification with his own hasidic ancestors, invest R. Kalonymus' work with vitality. Yet they also burden the author himself with a prophetic mission that offers no escape. This facet of self-understanding, I will suggest, endures as a crucial facet of the Piaseczner Rebbe's later activity as well. Moreover, it underlies the urgency with which he related to the tasks of writing and preserving his manuscripts during the Holocaust, and to vouchsafing their publication in the unknown future. I will return to this point later on.

Winter, 1940. The largest concentration of Jews in all of Nazi-occupied Europe, some 400,000, were crammed into the 3.4 square kilometres of the Warsaw ghetto. In the words of one ghetto diarist, Abraham Lewin:

The proportions of life and death have radically changed. Times were when life occupied the primary place, when it was the main and central concern, while death was a side phenomenon, secondary to life, its termination. Nowadays death rules in all its majesty, while life hardly glows under a thick layer of ashes. Even this faint glow of life is feeble, miserable and weak, poor, devoid of any free breath, deprived of any spark of spiritual content. The very soul, both in the individual and in the community, seems to have starved and perished, to have dulled and atrophied. There remain only the needs of the body; and it leads merely an organic-physiological existence.[153]

It was in these inhuman circumstances, amidst communal devastation, after having lost most of his family, that the Piaseczner Rebbe composed his *derashot*. By May 1943 most of those who had not already perished had been deported from the ghetto and murdered in Treblinka and other surrounding death camps. Near the end of the ghetto revolt, which took place in April–May of the same year, R. Kalonymus was taken to the Trawniki labour camp in the Lublin district. He was apparently murdered there in November 1943.[154] His manuscripts were unearthed from the rubble of the destroyed ghetto in December 1950, along with thousands of other documents that had been buried in the Emanuel Ringelblum 'Oyneg Shabbes' underground archive. The ghetto sermons were redacted and published in 1960 in Israel

[153] 'Eulogy in Honor of Yitshak Meir Weissenberg, September 13, 1941', in Lewin, *A Cup of Tears*, 243.

[154] According to Polen (*The Holy Fire*, 155–6); for other views see Leshem, 'Between Messianism and Prophecy' (Heb.), 11 n. 4.

under the title *Esh kodesh*, or 'Holy Fire'. They are 'a rare and vital testament to efforts in consoling followers . . . a record of an extended existential struggle to wrest religious meaning out of the most extreme experience of suffering imaginable'.[155]

For scholars, *Esh kodesh* is invaluable as an authentic and extensive (Orthodox) Jewish response to the Holocaust, written in real time.[156] These sermons attest to their author's struggle with weighty issues, such as the meaning of suffering, the nature of evil, the dialectics of faith and doubt, perhaps even the need for theological protest of God's design. Scholars have also attempted to correlate historical conditions and events in the Warsaw ghetto with the Rebbe's changing ideological stance, and have scrutinized his private spiritual world. Was he a mystic or a realist? Did he undergo a spiritual crisis?[157] We must keep in mind, however, that the sermons collected in *Esh kodesh* were not composed as discursive theology, religious philosophy, or autobiography. Reading the Rebbe's sermons as what they were—part of the traditional Jewish genre of homiletics—with an eye to their hermeneutical and literary aspects, might help us catch sight of other important facets of meaning.

The Piaseczner Rebbe's early writings, as we have seen, articulate his vision of hasidism and its meta-historical role. They set out his own project to actualize the redemptive potential of hasidic teaching and underscore its urgency here and now. *Esh kodesh* must be read as part of that effort. Many of the ghetto sermons could illustrate this; I have chosen one *derashah* as a test case of sorts. Reading it, the hermeneutical issues that have concerned us throughout this book will be at the fore. How does R. Kalonymus creatively

[155] Diamond, 'The Warsaw Ghetto Rebbe', 299, 307. On the discovery of the manuscripts, see Reiser, '*Esh Kodesh*: A New Evaluation', 80.

[156] In his essay 'Concerning Authentic and Unauthentic Responses to the Holocaust', Emil Fackenheim stresses the importance of texts of this nature: 'To find a meaning in the Holocaust will forever be impossible, but to find authentic responses is an imperative which brooks no compromise. The nature of the dilemmas involved makes this task at once profound, formidable, and perilous' (p. 66).

[157] On the 'theology of protest' as an inherent part of Jewish tradition, see Dov Weiss, *Pious Irreverence: Confronting God in Rabbinic Judaism* (Philadelphia, 2017); Anson Laytner, *Arguing With God: A Jewish Tradition* (Lanham, 1990), esp. 179–89; in Holocaust studies, see David Blumenthal, *Facing the Abusing God: A Theology of Protest* (Westminster, 1993); on the disputed question of 'theological protest' in *Esh kodesh* see Diamond, 'The Warsaw Ghetto Rebbe'. The most thorough treatment in English of *Esh kodesh*, with translation and commentary on parts of many sermons, along with extensive biographical and historical material, remains Polen, *The Holy Fire*.

reconfigure traditional religious sources to address the needs of the present moment? What is he trying to communicate to his listeners, his own hasidim, and to future readers?[158] Where are the crossroads found—those charged places where interpreting texts, making sense of the world, and the author's self-understanding intersect? The following *derashah*, on the Torah portion 'Va'era', was written in mid-January 1942.

'God [Elohim] spoke to Moses and said to him, I am YHVH. I appeared to Abraham, to Isaac, and to Jacob as El Shadai, but with My name YHVH I did not make Myself known to them. . . . And so say to the Children of Israel, "I am YHVH and I shall take you out from under the burdens of Egypt; I shall rescue you . . . I shall redeem you"' [Exod. 6: 2–8].

In the Talmud [*Arakh.* 10*b*], Rabah bar Shela said in the name of Rav Matnah, from Samuel: There was an [instrument called] *magrefah* in the holy Temple, etc. It had ten holes and each of them made one hundred melodies—in all, one thousand different melodies. Rashi comments: 'the *magrefah* that was used to rake the ashes from the altar'. Now, we must understand why the tool used for the ashes had to sing—and a song as mighty as the voice of a thousand people, so much louder than any other musical instrument. It even says in [Mishnah] *Tamid* [3: 8] that the sound of the *magrefah* could be heard as far away as Jericho. Yes, the Tosafists explained it otherwise; but we need to understand, after Rashi, what this means regarding our own reality. For in *Tamid* [2: 2] it is taught concerning the 'raising of the ashes' [*haramat hadeshen*] that on the pilgrimage festivals the ashes were not removed because they beautified the altar.[159] That is, they showed how very many sacrifices had been offered on it. Now we must apprehend what all this teaches us—that the ashes were testimony to the great number of sacrifices—for it surely means something.

All the sacrifices brought upon the altar were symbolically 'in place of his son', after the trial of our forefather Abraham. That is, those who sought atonement for their sins or brought a burnt offering as a gift were, in essence, offering up their souls as a sacrifice to God. The Torah, however, proposed another way—to sacrifice an animal [in place of oneself]. The animal sacrifices symbolize this: once they have been offered up, the ashes [*deshen*] that remain show how very numerous they were. And so it is when Jews have departed from us at God's will—because thus it arose in divine

---

[158] That readership in the unknown future was a powerful, real presence, as the Rebbe's final testament (written January 1943) makes clear. See below.

[159] See Lev. 6: 1–6; Mishnah *Tamid* 2: 2. Concerning the *magrefah*: the Tosafists contend, against Rashi, that two different objects share the name *magrefah*. Mishnah *Tamid* 3: 8 lists a series of musical instruments; there, the Tosafists define the *magrefah* as a tympanum. The tool called *magrefah* used to rake (*ligrof*) the ashes from the altar, the Tosafists held, was a perforated trowel. Rashi, in contrast, merges the two occurrences of the word. This merging results in a fantastical instrument that performs both tasks. In the course of the *derashah* it becomes clear why R. Kalonymus foregrounds Rashi's reading.

thought that they would be offered up as sacrifices to Him—only once they are gone do we realize their greatness. Great in number and so very precious. Before, while they were here, they were the light of our eyes, the spirit of our body and soul. But as much as we rejoiced and delighted in them, we did not realize how very much we had. We did not comprehend how good it was when they were still with us. And now that they are gone, may the Merciful One protect us, now we see how sorely we miss them. The heart yearns and the pain is beyond comfort, were it not for the words of the Holy One, blessed be He, to Moses: 'So did it arise in thought before Me' [BT *Men.* 29*b*].

The *magrefah* that was used for the ashes of the sacrifices: the melody it produced was so very powerful because, in the Temple, all the music and song served to make their voice heard on High, as it is written, 'You shall sound [the trumpets—*utekatem*] and it shall be a remembrance before the Lord, your God'.[160] This means that it is not only we who are moved by the ashes left from the sacrifices that were offered up. So it is on High as well. What they couldn't do when they were alive—now they have the power to arouse abundant mercy in Heaven, and to awaken salvation for the Jewish people, very soon and without delay.

This relates to what the Talmud says about Rabbi Yose, who went into one of the ruins of Jerusalem to pray. 'He heard the lament of an echoing voice: Woe is Me for I have destroyed My house' [*Ber.* 3*a*], etc. But why hadn't he heard that voice before? After all, Elijah the prophet told him that every day, when Jews gather in synagogues and study halls, the Blessed Holy One exclaims thus. Yet it is here, amidst the ruins of Jerusalem with ashes all around, that God's own sorrow and compassion, so to speak, are more intense as well, and so Rabbi Yose was able to hear what he had not heard before.

Let us pause here for a minute to take stock. In this first section, R. Kalony-mus has introduced the texts and thematic elements on which the *derashah* will be built. 'Va'era', the Torah portion that elicits these reflections, begins with a powerful moment of revelation and goes on to foretell the ultimate redemption of the Jewish people. Both events—revelation and redemption—are predicated on suffering. 'I am YHVH . . . I have heard the groans of the Children of Israel . . . and I shall rescue you.' R. Kalonymus cites the momen-tous opening verses of the *parashah* without comment. He then evokes another, equally unreal scenario: the Temple service in Jerusalem, mounds of ashes left on the bronze altar, and the mighty song of the *magrefah*. After pre-senting these two seemingly unrelated sources, he closes with a statement of

---

[160] After Num. 10: 9–10. The allusion seems to be to midrash *Tanḥuma*, 'Vayera', 23, where this chain of associations appears—'making their voice heard on High', sounding the *shofar* (*utekatem*), arousing remembrance and awakening redemption—along with the important image of 'the ashes of Isaac'. On that image, see below.

purpose: 'We need to understand, after Rashi, what this means regarding our own reality . . . Now we must apprehend what all this teaches us . . . for it surely means something.'

Ashes (*afar* or *deshen*)—the burnt remains of the ritual sacrifices—are the formative literary image in this sermon. To explain its meaning, R. Kalonymus recalls a primary religious tenet: the animal offerings that individuals brought to the Temple for atonement represent a crucial moment of displacement. The Akedah (the binding of Isaac) provides the paradigmatic instance in the ram that Abraham offered 'in place of his son' (Gen. 22: 13). On a straightforward reading, the biblical story thus introduces the notion of the animal sacrifice as a surrogate. But a second, subversive reading of the Akedah seems to be at work here as well. Midrashic and medieval sources recount a chilling counter-narrative in which 'Isaac's ashes remain piled on the altar to atone for Israel'.[161] 'Isaac's ashes', then, come to represent the countless times in Jewish history when the heavens did not miraculously open. The next lines of the *derashah* refer to that cruel reality playing out right now. 'And so it is when Jews have departed from us at God's will—because thus it arose in divine thought that they would be offered up as sacrifices to Him.'[162] Grief wells up—for the Piaseczner Rebbe's own heavy personal losses, for the recent, tragic death of so many dear ones, for the gaping empty space that is left.

On closer reading, the emblem of ashes seems to carry yet another meaning. R. Kalonymus dwells on its paradoxical nature. The ashes, in effect, embody absence, and yet they are an active presence. On this point, too, he draws on a late midrashic tradition: 'when the Jewish nation is in distress, the ashes of Isaac ascend and come before the Holy blessed One'.[163] The ashes here take on a powerful symbolic role—symbolic in the most literal sense.

[161] See BT *Ta'an.* 16*a* and textual parallels; Rashi on Gen. 22: 14. R. Tsedekiah ben Abraham Anav (1210–*c*.1280) writes in *Shibolei haleket*: 'When Father Isaac was bound on the altar and was reduced to ashes, and his sacrificial dust was cast on Mount Moriah, the Holy One, blessed be He, immediately brought upon him dew and revived him.' Cited in Spiegel, *The Last Trial*, 33.

[162] The image of the ashes here may or may not refer to real events. The sermon was delivered on 17 January 1942 and transcribed shortly afterwards. The first death camp had been established at Chelmno (70 km west of Łódź) less than a month earlier, in December 1941. 'On January 19, 1942 Jakob Grojanowski escaped from Chelmno and reached the Warsaw ghetto where he gave a detailed report about the extermination process to the staff of the Oneg Shabbat archive. The information circulated in the Warsaw ghetto and even appeared in the underground Jewish press there in February, 1942' (Ungar, *Reassessment of the Image of Mordechai Chaim Rumkowski*, 42).

[163] See Zohar iii. 33*a*; there the context is the death of Nadav and Avihu, but in a broader sense the death of 'holy ones' who perished in sanctification of God's name.

As Umberto Eco points out, 'originally, a symbol was a token, the present half of a broken tablet or coin or medal'; its very presence, though, evoked 'the ghost of its absent companion and of the original wholeness'.[164] Here, the ashes of Isaacs beyond number have a sacred mission: 'What they couldn't do when they were alive—now they have the power to arouse abundant mercy in Heaven, and to awaken salvation for the Jewish people, very soon and without delay.' This part of the *derashah* closes with the image of the second-century sage Rabbi Yose praying amidst the ruins of Jerusalem, with ashes all around. The site of desolation, like the ashes, proves to be a charged space of absent presence, a locus of memory and of unexpected encounter.[165] Both poetic images—the ashes and the silent ruin—speak of a duality that must be recognized. From the grief of absence, a deep sense of presence might emerge. We will leave this scene featuring Rabbi Yose for the moment. R. Kalonymus returns to it at the end of the *derashah*, where its full meaning comes to the fore. The next part of his sermon shifts to a new and important plane. How is all of this to manifest outwardly in religious action?

What it means for us in our serving God is this. As we know from *Sha'arei kedushah*, by the saintly R. Hayim Vital, the soul's evil inclination is rooted in the four elements: in fire—anger; in wind—pride, etc., and in dust—lethargy. Now, from the holy book *Imrei elimelekh* ('Toledot') we learn that hot lust for evil can be redirected towards holiness, to arouse a desire to do good.[166] But the cold evil that is embodied in Amalek—that cannot be transmuted to anything holy. This is because the evil inclination uses all four elements for evil. And dust serves the forces of Amalek, that 'dust-eating Snake' cursed by God.[167] ... The chilling force of evil strikes at a person's faith and turns everything else to evilness as well. In other words, so long as the husk of Amalek does not paralyse one with lethargy and heaviness, all four elements can still be channelled to holiness. But once a person's faith has been frozen ... his spirit can no longer rise and join with anything sacred, above and beyond his own intellectual

[164] Eco, *The Limits of Interpretation*, 9.

[165] Richard Shusterman, writing at the turn of the twenty-first century in the still-haunted remains of East-West Berlin, reflects on this play of present absences in the urban landscape. 'Even its etymology (ab+esse—"away from being") reveals its link to the ancient philosophical puzzle of nonbeing, the paradoxical nature of "things" that don't exist or simply fail to be "here and now" (that is, present). Yet absence has also been regarded as something at the core of all being, as the crucial ground for whatever exists or is present' (*Performing Live*, 99).

[166] The author is R. Kalonymus' father, R. Elimelekh (*Imrei elimelekh*, 'Toledot', 20*b* (44)). R. Kalonymus cited this teaching in *Hakhsharat ha'avrekhim*, 9*b* and alluded to it in the passage we saw earlier in *Tsav veziruz*.

[167] After Isa. 65: 25. The figure of the Snake/Amalek/evil is linked already in the midrash with the verse in Prov. 16: 28, 'the inciter who estranges the Master'; see *Gen. Rab.* 20: 2.

understanding. Instead, lethargy and despair pull his heart, his mind, his whole body down so far that he hasn't the strength to rise again and join himself to holiness. And then his faith is damaged, Heaven forbid. After that, when grief and suffering come, they break him even more and cast him still lower. His heart and brain turn to stone . . . until dark, blemished thoughts begin to invade his mind. Thus, when the Jewish people offered up sacrifices and they were consumed in the flames of holiness, ashes were left behind. The ashes are that heaviness of elemental dust which could not join itself to holiness. And so the ashes needed to be raised by other means. Now, how was that done? By the *magrefah*, with its manifold voice singing the joyful deliverance of Israel. For with that joy, the happiness of salvation, everything can be redeemed and darkness itself is transformed into light.

The focus in this part of the *derashah* has changed to another realm of experience: from the tragedy of human sacrifices to the psyche of those left among the living. As we saw in his earlier works, R. Kalonymus knew well how to portray the foundering and gradual disintegration of religious faith; he did so with empathy and unflinching honesty. Similar observations appear here. This time he grounds the process in kabbalistic and hasidic sources, in which 'cold' figures as a metaphor of emotional deadening, apathy, lethargy, defeat, hopelessness. Other correspondences are affirmed as well, linking emotional, psychological, and existential states to the element of dust (*afar*). The anti-hero behind it all is named: it is 'the husk of Amalek', the snakelike, cursed eater of dust, archetype of evil.[168] A final hermeneutical gesture recalls the trope of ashes (*efer*)—the heavy, seemingly unredeemable remains of the offering that the altar's holy fire did not consume, left below, littering the altar.

'And so they needed to be raised by other means.' In a literal sense, the ancient Temple ritual called *terumat hadeshen* (raising of the ashes) did just that. But in the exegetical imagination of the hasidic masters that act means much more: it is reimagined as a founding element of hasidic teaching. R. Kalonymus reflected on this already in his interwar writings. He cited R. Elimelekh of Lizhensk on the biblical verses that prescribe it: "And he raised up the ashes left after the consuming flames" [Lev. 6: 3]. For no one can break all the negative forces planted in the self from birth. Rather, they must be elevated and brought to holiness. . . . That is the labour called hasidism

---

[168] Needless to say, Amalek in contemporary parlance referred to the Nazi oppressors. So, for instance, Yehoshue Perle wrote, 'It happened in the year 1942 in the month of Tishrei, in the land of Poland, in the city of Warsaw. Under the savage rule of Amalek—may his name and memory be blotted out' (cited in Roskies, *The Literature of Destruction*, 450).

(*avodat haḥasidut*).' In his own voice, R. Kalonymus added, 'Indeed, it was the Ba'al Shem Tov who taught how it is to be done. He revealed that the vessels themselves are holy, and that they, too, must be transformed.'[169]

This part of the sermon is informed by a second seminal innovation of hasidism. It comes to the fore most clearly in the final lines of the passage, in the end point they envision: 'for everything can be redeemed and darkness itself transformed into light'. R. Kalonymus touched on that dialectic in his presentation of the Ba'al Shem Tov's 'Holy Epistle' in *Mavo hashe'arim*. Reading on, though, we see that the notions of radical transformation and total reversal are, in fact, a central theme in that work as a whole. Remember that *Mavo hashe'arim*, the last work that the Rebbe of Piaseczno wrote before the Holocaust, is devoted in large part to presenting the essentials of hasidic teaching. Repeatedly, he underlines the role of hasidism in heralding the messianic era. And so his treatment there of these themes—darkness giving way to light, transformation, and redemption—demands closer attention. To explain them R. Kalonymus draws on the thought of Habad hasidism, with its reconfiguration of kabbalistic motifs. He cites R. Shneur Zalman of Lyady: 'In the first chapters of the *Tanya*: to turn evil to good, darkness to light, bitterness to sweetness—that is the level of perfect *tsadikim*.' A second work by R. Shneur Zalman, *Likutei torah*, comes to affirm that this inner process of spiritual rectification is 'not only for great *tsadikim*, but for everyone'. The key concepts here, he notes, are called *itkafya* and *ithapekha*, and he adds in explanation: '*itkafya* means merely to subdue the evil inclination and impede its action. But *ithapekha* means transforming it into holiness, so that the evil inclination, too, will come to serve God.'[170] After this discursive and rather abstract presentation, however, he summons a second speaker— R. Aaron ben Asher of Karlin (1802–72)—and a very different rhetorical voice to drive his point home:

As it is written in the holy book *Beit aharon* on Pesach: 'My dear friends, my brothers, you must believe me, for all the books are filled with it. What the first *tsadikim* needed days and months to accomplish, now it is possible to repair in a single hour, for the

[169] *Mevo hashe'arim*, 50*b*, 53*a*, citing *No'am elimelekh*, 'Tsav'. In that context he also cites R. Hayim Vital's *Sha'arei kedushah* 1: 2—the same source noted in the passage from *Esh kodesh* that we are now reading.

[170] *Mevo hashe'arim*, 53*a*. In the printed version these lines appear as a marginal addition. In the original manuscript, held in the archives of the Jewish Historical Institute in Warsaw, they are written between square brackets in the body of the text. Żydowski Instytut Historyczny (ŻIH), Ring. II/432b (fo. 23*b*) [MS-133/145]. My gratitude to Daniel Reiser for enabling me to examine the manuscript. Cf. *Tanya*, 1: 27.

world is at a lower level, etc. God had mercy on His world and allowed His holiness to descend into the world.' So he wrote. But we can say even more. God causes His holiness to move lower and lower along with the decline of the generations. And thus our *tsadikim* adapted the work to be done [*ha'avodah*] to each generation, in order to elevate them and to make them holy. And now we, too, must follow their path. In all that we say and in all that we write, the main thing now must be to draw down holiness and to broaden its influence. And if it is hard for us, as ordinary people [*beinonim*], to conquer the Other Side of evil, we must at the very least wrest the elements of our soul—our strengths and our emotions—from its grasp and harness them for holiness. We shall subordinate our inner drives not by force, in the sense of *itkafya* . . . No, most essentially, we must bring about a total transformation, in the sense of *ithapekha*—so that something of them might actually be transmuted into holiness.[171]

Returning to the *derashah* at hand: here, it seems, is the Piaseczner Rebbe's own attempt, from the depths of unimaginable suffering, to live out these founding ideals. In his unspoken role as *tsadik*, or at the very least as an 'ordinary person', he speaks as one 'responsible for the needs of all of Israel', 'to illuminate them in the ways of God, to elevate them and bring them to holiness'. This part of the sermon thus outlines the spiritual effort or *avodah* that might help 'this generation'—his own listeners and perhaps the Rebbe along with them—to wrest themselves from the iron grip of despair and to rise, in spirit at least, towards something more pure and free. In the darkness of the Warsaw ghetto, the toil of the heart that he counsels is a heroic, defiant refusal to surrender to the evil inclination, the 'Other Side' of evil, the primordial Snake seeking Israel's destruction.

The next part of the *derashah* slips into a lyrical, mystical mode. Its language is allusive, its images fleetingly elusive. In that unreal landscape alone, it seems, can the secret moment of reversal, of transformation and redemption, be told.

Yet perhaps we can understand a bit more, even with our bounded comprehension. It is known that the four elements are drawn from the four letters of the divine Name YHVH. 'Dust' stems from the last letter, *heh*—that is, the *sefirah* of Malkhut. And so when she is estranged and cut off, Heaven forbid, from the Name and falls, 'He who disunites the One will be bereft of light'. So, too, the moon, who brought darkness upon herself. But when she awakens to unite with her beloved, then she sings—this we know, for it is written, 'to arouse the Lily of Sharon to sing etc. and rejoice in gladness'. And then all is reversed [*aderaba*]: the very separation that she first endured is

---

[171] *Mevo hashe'arim*, 55b–56a, citing *Beit aharon*, 'Pesach', 87a (p. 173). The author of that work, R. Aaron Perlov 'the Second' of Karlin-Stolin, was the grandson of R. Aaron 'the Great', the founder of the Karlin dynasty and disciple of the Magid of Mezhirech.

what arouses her desire, her song, and her longing for oneness. Indeed, the Song of Songs tells of it—that play of remoteness and intimacy: 'My beloved slipped away', and then, 'my soul went out with his words' [S. of S. 5: 6]. From that distance her song is awakened with a flood of longing and love. We see this, too, between father and child. When they are parted, their love for one another grows more intense. This, then, is the meaning of the mighty voice of the *magrefah* and the ashes: their very heaviness as elemental dust was what aroused that immense yearning and its vibrant song—so much so that on the festivals the ashes were not removed. For then they beautified the altar and the unity they engendered was greater still.[172]

The agonies of the ghetto have receded into the distance. These lines evoke deep mysteries taking place in hidden realms: 'He who disunites the One will be bereft of light' refers to the primordial agent of disunity, the Snake, who cut humanity off from the source of holiness. The kabbalists envisioned it graphically. The unity of the divine name YHVH was violated; the last letter, the final *heh*—symbolizing the *sefirah* of Malkhut, the moon, the Shekhinah— was cast down into the dust. Yet it is here that the crucial moment of reversal occurs. From distance, sorrow, and absence, longing is aroused. A second, cosmic process of healing is set in motion. The promise, unarticulated, still unfulfilled, is of a commensurate 'awakening from Above'. Finally, repair and reunion beyond the sorrows of this world, 'the joyful deliverance of Israel'. Translated to spiritual action, this passage affirms the task of every Jew to 'raise the Shekhinah from the dust, to aid her ascent, to reunite her with her beloved'.[173] Heaviness and despair can be transformed, the Rebbe suggests —that is the song of the *magrefah*, of desire in the ashes. Something of it, perhaps, is enacted in the telling.[174]

[172] Among the allusions at work in this passage: the connection between the four elements and God's four-letter name is made in the same kabbalistic work on which this sermon is founded, *Sha'arei kedushah* 3: 1; 'Who disunites the One' alludes to the kabbalistic *piyut* 'El mistater' by R. Abraham Maimon, a student of R. Moses Cordovero, which hasidim traditionally sing at the third sabbath meal. The words that R. Kalonymus cites are from its last verse and refer to the tenth *sefirah*, Malkhut. On the moon, see BT *Ḥul.* 60b. 'To arouse the Lily of Sharon'—from the kabbalistic prayer ('Yehi ratson') said before reciting the Song of Songs. Much of the imagery and a number of thematic elements in this passage appear in Zohar ii. 184a, e.g. the diminishment of the moon, her luminosity regained; the Snake as attacker; the overcoming (*itkafya*) of the Other Side and its ultimate transformation (*ithapekha*); light emerging from darkness and good from evil; the sounding of the shofar that arouses compassion on High; 'arousal from below', 'arousal from above'.

[173] Citing *Imrei elimelekh*, 'Aḥarei mot', 112b.

[174] I allude here to a famous hasidic story: 'When the Baal Shem had a difficult task before him, he would go to a certain place in the woods, light a fire and meditate in prayer—and what he had set out to perform was done. When a generation later the 'Maggid' of Meseritz was faced

The *derashah* closes in classic homiletical style, circling back to the primary texts with which it began:

We return now to what we talked about earlier: In the ruin Rabbi Yose heard more, for divine sorrow and compassion for the suffering of the Jewish people are aroused there most of all. 'God [Elohim] spoke etc., I am YHVH' [Exod. 6: 2]. After the aspect of rigour, Elohim, then compassion, YHVH, is revealed. 'I appeared to the forefathers but I did not fulfil My promise to them', as Rashi explains. But now, an awakening. 'Alas [*haval*] for those who are gone, no longer to be found!' And now, from the arousal of 'alas' [*hitorerut hahaval*] redemption awakens. 'And I shall take you out'.[175]

These final lines retell the drama of estrangement, arousal, and freedom from oppression that are meant to take place sometime in the unseen future. In a general sense, they are one more instance of the Rebbe's sustained and heroic effort to console his listeners, to remind them of God's infinite, hidden suffering for the Jewish people, and to succour them with the promise that salvation is near. Sacred history, recounted in the week's Torah portion, does foresee the optimistic trajectory from exile to redemption and offers a reassuring precedent of sorts. As in many of the sermons in *Esh kodesh*, the hasidic concept of arousal, from below and from above, figures here as a central motif.[176]

A closer look at these lines, however, reveals an additional and crucial plane of meaning. Here is a striking self-referential moment—and one that offers compelling testimony to the Rebbe's belief in the power of words to

---

with the same task he would go to the same place in the woods and say: We can no longer light the fire, but we can still speak the prayers—and what he wanted became reality. Again a generation later Rabbi Moshe Leib of Sassov had to perform this task. And he too went into the woods and said: We can no longer light a fire, nor do we know the secret meditations belonging to the prayer, but we do know the place in the woods to which it all belongs—and that must be sufficient, and sufficient it was. But when another generation had passed and Rabbi Israel of Rishin was called upon to perform the task, he sat down on his golden chair in his castle and said: We cannot light the fire, we cannot speak the prayers, we do not know the place, but we can tell the story of how it was done. And, the story-teller adds, the story which he told had the same effect as the actions of the other three.' Cited by Gershom Scholem 'as I have heard it told by that great Hebrew novelist and story-teller, S. J. Agnon', *Major Trends in Jewish Mysticism*, 349–50.

[175] *Esh kodesh*, 146–9.

[176] Polen formulates this idea in reference to other sermons in *Esh kodesh*: 'Also striking is the notion that it is precisely from catastrophe that a new revelation may emerge' (*The Holy Fire*, 118); 'as [R. Shapiro] himself taught . . . it was a time for *itarurta deletata*, the "arousal from below", the human reaching for relationship with the divine, not as a response to the favorable stimulus from above, but initiated by one's own capacity for self-awakening out of the darkness' (ibid. 146).

affect reality. R. Kalonymus cites Rashi's famous commentary on the Bible as the linchpin of his reading. But there is a subtext underlying Rashi's biblical gloss; it appears in his more extensive commentary on the Talmud (*San.* 111a). This composite reading radically transforms the biblical narrative. Here is the talmudic text, with Rashi's commentary superimposed on it in italics:

> It has been taught: Rabbi Eleazar, son of Rabbi Yose, said: I once visited Alexandria of Egypt and found an old man there, who said to me, 'Come and I will show you what my ancestors did to yours. Some of them they drowned in the sea, some they slew by the sword, and some they crushed in the buildings.'[177] Now, for this Moses was punished—*when he saw the suffering of the Jewish nation he was deeply disturbed and his faith in the Holy blessed One was shaken.* 'Moses reproached God: Ever since I came to Pharaoh to speak in Your name, he has done evil to this nation, and still You have not saved Your people at all!' [Exod. 5: 23]. God exclaimed, 'Alas for those who are gone, no longer to be found! *Such a grievous loss! Those great men are here no longer and I cannot find any righteous ones like them. You are nothing like Abraham, Isaac, and Jacob.* For they never questioned My character. . . . But you—*first you asked Me*, 'What is Your Name?' [Exod. 3: 13] *and now you doubt Me*, saying, 'Neither have You saved Your people at all' [Exod. 5: 23]. But now—'now you shall see what I will do to Pharaoh' [Exod. 6: 1].[178]

Moses, in this astonishing portrait, appears in all his dialectical ambivalence. He is God's chosen, loyal servant, emboldened to protest and challenge, humbled when his faith is shaken. Read through the prism of a hasidic sensibility, this dialogue also avers that Moses, as a religious leader, has been granted the power to sweeten harsh judgements, to affect God's ways through his own spiritual efforts. He bears the burden of all of Israel; his trials and his failings are for their sake. Refracted backward on the *derashah* as a whole, it seems that R. Kalonymus has telescoped the experience of three spiritual masters— Rabbi Yose, Moses, and himself—and merged them in these closing lines. This, I think, is what they mean. 'Va'era'—I revealed Myself, but not completely; the forefathers did not know My name. Nonetheless, they trusted in My promises without question; their faith did not falter. Alas for their loss! How the generations have declined! Those first great, righteous ones are gone. Now Moses, or the Rebbe, needs reassurance. But the suffering of the

---

[177] *Dikdukei soferim* adds these lines (absent in the Vilna edition of the Talmud): 'He showed him the bones and hair that [the Egyptians] had ground into the bricks of the building.'

[178] Cf. BT *San.* 111a and Rashi ad loc. In his commentary on the Torah (Exod. 5: 22–6: 7), Rashi distributes his talmudic glosses on this passage selectively among the relevant verses in the biblical narrative. Parallels to the talmudic passage are found in *Exod. Rab.* 6: 4; *Yalkut shimoni* on Exodus, 176: 7.

Jewish people is immense. God is silent. Despair weighs heavy. Whose faith wouldn't falter?

But R. Kalonymus seems to be saying still more. 'Alas for their loss!' mourns not only the long dead. God himself, as it were, grieves the sacrifice, here and now, of so many precious lives. And from that truly boundless sorrow —divine suffering for 'dust and ashes', our anguish for our lost ones, my longing for Your presence—'from the arousal of "alas", redemption awakens'.

The *derashah* that has concerned us here does not instance the wrenching existential screams or the radical theological tensions that many scholars have focused on in analysing the Piaseczner Rebbe's ghetto sermons. I have quite deliberately tried to read in another register, to listen from a different perspective, and to approach these texts with alternative tools and assumptions. Above all, I have tried to be attentive to the hermeneutical and literary valences in the Rebbe's writings. With those elements in mind, my aim was to understand the ways he sought, through his *derashot*, to continue his life's work.

The self-referential dimensions that I've touched on in these pages give voice to the Rebbe's ever-present struggles as a solitary religious leader, at times painfully inadequate yet burdened, like his own hasidic ancestors, with 'the needs of all of Israel'. His primary concern, even now, is with the souls of individuals and of the community, 'starved and perished, dulled and atrophied' though they are. He continues to believe in the possibility of spiritual and moral growth. He reminds those around him of their identity, bound up with Jewish tradition and history, and envisions a place of intimacy where holiness can still be found.

In a more encompassing sense, R. Kalonymus' ghetto sermons are meant to further the project that concerned him from the outset. Its motivating force was the profound conviction that 'hasidism is the final stage of revelation before the coming of the messiah, and that it brings the first rays of his luminous holiness'. The task to transform the world through hasidic teaching requires the *tsadik* to adapt the work to be done to his generation. R. Kalonymus takes up that task—now to 'draw down holiness' even into the depths of misery. There, perhaps most of all, might the power of hasidic teaching be revealed—'For everything can be redeemed and darkness itself transformed to light'.

In the face of his own imminent death, the Rebbe sought to further that 'final stage of revelation' by means of his own writings. This mission is what charges his final testament with such extraordinary urgency. He implores relatives and friends in far-off Palestine to publish his manuscripts, to distribute them widely, and to include in each of his works the request that 'every Jew should study my books'.[179] Beyond himself, their words might help his readers ready themselves for the messianic future just beginning to dawn.

[179] Printed at the beginning of *Esh kodesh*, unnumbered page; MSS, ŻIH, Ring. II/370 (cited by Reiser in '*Esh Kodesh*: A New Evaluation', n. 50). Reiser posits that 'the *Rebbe*'s writings were given over to the "Oneg Shabbat" Archives between January 3 and February 1943, when the second part of the archive was interred' (ibid. 80). On the publishing of hasidic works as part of the messianic project of 'spreading the wellsprings', see Loewenthal, *Communicating the Infinite*, 4–28; Tishby, 'The Messianic Idea and Messianic Trends' (Heb.), 39–41; Wolfson, *Open Secret*, 34, 273.

Postscript

On the Mishnah: 'Know what is above you: A seeing eye, a hearing ear, and all your deeds are written in the book.' At the time of the First Temple they knew what was happening above by looking at the *urim* and *tumim*.[1] By the time of the Second Temple they no longer had the *urim* and *tumim*, but they knew what was above by listening to the echoing voice [*bat kol*]. That, too, is no more. But still, 'all your deeds are written in the book'. Even now, you can know what is wanted of you: there it is, written in the books you learn.[2]

The books you learn. Which books? What gives certain books such power and such mystery? Books worth reading, the Rebbe of Piaseczno says, are those written by a *meḥaber*—an author in whom heaven meets earth, who can draw vision down into the shadows, whose words show the way to worlds beyond.[3] Readers worthy of such books are those who bring their questions and their search over the threshold of the open page. What stands to be gained, the Rebbe suggests, is a glimpse of something from above, of 'knowing what is wanted of you'. That manner of knowing is a redemptive moment of repair and healing. The *tsadik*, the author, mediates it. He conveys it, always by indirection, in the Torah he learns and teaches. Real presence, even now, can be found written in the books.

---

[1] The *urim* and *tumim* are associated with the breastplate worn by the High Priest. When the Jewish people were in great need, the *urim* and *tumim* could be consulted to reveal God's will (Rashi on Num. 27: 21). Nahmanides recognized the *urim* and *tumim* as one of the levels of divine inspiration—lower than prophecy but higher than the heavenly voice (*bat kol*); see Nahmanides on Exod. 28: 30.

[2] R. Kalonymus Kalman Shapira cites this teaching in the name of R. Israel, the Magid of Kozienice, in a sermon from 1929; see *Derekh hamelekh*, 'Shemot', 79. His citation differs in some significant ways from the original version in R. Israel's commentary on *Pirkei avot*—differences that I will not discuss here. See *Beit yisra'el* on *Pirkei avot*, 5a.

[3] In its primary sense, the word *meḥaber* means 'author'; a second, metaphorical, meaning is 'connector': see Zohar i. 32a. R. Kalonymus plays on both meanings here. He alludes, as well, to the image of the *tsadik* in kabbalistic and hasidic teaching as one who 'joins heaven and earth'.

I conclude with a hasidic story. Its message is at the heart of what I've been trying to say. R. Gedaliah Rabinowitz, the *admor* of Monastyrishche in Jerusalem, told me this story, which he heard from his father, R. Isaac Joel.

The first time that the two holy brothers, Reb Shmelke and Reb Pinhas, came to the Great Magid of Mezhirech, they spent some days there but the ways of the Magid did not please them. Finally they went to the master to take leave of him. The Magid asked what they thought of his teaching. Stuttering and stammering, they avoided the question, and so the Magid understood that they weren't drawn to his path. As a final request before they went on their way, he asked them to stop in at the *beit midrash* and look there for his disciple Reb Zusha, and ask him for a word of Torah, some insight he could share with them. So they went to the house of study and asked where Reb Zusha might be. There he was, sitting behind the oven, a beggar dressed in tattered rags, reading Psalms. The brothers approached him and said: 'The Magid told us to come and receive a word of Torah from you before we leave here.' Reb Zusha gazed back at them in astonishment and asked, 'What can I teach you—two great Torah scholars? And what am I—a simple Jew who's learned nothing and understands even less? But Reb Shmelke and Reb Pinhas argued and insisted until Reb Zusha saw that his efforts were in vain. They wouldn't leave him in peace until he had taught them something. So he told them that once he had learned *Berakhot*—if they'd like, they could sit and learn with him.

Opening the tractate, they came upon the discussion about 'nine [men] and the holy ark combine [to form a quorum of ten]' [*Ber. 47b*]. And Reb Zusha reads and explains the text simply, innocently, saying that nine people and a cabinet full of Torah scrolls combine together to make a *minyan*. Then he gets to the question the Talmud raises: 'But is the holy ark a person?!' Reb Zusha remarks that he's always wondered what kind of a question that is at all—doesn't the Talmud already know that the holy ark isn't a person? He adds that he thinks maybe it can be explained according to something we know from *halakhah*: If there's one person missing to form a *minyan*, you can take a child and have him hold a Torah scroll, and altogether that will make a quorum.[4] So with that in mind the Gemara infers: If we can include a child holding one Torah scroll to form a *minyan*, all the more so we could include the holy ark, as it is full of Torah scrolls. Now, based on that reasoning of 'all the more so' the Gemara challenges: But no—what good are all those sacred scrolls? Where's the person, the *mentsh*? We still need a *mentsh*! [*Vu iz der mentsh? Men darf dokh hobn dem mentsh!*]

Then the two holy brothers, Reb Shmelke and Reb Pinhas, understood his message. This is what hasidism teaches you—how to be a *mentsh*. So they stayed there with the Great Magid of Mezhirech to receive his wisdom and learn his ways.

[4] See 'Ba'er heitev' on *Shulḥan arukh*, 'Oraḥ ḥayim', 55:7.

Bibliography

Kabbalistic and Hasidic Works

Avodat yisra'el. Israel Hofstein of Kozienice (Józefów, 1842; Benei Berak, 1996).

Beit aharon. Aaron Perlov (Brody, 1875).

Beit ya'akov. Jacob Leiner. 4 vols. (vol. i: Warsaw, 1881; Jerusalem, 1998; vol. ii: Lublin, 1904; Jerusalem, 1998; vol. iii: Lublin, 1937; Jerusalem, 1998; vol. iv: *Beit ya'akov al hatorah im sefer hazemanim* (Lublin, 1903; Jerusalem, 1976)).

Beit yisra'el. Israel Hofstein of Kozienice, in *Pirkei avot* (Bardejov, 1905).

Ben porat yosef. Jacob Joseph of Polonnoye (Korets, 1781; Jerusalem, 1971).

Benei yisaskhar. Tsevi Elimelekh Shapira (Żółkiew, 1846; 2 vols. Jerusalem, 1997).

Degel mahaneh efrayim. Moses Hayim Ephraim of Sudilkov (Korets, 1810; Jerusalem, 1994).

Derekh hamelekh. Kalonymus Kalman Shapira (Tel Aviv, 1976; Jerusalem, 1992).

Divrei elimelekh. Elimelekh of Grodzisk (Warsaw, 1890).

Divrei yehoshua. Joshua Heschel Rabinowitz (Berdichev, 1899–1907; Jerusalem, 1981).

Dover tsedek. Tsadok Hakohen (Piotrków, 1911; Benei Berak, 1973).

Erekh avot. Joshua Heschel Rabinowitz, in *Masekhet avot im biur torat avot* (New York, 1926; Jerusalem, 1990).

Esh kodesh. Kalonymus Kalman Shapira (Jerusalem, 1960); ed. D. Reiser as *Sermons from the Years of Rage* (Jerusalem, 2017).

Ets hayim. Hayim Vital (Korets, 1784; Benei Berak, 1986).

Hakhsharat ha'avrekhim. Kalonymus Kalman Shapira (Jerusalem, 1966).

Hidushei harim al hatorah. Isaac Meir Alter, ed. Judah Leib Hakohen Levin (Jerusalem, 1965).

Hovat hatalmidim. Kalonymus Kalman Shapira (Warsaw, 1932).

Igerot kodesh, ed. Dov Ber Levin (Brooklyn, 1980).

Imrei elimelekh. Elimelekh of Grodzisk (Warsaw, 1876).

Kedushat levi. Levi Isaac of Berdichev (Slavuta, 1798).

Kedushat levi hashalem. Levi Isaac of Berdichev (Jerusalem, 1978).

Keter shem tov. Collected by Aaron ben Tsevi Hirsch Kohen of Opatów, 2 vols. (Żółkiew, 1784–5); Kehat edn. (Brooklyn, 1981).

Ketonet pasim. Jacob Joseph of Polonnoye (Lemberg, 1866); ed. Gedalyah Nigal (Jerusalem, 1985).

Kol simhah. Simhah Bunim of Przysucha (Breslau, 1859).

Likutim yekarim (Lemberg, 1792; Jerusalem, 1974).

Magid devarav leya'akov. Dov Baer of Mezhirech (Korets, 1781); ed. Rivka Schatz-Uffenheimer (Jerusalem, 1976).

Magid meisharim. Joseph Karo (Lublin, 1646; Jerusalem, 1960).

Ma'or vashemesh. Kalonymus Kalman Halevi Epstein (Breslau, 1842; Jerusalem, 2007).

Mei hashilo'aḥ. Mordecai Joseph Leiner, 2 vols. (vol. i: Vienna, 1860; vol. ii: Lublin, 1922).

Me'or einayim. Menahem Nahum of Chernobyl (Slavuta, 1798; Jerusalem, 1999).

Mevo hashe'arim. Kalonymus Kalman Shapira (Jerusalem, 1966).

No'am elimelekh. Elimelekh of Lizhensk (Lemberg, 1788; Jerusalem, 1952).

Or hame'ir. Ze'ev Wolf of Zhitomir (Korets, 1798; Warsaw, 1883; Jerusalem, 1968).

Peri tsadik. Tsadok Hakohen (Lublin, 1907).

Ramatayim tsofim. Samuel of Shinova (Warsaw, 1882; Jerusalem, 2003).

Seder hadorot. Jehiel Heilprin (Karlsruhe, 1769).

Sefat emet. Judah Leib Alter of Ger, 5 vols. (Piotrków–Kraków, 1905–8; Tel Aviv, 1988).

Sefer ḥaredim. Elazar Azikri (Venice, 1601; Jerusalem, 1990).

Sefer hazekhut. Isaac Meir Alter (Piotrków, 1923).

Sha'ar hapesukim. Hayim Vital (Jerusalem, 1988).

She'erit yisra'el. Israel of Kozienice (Lublin, 1895).

Shenei luḥot haberit. Isaiah Horowitz (Amsterdam, 1649; Haifa, 1990).

Shevet musar. Elijah Hakohen Itamari (Constantinople, 1712; Piotrków, 1889).

Shivḥei ha'ari. Solomon Dresnitz; first printed in Joseph Delmedigo, *Ta'alumot ḥokhmah*, 2 vols. (Basle, 1629, 1631).

Shivḥei habesht, ed. Israel Jaffe (Kopys, 1814); ed. B. Mintz (Jerusalem, 1969); facsimile edn., ed. Y. Mondshine (Jerusalem, 1982); annotated edn., ed. A. Rubinstein (Jerusalem, 1992); English edn., *In Praise of the Baal Shem Tov*, ed. and trans. D. Ben-Amos and J. R. Mintz (Bloomington, 1970).

Sod yesharim: rosh hashanah, yom kipur, sukot. Gershon Hanokh Henikh of Radzyn (Warsaw, 1902; Brooklyn, 1992).

Tanya—Likutei amarim. Shneur Zalman of Lyady (Slavuta, 1797; Kefar Habad, 1980).

Teshuot ḥen. Gedaliah of Linits (Berdichev, 1816; Ashdod, 2012).

Tiferet shelomoh. Solomon Hakohen Rabinowicz (Piotrków, 1890; Jerusalem, 1992).

Toledot ya'akov yosef. Jacob Joseph of Polonnoye (Korets, 1780; Jerusalem 1973).

Torah or. Shneur Zalman of Lyady (Kopys, 1836; Vilna, 1899; Brooklyn, 1978).

Torat simḥah. Simhah Bunim of Przysucha, ed. Israel Berger, in *Simḥat yisra'el* (Piotrków, 1910–11).

Tsav veziruz. Kalonymus Kalman Shapira (Jerusalem, 1966).

Yedei mosheh. Moses Kahlenberg, ed. Esther Farbstein (Jerusalem, 2005).

Secondary Works

ABRAMS, M. H., *The Mirror and the Lamp: Romantic Theory and the Critical Tradition* (Oxford, 1953).

ALTSHULER, MOR, *The Messianic Secret of Hasidism*, trans. Rachel Yarden (Leiden, 2006).

ARENDT, HANNAH, *Eichmann in Jerusalem: A Report on the Banality of Evil* (New York, 1963).

—— *The Human Condition* (Chicago, 1958).

ASSAF, DAVID, 'Hasidism', in *The YIVO Encyclopedia of Jews in Eastern Europe*, <http://www.yivoencyclopedia.org/article.aspx/hasidism/historical_overview>.

—— *The Regal Way: The Life and Times of R. Israel of Ruzhin and His Place in the History of Hasidism*, trans. David Louvish (Stanford, Calif., 2002).

—— *Untold Tales of the Hasidim: Crisis and Discontent in the History of Hasidism*, trans. Dena Ordan (Waltham, Mass., 2010).

BAKHTIN, MIKHAIL, *Problems of Dostoevsky's Poetics*, ed. and trans. Caryl Emerson (Minneapolis, 1984).

BARNAI, JACOB (ed.), *Hasidic Letters from the Land of Israel: From the Second Half of the Eighteenth Century and the Early Nineteenth Century* [Igerot ḥasidim me'erets yisra'el min hamaḥatsit hasheniyah shel hame'ah hashemoneh-esreh umereshit hame'ah hatesha-esreh] (Jerusalem, 1980).

BAUMINGER, M. S., 'Letters of our Rabbi Israel Ba'al Shem Tov and his Son-in-Law R. Yehiel Mikhel to Rabbi Abraham Gershon of Kutow' (Heb.), *Sinai*, 71 (1972), 248–69.

BENJAMIN, WALTER, 'The Task of the Translator', in Hannah Arendt (ed.), *Illuminations* (New York, 1969), 69–82.

BERLIN, ISAIAH, *The Roots of Romanticism*, ed. Henry Hardy (Princeton, 1999).

—— *Two Concepts of Liberty* (Oxford, 1958).

BERNASCONI, ROBERT, 'The Trace of Levinas in Derrida', in Martin McQuillan (ed.), *Deconstruction: A Reader* (New York, 2001), 431–42.

BIALE, DAVID, *Not in the Heavens: The Tradition of Jewish Secular Thought* (Princeton, 2010).

BIRNBAUM, PIERRE, *Geography of Hope: Exile, the Enlightenment, Disassimilation* (Stanford, 2008).

BLAKE, WILLIAM, *The Complete Poetry and Prose of William Blake*, ed. David Erdman (Berkeley, 1982).

BLOOM, HAROLD, *The Anxiety of Influence: A Theory of Poetry* (New York, 1973).

—— *A Map of Misreading* (New York, 1975).

BOYARIN, DANIEL, 'Old Wine in New Bottles: Intertextuality and Midrash', *Poetics Today*, 8 (1987), 539–56.

BRENNER, MICHAEL, *Prophets of the Past: Interpreters of Jewish History* (Princeton, 2010).

BRILL, ALAN, 'Grandeur and Humility in the Writings of R. Simhah Bunim of Przysucha', in Yaakov Elman and Jeffrey S. Gurock (eds.), *Ḥazon naḥum: Studies in Jewish Law, Thought, and History Presented to Dr. Norman Lamm* (New York, 1997), 419–48.

BRILL, ALAN, 'The Spiritual World of a Master of Awe: Divine Vitality, Theosis and Healing in the *Degel Mahaneh Ephraim*', *Jewish Studies Quarterly*, 8/1 (2001), 27–65.

—— *Thinking God: The Mysticism of Rabbi Zadok of Lublin* (New York, 2002).

BRINKER, MENACHEM, *Narrative Art and Social Thought in Y. H. Brenner's Work* [Ad hasimtah hateveryanit: ma'amar al sipur umaḥshavah biyetsirat brenner] (Tel Aviv, 1991).

BUDNITSKII, OLEG, *Russian Jews: Between the Reds and the Whites, 1917–1920* (Philadelphia, 2012).

CARUTH, CATHY, *Unclaimed Experience: Trauma, Narrative and History* (Baltimore, 1996).

CASSIRER, ERNST, *An Essay on Man: An Introduction to a Philosophy of Human Culture* (New York, 1944).

CLARK, TIMOTHY, *The Theory of Inspiration: Composition as a Crisis of Subjectivity in Romantic and Post-Romantic Writing* (Manchester, 2001).

DAN, JOSEPH, 'Hasidism: The Third Century', in Ada Rapoport-Albert (ed.), *Hasidism Reappraised* (London, 1996), 415–26.

—— *Hebrew Ethical and Homiletical Literature* [Sifrut hamusar vehaderush] (Jerusalem, 1975).

—— 'Is Midrash Exegesis?', in Howard Kreisel (ed.), *Study and Knowledge in Jewish Thought* (Be'er Sheva, 2006), 81–99.

—— 'Some Notes on Homiletic Literature in Jewish Medieval and Early Modern Culture' (Heb.), in B. Z. Kedar (ed.), *Jewish Folk Culture* [Hatarbut ha'amamit] (Jerusalem, 1996), 141–54.

DE VRIES, HENT (ED.), *Religion: Beyond a Concept* (New York, 2008).

DEUTSCH, NATHANIEL, *The Jewish Dark Continent: Life and Death in the Pale of Settlement* (Cambridge, Mass., 2011).

DIAMOND, JAMES, 'The Warsaw Ghetto Rebbe: Diverting God's Gaze from a Utopian End to an Anguished Now', *Modern Judaism*, 30/3 (Oct. 2010), 299–331.

DILLARD, ANNIE, *Pilgrim at Tinker Creek* (New York, 1999).

DORAN, SABINE, *The Culture of Yellow; or, The Visual Politics of Late Modernity* (New York, 2013).

DUBNOW, SIMON, *History of Hasidism* [Toledot haḥasidut] (Tel Aviv, 1931).

DYNNER, GLENN, 'The Garment of Torah: Clothing Decrees and the Warsaw Career of the First Gerer Rebbe', in G. Dynner and François Guesnet (eds.), *Warsaw: The Jewish Metropolis. Essays in Honor of the 75th Birthday of Professor Antony Polonsky* (Leiden, 2015), 91–127.

—— 'The Hasidic Conquest of Small-Town Central Poland, 1754–1818', in Antony Polonsky (ed.), *The Shtetl: Myth and Reality*, Polin: Studies in Polish Jewry 17 (2004), 51–81.

—— *Men of Silk: The Hasidic Conquest of Jewish Polish Society* (New York, 2006).

——'Merchant Princes and Tsadikim: The Patronage of Polish Hasidism', *Jewish Social Studies*, 12/1 (2005), 64–110.

——and MARCIN WODZIŃSKI, 'The Kingdom of Poland and Her Jews: An Introduction', in Glenn Dynner, Antony Polonsky, and Marcin Wodziński (eds.), *Jews in the Kingdom of Poland, 1815–1918*, Polin: Studies in Polish Jewry 27 (Oxford, 2015), 3–44.

ELIOR, RACHEL, 'Messianic Expectations and Spiritualization of Religious Life in the Sixteenth Century', *Revue des études juives*, 145 (1986), 35–49; repr. in David B. Ruderman (ed.), *Essential Papers on Jewish Culture in Renaissance and Baroque Italy* (New York, 1992), 283–98.

—— *The Mystical Origins of Hasidism* (Oxford, 2006).

—— *The Paradoxical Ascent to God: The Kabbalistic Theosophy of Habad Hasidism*, trans. Jeffrey Green (Albany, 1993).

ELMAN, YAAKOV, 'The History of Gentile Wisdom According to R. Zadok Hakohen of Lublin', *Journal of Jewish Thought and Philosophy*, 3/1 (1993), 153–87.

ELYASHIV, MENASHE, 'Tefillin Times Two', Bar-Ilan University's Parashat Hashavua Study Center, Parashat Ekev 5765/27 Aug. 2005, <http://www.biu.ac.il/JH/Parasha/eng/ekev/ely.html>.

ETKES, IMMANUEL, *Ba'al Hatanya: Rabbi Shneur Zalman and the Origins of Habad Hasidism* [Ba'al hatanya: rabi shne'ur zalman miladi vereshitah shel ḥasidut ḥabad] (Jerusalem, 2011).

—— *The Besht: Magician, Mystic, and Leader*, trans. Saadya Sternberg (Waltham, Mass., 2005).

——'Research in Hasidism: Trends and Directions' (Heb.), *Mada'ei hayahadut*, 31 (1991), 5–21.

FACKENHEIM, EMIL L., 'Concerning Authentic and Unauthentic Responses to the Holocaust', *The Solomon Goldman Lectures*, 1 (1977), 65–85.

FAFLAK, JOEL, and JULIA M. WRIGHT, 'Introduction', in Joel Faflak and Julia M. Wright (eds.), *A Handbook of Romanticism Studies* (Chichester, 2012), 1–15.

FAIERSTEIN, MORRIS, *All Is in the Hands of Heaven: The Teachings of Rabbi Mordecai Joseph Leiner of Izbica* (New York, 1989).

——'Charisma and Anti-Charisma in Safed: Isaac Luria and Hayyim Vital', <http://www.academia.edu/1425548/Charisma_and_Anti-Charisma_in_Safed_Isaac_Luria_and_Hayyim_Vital>.

——'Personal Redemption in Hasidism', in Ada Rapoport-Albert (ed.), *Hasidism Reappraised* (London, 1996), 214–24.

FARBSTEIN, ESTHER, '"His Hands Were Steady": The Sermons of Rabbi Moses Kahlenberg' (Heb.), in Esther Farbstein (ed.), *Yedei Mosheh: Holocaust Era Sermons* [Yedei mosheh: ketavim miyemei hasho'ah] (Jerusalem, 2005), 47–93.

——'Sermons Speak History: Rabbinic Dilemmas in Internment between Metz and Auschwitz', *Modern Judaism*, 27/2 (2007), 146–72.

FINE, LAWRENCE, *Physician of the Soul, Healer of the Cosmos: Isaac Luria and His Kabbalistic Fellowship* (Stanford, Calif., 2003).

FISH, STANLEY, *Is There a Text in This Class? The Authority of Interpretive Communities* (Cambridge, Mass., 1980).

FISHBANE, MICHAEL, *The Garments of Torah: Essays in Biblical Hermeneutics* (Bloomington, 1989).

—— *Michael Fishbane: Jewish Hermeneutical Theology*, ed. Hava Tirosh-Samuelson and Aaron W. Hughes (Leiden, 2015).

—— *Sacred Attunement: A Jewish Theology* (Chicago, 2008).

FRANKEL, ESTELLE, *Sacred Therapy: Jewish Spiritual Teachings on Emotional Healing and Inner Wholeness* (Boston, 2003).

FRANKEL, JONATHAN, *Crisis, Revolution, and Russian Jews* (Cambridge, 2009).

—— *Prophecy and Politics: Socialism, Nationalism, and the Russian Jews, 1862–1917* (Cambridge, 1981).

—— 'S. M. Dubnov: Historian and Ideologist', introductory essay, in Sophie Dubnov-Erlich, *The Life and Work of S. M. Dubnov: Diaspora Nationalism and Jewish History*, trans. Judith Vowles, ed. Jeffrey Shandler (Bloomington, 1991), 1–33.

—— 'Yosef Haim Brenner, the "Half-Intelligentsia," and Russian-Jewish Politics', in Benjamin Nathans and Gabriella Safran (eds.), *Culture Front: Representing Jews in Eastern Europe* (Philadelphia, 2008), 145–75.

FREUD, SIGMUND, *The Interpretation of Dreams* (Philadelphia, 2010).

FRIEDMAN, PHILIP, 'The Jewish Badge and the Yellow Star in the Nazi Era', *Judaica Historia* (1955), 41–70; repr. in Ada Friedman (ed.), *Roads to Extinction: Essays on the Holocaust* (New York, 1980), 11–33.

GADAMER, HANS GEORG, *Truth and Method*, trans. Joel Weinsheimer and Donald G. Marshall (New York, 1994).

GELLMAN, JEROME I., *The Fear, the Trembling, and the Fire: Kierkegaard and Hasidic Masters on the Binding of Isaac* (Lanham, Md., 1994).

✳ GINZBURG, CARLO, 'Clues: Roots of an Evidential Paradigm', in Carlo Ginzburg, *Clues, Myths, and the Historical Method*, trans. John and Anne C. Tedeschi (Baltimore, 1989), 96–125; 200–14 (notes).

GOETSCHEL, ROLAND, '*Torah lishmah* as a Central Concept in the *Degel mahaneh Efrayim* of Moses Hayyim Ephraim of Sudylkow', in Ada Rapoport-Albert (ed.), *Hasidism Reappraised* (London, 1996), 258–67.

GREEN, ARTHUR, *A Guide to the Zohar* (Stanford, 2004).

—— *The Language of Truth: The Torah Commentary of the Sefat Emet, Rabbi Yehudah Leib Alter of Ger* (Philadelphia, 1998).

—— 'On Translating Hasidic Homilies', *Prooftexts*, 3 (1983), 63–72.

—— 'Three Warsaw Mystics', *Jerusalem Studies in Jewish Thought*, 13 (1996), 1–58.

——*Upright Practices: The Light of the Eyes—Menahem Nahum of Chernobyl* (New York, 1982).

——'The Zaddik as *Axis Mundi*', *Journal of the American Academy of Religion*, 45 (1997), 327–47.

——with EBN LEADER, ARIEL EVAN MAYSE, and OR N. ROSE, *Speaking Torah: Spiritual Teachings from around the Maggid's Table*, 2 vols. (Woodstock, Vt., 2013).

GREENBERG, GERSHON, 'Hasidic Thought and the Holocaust (1933–1947): Optimism and Activism', *Jewish History*, 27 (2013), 353–75.

GRIES, ZEEV, 'Between History and Literature: The Case of Jewish Preaching', *Journal of Jewish Thought and Philosophy*, 4/1 (1994), 113–22.

——*The Book in Early Hasidism: Genres, Authors, Scribes, Managing Editors and Its Review by Their Contemporaries and Scholars* [Sefer sofer vesipur bereshit haḥasidut: min habesht ve'ad menaḥem mendel mikotsk] (Tel Aviv, 1992).

——*The Book in the Jewish World, 1700–1900* (Oxford, 2007).

——*The Conduct Literature: Its History and Role in the Lives of the Followers of R. Israel Ba'al Shem Tov* [Sifrut hahanhagot: toledoteiha umekomah beḥayei ḥasidei rabi yisra'el ba'al shem tov] (Jerusalem, 1990).

——'The Hasidic Managing Editor as an Agent of Culture', in Ada Rapoport-Albert (ed.), *Hasidism Reappraised* (London, 1996), 141–55.

—— 'Hasidism: The Present State of Research and Some Desirable Priorities', *Numen*, 34/1 (1987), 97–108; 34/2 (1987), 179–213.

——'R. Israel ben Shabetai of Kozienice and His Commentary on the Tractate *Avot*' (Heb.), in Israel Bartal, Rachel Elior, and Chone Shmeruk (eds.), *Hasidism in Poland* [Tsadikim ve'anshei ma'aseh] (Jerusalem, 1994), 127–65.

GRONDIN, JEAN, 'Hermeneutics', in M. C. Horowitz (ed.), *New Dictionary of the History of Ideas* (New York, 2005), iii. 982–7.

HACOHEN, AVI'EZER, 'I Wanted to Write a Book . . .' (Heb.), *Dimui*, 28 (2006) 4–18, 86.

HALLAMISH, MOSHE, *An Introduction to the Kabbalah* (New York, 1999).

HANDELMAN, SUSAN, *Fragments of Redemption: Jewish Thought and Literary Theory in Benjamin, Scholem, and Levinas* (Bloomington, 1991).

——*Make Yourself a Teacher: Rabbinic Tales of Mentors and Disciples* (Seattle, 2011).

—— 'The Philosopher, the Rabbi, and the Rhetorician', *College English*, 72/6 (July 2010), 590–607.

HERCENBERG, B. DOV, 'La Transcendance du regard et la mise en perspective du *tekhelet* ("bleu" biblique)', *Revue d'histoire et de philosophie religieuse*, 78/4 (Oct.–Dec. 1998), 387–411.

HERSHKOWITZ, ISAAC, '*Ge'ulat yisra'el* by the Koznitzer Maggid: A Hasidic Ambivalent Attitude to Rabbi Loew of Prague' (Heb.), *Da'at*, 68–9 (2010), 15–31.

Holzer, Elie, 'Educational Aspects of Hermeneutical Activity in Text Study', in Jonathan Cohen and Elie Holzer (eds.), *Modes of Educational Translation*, Studies in Jewish Education 13 (2008), 205–39.

——'Ethical Dispositions in Text Study: A Conceptual Argument', *Journal of Moral Education*, 36/1 (March 2007), 37–49.

Hopkins, Gerard Manley, *The Letters of Gerard Manley Hopkins to Robert Bridges*, ed. Claude Colleer Abbott (London, 1955).

Hughes, H. S., *Consciousness and Society: Reorientation of European Social Thought* (New York, 1977).

Hundert, Gershon David, *Jews in Poland-Lithuania in the Eighteenth Century: A Genealogy of Modernity* (Berkeley, Calif., 2004).

Huss, Boaz, 'Admiration and Disgust: The Ambivalent Re-canonization of the Zohar in the Modern Period', in Howard Kreisel (ed.), *Study and Knowledge in Jewish Thought* (Be'er Sheva, 2006), 203–37.

Idel, Moshe, *Absorbing Perfections: Kabbalah and Interpretation* (New Haven, 2002).

——*Ascensions on High in Jewish Mysticism: Pillars, Lines, Ladders* (Budapest, 2005).

——'"The Besht Passed His Hand over His Face": On the Besht's Influence over His Followers—Some Remarks', in Philip Wexler and Jonathan Garb (eds.), *After Spirituality: Studies in Mystical Traditions* (2012), 79–106.

——'East European Hasidism: The Emergence of a Spiritual Movement', *Kabbalah: Journal for the Study of Jewish Mystical Texts*, 32 (2014), 36–61.

——'The Hasidic Revival: An Interpretation of the Emergence of a Spiritual Movement', in Yohanan Friedmann (ed.), *Religious Movements and Transformations in Judaism, Christianity and Islam* (Jerusalem, 2016), 51–82.

——*Hasidism: Between Ecstasy and Magic* (New York, 1995).

——*Hasidism: New Perspectives* (New Haven, 1988).

——'Hermeneutics in Hasidism', *Journal for the Study of Religions and Ideologies*, 9/25 (Spring 2010), 4–16.

——*Messianic Mystics* (New Haven, 1988).

——'Multiple Forms of Redemption in Kabbalah and Hasidism', *Jewish Quarterly Review*, 101/1 (Winter 2011), 27–70.

——'White Letters: From R. Levi Isaac of Berditchev's Views to Postmodern Hermeneutics', *Modern Judaism*, 26/2 (2006), 169–92.

Iser, Wolfgang, *The Implied Reader* (Boston, 1974).

Jacobs, Louis, 'Pesach and the Exodus in the Thought of Two Hasidic Masters', *Judaism Today*, 1 (1995), 19–24.

——*Their Heads in Heaven: Unfamiliar Aspects of Hasidim* (London, 2005).

Johnson, Christopher, *Memory, Metaphor, and Aby Warburg's Atlas of Images* (New York, 2012).

KAHLENBERG, HAIM MORDEKHAI, 'Divrei ḥayim' (Heb.), in Esther Farbstein (ed.), *Yedei mosheh* (Jerusalem, 2005), 27–42.

KARLINSKY, NAHUM, *Counter-History: The Hasidic Epistles from the Land of Israel—Text and Context* [Historyah shekeneged: igerot ḥasidim me'erets yisra'el, hatekst vehakontekst] (Jerusalem, 1999).

KASIRER, SHLOMO, '"Souls as Mirrors": Psychological Aspects of the Final Dispute between R. Yohanan and Resh Lakish, according to R. Tsadok Hakohen of Lublin' (Heb.), *Michlol*, 29 (2013), 141–60.

KATZ, STEVEN, 'Mysticism and the Interpretation of Sacred Scripture', in Steven Katz (ed.), *Mysticism and Sacred Scripture* (New York, 2000), 7–67.

KEARNEY, RICHARD, 'Paul Ricoeur and the Hermeneutics of Translation', *Research in Phenomenology*, 37 (2007), 147–59.

KENEZ, PETER, 'Pogroms and White Ideology in the Russian Civil War', in John D. Klier and Shlomo Lambroza (eds.), *Pogroms: Anti-Jewish Violence in Modern Russian History* (New York, 1992), 293–313.

KERMODE, FRANK, *The Uses of Error* (Cambridge, Mass., 1991).

KISCH, GUIDO, 'The Yellow Badge in History', *Historia Judaica*, 4/2 (Oct. 1942), 95–144.

LAKOFF, GEORGE, and MARK JOHNSON, *The Metaphors We Live By* (Chicago, 1980).

LAMM, NORMAN, *The Religious Thought of Hasidism* (New York, 1999).

LEDERBERG, NETANEL, *The Gateway to Infinity: Rabbi Dov Baer, the Magid Meisharim of Mezhirech* [Hasha'ar le'ayin: Torat haḥasidut behaguto shel rabi dov ber, hamagid mimezeritch] (Jerusalem, 2011).

—— *Rabbi Israel Ba'al Shem Tov: His Spiritual Character and Social Leadership* [Sod hada'at: Demuto haruḥanit vehanhagato haḥevratit shel rabi yisra'el ba'al shem tov] (Jerusalem, 2007).

LESHEM, ZVI, 'Between Messianism and Prophecy: Hasidism According to the Piaseczner Rebbe' [Bein meshiḥiyut linevuah: haḥasidut al pi ha'admor mipiaseczna], Ph.D. diss. (Bar-Ilan University, 2007).

LEVINAS, EMMANUEL, *Difficult Freedom: Essays on Judaism*, trans. Sean Hand (London, 1990).

—— *Otherwise than Being or Beyond Essence*, trans. Alphonso Lingis (Dordrecht, 1978).

—— *Totality and Infinity: An Essay on Exteriority*, trans. Alphonso Lingis (Pittsburgh, 1969).

LEVINE, HILLEL, '"Should Napoleon Be Victorious …": Politics and Spirituality in Early Modern Jewish Messianism', *Jerusalem Studies in Jewish Thought*, 16–17 (2001), pp. lxv–lxxxiii.

LEWIN, ABRAHAM, *A Cup of Tears: A Diary of the Warsaw Ghetto*, ed. Antony Polonsky, trans. Christopher Hutton (Oxford, 1988).

LEYMAN, SHNAYER Z., 'Dwarfs on the Shoulders of Giants', *Tradition*, 27 (1993), 90–4.

LIEBES, YEHUDA, *Sections of the Zohar Lexicon* [Perakim bemilon sefer hazohar] (Jerusalem, 1982).

LIWER, AMIRAH, 'Oral Torah in the Writings of R. Tsadok Hakohen of Lublin' [Torah shebe'al pe bekhitvei rav tsadok milublin], MA thesis (Hebrew University of Jerusalem, 1993).

LOEWENTHAL, NAFTALI, *Communicating the Infinite: The Emergence of the Habad School* (Chicago, 1990).

——'Finding the Radiance in the Text: A Habad Hasidic Interpretation of the Exodus', in Deborah A. Green and Laura S. Lieber (eds.), *Scriptural Exegesis: The Shapes of Culture and the Religious Imagination. Essays in Honour of Michael Fishbane* (Oxford, 2009), 299–309.

——'Midrash in Habad Hasidism', in Michael Fishbane and Joanna Weinberg (eds.), *Midrash Unbound: Transformations and Innovations* (Oxford, 2013), 429–55.

MAGID, SHAUL, 'Hasidism: Mystical and Nonmystical Approaches to Interpreting Scripture', in Frederick Greenspahn (ed.), *Jewish Mysticism and Kabbalah: New Insights and Scholarship* (New York, 2001), 139–58.

—— *Hasidism on the Margin: Reconciliation, Antinomianism, and Messianism in Izbica and Radzin Hasidism* (Madison, Wis., 2003).

——'The Intolerance of Tolerance: *Mahaloket* (Controversy) and Redemption in Early Hasidism', *Jewish Studies Quarterly Review*, 8 (2001), 326–68.

MAHLER, RAPHAEL, *Hasidism and the Jewish Enlightenment: Their Confrontation in Galicia and Poland in the First Half of the Nineteenth Century* (New York, 1985).

MAIMON, SOLOMON, *Lebensgeschichte* [Autobiography], ed. R. P. Moritz, 2 vols. (Berlin, 1792–3); English edn., *Solomon Maimon: An Autobiography*, trans. J. Clark-Murray (Oxford, 1954; repr. Urbana, Ill., 2001).

MAIMONIDES, MOSES, *Moreh nevukhim* [The Guide of the Perplexed], trans. into Heb. and commentary by Michael Schwartz, 2 vols. (Tel Aviv, 2002).

MAISELS, JAMES, *The Self and Self-Transformation in the Thought and Practice of Rabbi Kalonymus Kalmish Shapira*, Ph.D. diss. (University of Chicago, 2014).

MAYSE, ARIEL EVAN, 'Beyond the Letters: The Question of Language in the Teachings of Rabbi Dov Baer of Mezritch', Ph.D. diss. (Harvard University, 2015).

—— 'Of Letters and Leadership: Some Thoughts on the Teachings and Image of Rabbi Levi Yitzhak of Berditchev', <https://hebrewcollege.academia.edu/Ariel-Mayse>.

——and REISER, DANIEL, 'Sefer Sefat Emet, Yiddish Manuscripts and the Oral Homilies of R. Yehudah Aryeh Leib of Ger', *Kabbalah: Journal for the Study of Jewish Mystical Texts*, 33 (2015), 9–43.

MEIR, JONATAN, *Literary Hasidism: The Life and Works of Michael Levi Rodkinson*, trans. Jeffrey G. Amshalem (Syracuse, 2016).

MEIR, NATAN, "'The Sword Hanging Over Their Heads": The Significance of Pogrom for Russian Jewish Everyday Life and Self-Understanding (The Case of Kiev)', in J. Dekel-Chen, D. Gaunt, N. Meir, and I. Bartal (eds.), *Anti-Jewish Violence: Rethinking the Pogrom in East European History* (Bloomington, 2011), 111–28.

MELAMED, ABRAHAM, *On the Shoulders of Giants: The Debate between Moderns and Ancients in Medieval and Renaissance Jewish Thought* [Al kitfei anakim: toledot hapulmus bein aharonim lerishonim bahagut hayehudit biyemei habeinayim uvereshit ha'et hahadashah] (Ramat Gan, 2003).

MONDSHINE, YEHOSHUA, *In Praise of the Ba'al Shem Tov: A Manuscript* [Shivhei habesht: Faksimil miketav yad hayehidi hanoda lanu veshinuyei nusahav le'umat nusah hadefus] (Jerusalem, 1982).

MORAN, DERMOT, 'Gadamer and Husserl on Horizon, Intersubjectivity, and the Lifeworld', in Andrzej Wierciński (ed.), *Gadamer's Hermeneutics and the Art of Conversation*, International Studies in Hermeneutics and Phenomenology 2 (Münster, 2011), 73–94.

MORSON, GARY SAUL, and CARYL EMERSON, *Mikhail Bakhtin: Creation of a Prosaics* (Stanford, 1990).

NADLER, ALLAN, *The Faith of the Mithnagedim: Rabbinic Responses to Hasidic Rapture* (Baltimore, 1997).

—— 'The Gaon of Vilna and the Rabbinic Doctrine of Historical Decline', in David Assaf and Ada Rapoport-Albert (eds.), *'Let the Old Make Way for the New': Studies in the Social and Cultural History of Eastern European Jewry, Presented to Immanuel Etkes* [Yashan mipenei hadash: mehkarim betoledot yehudei mizrah eiropah uvetarbutam, shai le'imanu'el etkes] (Jerusalem, 2009), ii. 151–61.

—— 'Rationalism, Romanticism, Rabbis and Rebbes', Inaugural lecture, YIVO Institute for Jewish Research (New York, 1992), 1–24.

NEHER, ANDRE, *They Made Their Souls Anew*, trans. David Maisel (New York, 1990).

OGDEN, THOMAS, 'Fear of Breakdown and the Unlived Life', *International Journal of Psychoanalysis*, 95 (2014), 205–23.

PAISOT-BEAL, SOPHIE, 'Le Camp de La Lande,' *Le Monde Juif*, 153 (Jan.–Apr. 1995), 143–77.

PALMER, PARKER, *The Courage to Teach: Exploring the Inner Landscape of a Teacher's Life* (San Francisco, 1998).

—— *To Know as We Are Known: Education as a Spiritual Journey* (San Francisco, 1980).

PALMER, RICHARD, *Hermeneutics* (Evaston, 1969).

—— 'The Liminality of Hermes and the Meaning of Hermeneutics', *Proceedings of the Heraclitean Society: A Quarterly Report on Philosophy and Criticism of the Arts and Sciences*, 5 (1980), 4–11.

PASTOUREAU, MICHEL, *Blue: The History of a Color* (Princeton, 2001).

PEDAYA, HAVIVA, 'The Ba'al Shem Tov, R. Jacob Joseph of Polonnoye, and the Magid of Mezhirech: Outlines for a Religious Typology' (Heb.), *Da'at*, 45 (2000), 25–73.

—— 'The Ba'al Shem Tov's *Holy Epistle*' (Heb.), *Zion*, 70/3 (2005), 311–54.

—— 'Two Types of Ecstatic Experience in Hasidism' (Heb.), *Da'at*, 55 (2005), 73–108.

PETROVSKY-SHTERN, YOCHANAN, '"*Hasidei de'ar'a* and *Hasidei dekokhvaya*": Two Trends in Modern Jewish Historiography', *AJS Review*, 32/1 (2008), 141–67.

—— '"We are too late": An-sky and the Paradigm of No-Return', in Gabriella Safran and Steven J. Zipperstein (eds.), *The Worlds of S. An-sky: A Russian Jewish Intellectual at the Turn of the Century* (Stanford, Calif., 2006), 83–102.

PIEKARZ, MENDEL, *The Beginning of Hasidism: Ideological Trends in Derush and Musar Literature* [Biyemei tsemiḥat haḥasidut: megamot ra'ayoniyot besifrei derush umusar] (Jerusalem, 1997).

—— *The Hasidic Leadership: Authority and Faith in Zadikim as Reflected in the Hasidic Literature* [Hahanhagah haḥasidit: samḥut ve'emunat tsadikim be'aspaklaryat sifrutah shel haḥasidut] (Jerusalem, 1999).

—— *Ideological Trends of Hasidism in Poland During the Interwar Period and the Holocaust* [Ḥasidut polin: megamot ra'ayoniyot besifrei derush umusar] (Jerusalem, 1978).

—— '"The Inner Point" of the Admorim of Gur and Alexander as a Reflection of Their Ability to Adjust to Changing Times' (Heb.), in Joseph Dan and Joseph Hacker (eds.), *Studies in Jewish Mysticism, Philosophy, and Ethical Literature, Presented to Isaiah Tishby* [Meḥkarim bekabalah, befilosofyah hayehudit uvesifrut hamusar vehehagut] (Jerusalem, 1986), 617–60.

PINSKER, SHAHAR, *Literary Passports: The Making of Modernist Hebrew Fiction in Europe* (Stanford, Calif., 2010).

POLEN, NEHEMIA, 'Hasidic *Derashah* as Illuminated Exegesis', in Michael Zank and Ingrid Anderson (eds.), *The Value of the Particular: Lessons from Judaism and the Modern Jewish Experience. Festschrift for Steven T. Katz on the Occasion of his Seventieth Birthday* (Boston, 2015), 55–70.

—— *The Holy Fire: The Teachings of Rabbi Kalonymus Shapira, the Rebbe of the Warsaw Ghetto* (Northvale, NJ, 1994).

—— 'Introduction', in Malkah Shapiro, *The Rebbe's Daughter: Memoir of a Hasidic Childhood* (Philadelphia, 2002), pp. xv–xlvi.

POLIAKOV, LÉON, *L'Étoile jaune* (Paris, 1949).

POLONSKY, ANTONY, *The Jews in Poland and Russia*, 3 vols. (Oxford, 2010).

POPE, ROB, *Creativity: Theory, History, Practice* (Routledge, 2005).

RABINOWICZ, TSEVI MEIR, *Between Przysucha and Lublin: Men and Approaches in Polish Hasidism* [Bein peshiskhah lelublin: ishim veshitot beḥasidut polin] (Jerusalem, 1997).

RABINOWITSCH, ZE'EV, *Lithuanian Hasidism from its Beginnings to the Present Day*, trans. M. B. Dagut (New York, 1971).

RAMBERG, BJØRN, and KRISTIN GJESDAL, 'Hermeneutics', in Edward N. Zalta (ed.), *The Stanford Encyclopedia of Philosophy* (Summer 2013), available online at <http://plato.stanford.edu/archives/sum2013/entries/hermeneutics>.

RAPOPORT-ALBERT, ADA, 'God and the Zaddik as the Two Focal Points of Hasidic Worship', *History of Religions*, 18/4 (1979), 296–325.

——'Hasidism after 1772: Structural Continuity and Change', in Ada Rapoport-Albert (ed.), *Hasidism Reappraised* (London, 1996), 76–140.

RAWIDOWICZ, SIMON, 'On Interpretation', in Nahum Glazer (ed.), *Studies in Jewish Thought* (Philadelphia, 1974), 45–80.

REISER, DANIEL, '*Esh Kodesh*: A New Evaluation in Light of a Philological Examination of the Manuscript,' *Yad va-Shem Studies*, 44/1 (2016), 65–97.

——*Rabbi Kalonymus Kalman Shapira: Sermons from the Years of Rage* [Rabi kalonymus kalmish shapira: derashot mishenot haza'am] (Jerusalem, 2017).

——and ARIEL EVAN MAYSE, 'The Last Sermon of R. Judah Leib Alter of Ger and the Role of Yiddish for the Study of Hasidic Sermons' (Heb.), *Kabbalah: Journal for the Study of Jewish Mystical Texts*, 30 (2013), 127–60.

RICHARDS, I. A., *The Philosophy of Rhetoric* (Oxford, 1936); repr. in M. Johnson (ed.), *Philosophical Perspectives on Metaphor* (Minneapolis, 1981), 48–62.

RICOEUR, PAUL, 'The Bible and the Imagination' (1981), repr. in id., *Figuring the Sacred*, 144–66.

—— *Figuring the Sacred: Narrative, Religion, and Imagination*, trans. David Pellauer, ed. Mark Wallace (Minneapolis, 1995).

—— *Interpretation Theory: Discourse and the Surplus of Meaning* (Fort Worth, Tex., 1976).

——'The Metaphorical Process as Cognition, Imagination, and Feeling', *Critical Inquiry*, 5/1 (1978), 143–59.

—— *Oneself as Another*, trans. Kathleen Blamey (Chicago, 1992).

—— *A Ricoeur Reader: Reflection and Imagination*, ed. Mario J. Valdes (Toronto, 1991).

—— *The Rule of Metaphor: Multi-Disciplinary Studies in the Creation of Meaning in Language*, trans. Robert Czerny with Kathleen McLaughlin and John Costello (London, 1978).

ROSEN, MICHAEL, *The Quest for Authenticity: The Thought of Reb Simhah Bunim* (Jerusalem, 2008).

ROSKIES, DAVID, *A Bridge of Longing: The Lost Art of Yiddish Storytelling* (Cambridge, Mass., 1995).

ROSMAN, MOSHE, *Founder of Hasidism: A Quest for the Historical Ba'al Shem Tov* (Berkeley, Calif., 1996).

——'Hasidism as a Modern Phenomenon: The Paradox of Modernization Without Secularization', *Jahrbuch des Simon-Dubnow-Instituts*, 6 (2007), 215–24.

ROSMAN, MOSHE, 'Hasidism: The Verdict of Israeli Historiography' (Heb.), *Zion*, 74 (2009), 141–75.

ROSS, NIHAM, *A Beloved-Despised Tradition: Modern Jewish Identity and Neo-Hasidic Writing* [Masoret ahuvah usenuah: zehut yehudit modernit ukhetivah neo-ḥasidit befetaḥ hame'ah ha'esrim] (Be'er Sheva, 2010).

ROTENBERG, MORDECHAI, *Dialogue with Deviance: The Hasidic Ethic and the Theory of Social Contraction* (Philadelphia, 1983).

——*Hasidic Psychology: Making Space for Others* (New Brunswick, 2003).

SAPERSTEIN, MARC, *Decoding the Rabbis: A Thirteenth-Century Commentary on the Aggadah* (Cambridge, Mass., 1980).

——*Jewish Preaching 1200–1800: An Anthology* (New Haven, 1989).

——'Your Voice Like a Ram's Horn': Themes and Texts in Traditional Jewish Preaching* (Cincinnati, 1996).

SCHOLEM, GERSHOM, *Major Trends in Jewish Mysticism*, trans. George Lichtheim (New York, 1941).

SCHULZ-FORBERG, HAGEN, *London–Berlin: Authenticity, Modernity, and the Metropolis in Urban Travel Writing from 1851 to 1939* (Brussels, 2006).

SCHWAB, JOSEPH J., 'Eros and Education: A Discussion of One Aspect of Discussion', in Ian Westbury and Neil J. Wilkof (eds.), *Science, Curriculum, and Liberal Education: Selected Essays* (Chicago, 1978), 105–32.

SCHWARZFUCHS, SIMON, 'The Long Road from Metz to Auschwitz' (Heb.), in Esther Farbstein (ed.), *Yedei mosheh* (Jerusalem, 2005), 11–23.

SCHWEID, ELIEZER, *From Ruin to Salvation* [Bein ḥurban liyeshuah: teguvot shel hagut ḥaredit lesho'ah bizemanah] (Tel Aviv, 1994).

SEEMAN, DON, 'Ritual Efficacy, Hasidic Mysticism and "Useless Suffering" in the Warsaw Ghetto', *Harvard Theological Review*, 101/3–4 (2008), 465–505.

SHAHAR, YESHAYAHU, *Criticism of Society and Leadership in the Musar and Derush Literature in Eighteenth-Century Poland* [Bikoret haḥevrah vehanhagat hatsibur besifrut hamusar vehaderush bepolin bame'ah hashemoneh-esreh] (Jerusalem, 1992).

SHAPIRA, ANITA, *Yosef Haim Brenner: A Life*, trans. Anthony Berris (Stanford, Calif., 2014).

SHERWIN, BYRON, *Mystical Theology and Social Dissent: The Life and Works of Judah Loew of Prague* (London, 1982).

SHONKOFF, SAM BERRIN, 'Michael Fishbane: An Intellectual Portrait', in *Michael Fishbane: Jewish Hermeneutical Theology*, ed. Hava Tirosh-Samuelson and Aaron W. Hughes (Leiden, 2015), 1–52.

SHOR, ABRAHAM ABISH, 'Rabbi Aaron the Great and the Hasidic Circle in Karlin' (Heb.), *Kovets beit aharon veyisra'el*, 9/1 (1994), 153–60.

SHUSTERMAN, RICHARD, *Performing Live: Aesthetic Alternatives for the Ends of Art* (Ithaca, NY, 2000).

SIFF, DAVID, 'Messianism, Revelation, and the Book: Rebbe Naḥman of Breslov and the Torah of Atiq', Ph.D. diss. (Jewish Theological Seminary, New York, 2009).

—— 'Shifting Ideologies of Orality and Literacy in Their Historical Context: Rebbe Nahman of Bratslav's Embrace of the Book as a Means for Redemption', *Prooftexts*, 30/2 (2010), 238–62.

SPIEGEL, SHALOM, *The Last Trial*, trans. Judah Goldin (Philadelphia, 1967).

STAMPFER, SHAUL, 'Hasidic Yeshivot in Inter-War Poland', *Families, Rabbis, and Education* (Oxford, 2010), 252–74.

—— 'How and Why Did Hasidism Spread?', *Jewish History*, 27/2–4 (2013), 201–19.

STEINER, GEORGE, *Real Presences* (Chicago, 1989).

TAYLOR, CHARLES, *Sources of the Self: The Making of the Modern Identity* (Cambridge, Mass., 1989).

TIROSH-SAMUELSON, HAVA, 'Interview with Michael Fishbane', in Tirosh-Samuelson and Aaron W. Hughes (eds.), *Michael Fishbane: Jewish Hermeneutical Theology* (Leiden, 2015), 219–69.

TISHBY, ISAIAH, 'The Messianic Idea and Messianic Trends in the Growth of Hasidism' (Heb.), *Zion*, 32 (1967), 1–45.

—— *Wisdom of the Zohar*, trans. David Goldstein, 3 vols. (Oxford, 1989).

TRILLING, LIONEL, 'Freud and Literature', *Horizon* (1947), 182–200.

—— *Sincerity and Authenticity* (Cambridge, Mass., 1972).

UNGAR, MENASHE, *A Fire Burns in Kotsk: A Tale of Hasidism in the Kingdom of Poland*, trans. Jonathan Boyarin (Detroit, 2015).

UNGAR, MICHAL, *Reassessment of the Image of Mordechai Chaim Rumkowski* (Jerusalem, 2004).

URBAN, MARTINA, *Aesthetics of Renewal: Martin Buber's Early Representation of Hasidism as Kulturkritik* (Chicago, 2008).

VEIDLINGER, JEFFREY, *Jewish Public Culture in the Late Russian Empire* (Bloomington, 2009).

WACKS, RON, *The Flame of the Holy Fire: Perspectives on the Teachings of Rabbi Kalonymous Kalmish Shapiro of Piaseczno* [Lahavat esh kodesh: sha'arim letorato shel ha'admor mipiaseczno] (Alon Shevut, 2010).

WALLACE, MARK, 'Introduction', in Paul Ricoeur, *Figuring the Sacred: Narrative, Religion, and Imagination*, trans. David Pellauer, ed. Mark Wallace (Minneapolis, 1995), 1–32.

WEIL, JIŘÍ, *Life with a Star*, trans. Ruzena Kovariskova with Roslyn Schloss (New York, 1989).

WEISS, JOSEPH, 'The Beginning of the Emergence of the Hasidic Path' (Heb.), in Avraham Rubinstein (ed.), *Studies in Hasidism* [Perakim betorat haḥasidut uvetoledoteiha] (Jerusalem, 1978), 122–81.

WEISS, JOSEPH, 'A Circle of Pneumatics in Pre-Hasidism', *Journal of Jewish Studies*, 8 (1957); repr. in id., *Studies in East European Jewish Mysticism and Hasidism* (Oxford, 1997), 27–42.

WELTSCH, ROBERT, *An der Wende des modernen Judentums: Betrachtungen aus fünf Jahrzehnten* (Tübingen, 1972).

WERBLOWSKY, RAFAEL JEHUDA ZWI, *Joseph Karo: Lawyer and Mystic* (London, 1962).

WIESE, CHRISTIAN, 'No "Love of the Jewish People"? Robert Weltsch's and Hans Jonas's Correspondence with Hannah Arendt on *Eichmann in Jerusalem*', in Christian Wiese and Martina Urban (eds.), *German-Jewish Thought Between Religion and Politics: Festschrift in Honor of Paul Mendes-Flohr* (Berlin, 2012), 387–431.

WILENSKY, MORDECAI L., 'Hasidic–Mitnaggedic Polemics in the Jewish Communities of Eastern Europe: The Hostile Phase', in Béla K. Király (ed.), *Tolerance and Movements of Religious Dissent in Eastern Europe* (New York, 1975), 89–113; repr. in Gershon Hundert (ed.), *Essential Papers on Hasidism: Origins to Present* (New York, 1991), 244–71.

——*Hasidim and Mitnagedim: On the History of Their Polemics, 1772–1815* [Ḥasidim umitnagedim: letoledot hapulmus shebeineihem bashanim 5532–5572], 2 vols. (Jerusalem, 1970).

WISKIND-ELPER, ORA, 'Hermeneutics and Hasidic Thought: The Izbica-Radzyn Reading of the Joseph Stories', *Tarbiz*, 80/5 (July–Sept. 2012), 595–622.

——'Rebbe Joshua Heschel Rabinowitz of Monastyrishche: Contemplations of a Hasidic Leader on Judaism in Troubled Times' (Heb.), *Jerusalem Studies in Jewish Thought*, 25 (2018), 157–204.

——*Tradition and Fantasy in the Tales of Reb Nahman of Bratslav* (Albany, NY, 1998).

——*Wisdom of the Heart: On the Teachings of Rabbi Ya'akov of Izbica-Radzyn* (Philadelphia, 2010).

WODZIŃSKI, MARCIN, *Hasidism and Politics: The Kingdom of Poland, 1815–1864* (Oxford, 2013).

——*Haskalah and Hasidism in the Kingdom of Poland: A History of Conflict* (Oxford, 2005).

——'War and Religion; or, How the First World War Changed Hasidism', *Jewish Quarterly Review*, 106/3 (Summer 2016), 283–312.

——and GLEN DYNNER, 'The Kingdom of Poland and her Jews: Introduction', in Glen Dynner, Antony Polonsky, and Marcin Wodziński (eds.), *Jews in the Kingdom of Poland: 1815–1918*, Polin: Studies in Polish Jewry 27 (Oxford, 2014), 3–44.

WOLFSON, ELLIOT, *Open Secret: Postmessianic Messianism and the Mystical Revision of Menaḥem Mendel Schneerson* (New York, 2009).

WUTTKE, DIETER, 'Nachwort des Herausgebers', in Aby Warburg, *Ausgewählte Schriften und Würdigungen*, ed. Dieter Wuttke (Baden-Baden, 1992), 601–38.

YERUSHALMI, YOSEF HAYIM, 'Toward a History of Jewish Hope', in David Myers and Alexander Kaye (eds.), *The Faith of Fallen Jews: Yosef Hayim Yerushalmi and the Writing of Jewish History* (Waltham, Mass., 2014), 299–318.

ZORNBERG, AVIVAH GOTTLIEB, *The Particulars of Rapture: Reflections on Exodus* ✳ (New York, 2001).

ZUCCOTTI, SUSAN, *The Holocaust, the French, and the Jews* (Lincoln, Nebr., 1999).

Index